The Lighting Art

The Lighting Art:
The Aesthetics of Stage
Lighting Design

RICHARD H. PALMER

College of William and Mary

Prentice-Hall, Inc., Englewood Cliffs, N.J. 07632

Library of Congress Cataloging in Publication Data
Palmer, Richard H.
  The lighting art

  Bibliography: p.
  Includes index.
  1. Stage lighting.   I. Title
PN2091.E4P35   1985   792'.025   84-9827
ISBN 0-13-536566-X

Editorial/production supervision and
  interior design: Barbara Kittle
Cover design: Wanda Lubelska
Manufacturing buyer: Barbara Kittle

Printed in the United States of America

10 9 8 7 6 5 4 3 2 1

ISBN 0-13-536566-X   01

Prentice-Hall International, Inc., *London*
Prentice-Hall of Australia Pty. Limited, *Sydney*
Editora Prentice-Hall do Brasil, Ltda., *Rio de Janeiro*
Prentice-Hall Canada Inc., *Toronto*
Prentice-Hall of India Private Limited, *New Delhi*
Prentice-Hall of Japan, Inc., *Tokyo*
Prentice-Hall of Southeast Asia Pte. Ltd., *Singapore*;
Whitehall Books Limited, *Wellington, New Zealand*

Contents

Illustrations

Foreword
for Teachers

Whether you use this book as a supplementary text for a beginning lighting design course or as a primary text for an advanced course will largely depend on whether you teach mechanics or design theory first. After having repeatedly tried both ways as well as various intermixtures, I think no one approach works inherently better than another. The function/mechanics/design scheme ultimately seems the most comfortable, I suspect, because most of us learned about lighting design in that order. The important point is that we must give our students thorough familiarity both with the practical tools of a lighting designer and with ways of intelligently using those tools.

This book makes no attempt to discuss lighting equipment or to prescribe specific instrumentation for transferring design concepts into lighting plots. A number of good texts, periodically updated and listed in the bibliography, discuss equipment and control and complement the present text. Many of these also touch on the history of stage lighting, a topic most fully covered in *Lighting in the Theatre*, by Gösta Bergman.

Just as it makes no attempt to replace a good standard text in lighting equipment and lighting methodology, *The Lighting Art* certainly requires the support of a good classroom teacher. Even though concrete examples constantly illustrate broader theory and principles, this book focuses on design *ideas*, concentrating on the process of developing a design concept and on the multiple factors the designer must consider in formulating that concept. Practical application always depends on the exigencies of the production situation: the lighting inventory and condition of instruments, mounting positions, control capabilities, money, time, the skill of electricians and operators, the specific scenic and costume designs, the director, and the working relationships of the production team. One of the problems with detailed, extended examples of lighting design in textbooks is that they would never work in *your* theatre!

This book addresses the eye and mind of the student designer. The transfer of these ideas into pratical designs requires an instructor who develops design projects as close to the real workaday conditions of an actual production as feasibility will allow. It would be particularly useful to support points made in this book by drawing design projects from plays discussed at some length in the text, such as *Oedipus Rex, A Streetcar Named Desire, Romeo and Juliet,* or *A Phoenix Too Frequent.* The section on lighting styles will particularly profit from design projects constructed around specific production styles. The plays cited in that section are suitable examples, or the instructor may choose other examples from his or her personal repertory.

Many of the lighting phenomena discussed in early chapters are difficult to describe but become immediately apparent when experienced. At the end of these chapters, a few practical demonstrations are described. The instructor will doubtlessly think of others. Most are relatively simple to set up and provide good projects for students for in-class demonstrations which will help to illustrate points made in the text.

Even though a full academic year allows time for a better intermixture of design theory and practical design projects, the material presented in this book can be covered in a semester or a quarter, allowing about a week to deal with each of the twelve chapters. An instructor anxious for students to begin developing lighting plots early in a term may find it useful, after covering Chapter 1, to jump to Chapters 10, 11, and 12, returning to material on psychophysics, composition, and style in the intervening chapters after initial design projects are underway.

In spite of its theoretical tone, this is a how-to-do-it text. The skills being developed are simply those of the mind and eye which should accompany skills of the hand. As with the mastery of any art form, lighting design depends on the master-apprentice relationship between the design teacher and the student. No book can replace the exemplar function or the experienced advice and guidance of the lighting designer/teacher.

Preface

If we judge theatrical lighting design by what has been written about it, we would conclude that stage lighting is mostly a matter of equipment and technical considerations. This orientation has several causes. All stage lighting texts have so far been written for beginners and assume that the first problem confronting the neophyte designer is how to use a wide array of complex equipment. Indeed, the last few decades saw rapid development in the technology of stage lighting, particularly in the area of dimmer control, and there has been an understandable fascination with lighting hardware.

There are thousands of people doing stage lighting who are "equipment freaks." The situation resembles the sound recording and reproduction industry, where legions of people who are obsessed with the technology of sound systems largely ignore the creative dimension of the sound being reproduced. We further confuse the issue by talking about the "state of the art" when we refer to sound or lighting technology. It is almost as if technical mastery of the equipment were the primary goal of the art form.

Certainly music is not threatened by its technology. Musicians and composers have been around for millennia—even musicologists have been around for centuries. Lighting design, however, is a relatively new art form, and even though some of its earlier theorists, Adolph Appia and Gordon Craig, predated its technical explosion, the aesthetic principles of lighting design were not clearly articulated before technology dominated.

This is not to say that lighting designers ignore the artistry in what they do. Obviously many fine artists design theatrical lighting. However, while volumes discuss lighting equipment, there has been only cursory or inadequate examination of the aesthetics of stage lighting, of the artistic principles which govern the use of lighting equipment.

Because of the lack of a well developed aesthetics of stage lighting, many colleges overlook this aspect of theatre education and produce graduates who know their electricity, electronics, optics, drafting, and equipment, but don't know how to design with light. The most consistent cause of failure by persons taking the lighting examinations with the United Scenic Artists is an inability to use lighting to create a viable design.

Aesthetic questions are not totally new to those concerned with stage lighting. Adolph Appia, Gordon Craig, Stanley McCandless, Antonin Artaud, Robert Edmond Jones, Jean Rosenthal, and others articulated important principles of theatrical lighting which we will discuss, but no one made a thoroughgoing investigation of lighting aesthetics based on current knowledge and the demands of contemporary theatre. The very newness of sophisticated, highly-flexible, and controllable techniques for stage lighting may partly account for the dearth of aesthetic investigation. Only in recent decades did theatrical lighting develop into an independent artistic endeavor with sufficient complexity to qualify as a sophisticated art form.

A large body of written material on lighting exists outside the field of stage lighting. Artists in other visual areas, particularly painting and photography, depend on the effects of light and have systematically examined its use. Perceptual psychologists and illumination engineers have done much basic research on the way lighting influences human perception, and their work yields much useful information for the stage lighting designer.

This book contains no detailed information on instruments, control devices, electricity, or optics. That material is essential knowledge for the practicing lighting designer who should seek it in any of the texts available or in the catalogues of equipment manufacturers. This book is intended to supplement that information, to pick up at the point the question is asked, "How do I use this equipment?" This book should also interest the threatregoer who wants to understand the elements of good lighting and know how the lighting design helps to shape the audience response to a production.

The lack of discussion on equipment should not create the impression that this investigation of aethetics will be only on an abstract level. We want to discover the most general principles governing the art of stage lighting design and expect the individual designer to apply these principles to specific production requirements with available equipment. At the same time, the writer is a practicing lighting designer and will illustrate the discussion throughout by references to specific design situations.

Because our seeing is influenced by so many psychological factors, which we will discuss, and because film has a unique and limited range of sensitivity to light, production photographs provide notoriously poor copies of stage lighting. We will use some photographs for the sake of the lighting they show, regardless of their accuracy as a record of the production, but often scene designs represent lighting more vividly than a production photograph and will be used to illustrate many of the elements of lighting discussed here.

I am indebted to a generation of students and audiences who have tolerated my experiments with lighting; to countless lighting designers who provided nu-

Introduction

In stage lighting design, the art of arranging light for a theatrical production, the lighting designer ultimately controls all visual aspects of any stage production not presented in daylight: the audience *must* have light in order to see. However, one large floodlight can create enough illumination for visibility. Illumination alone is neither a design nor an art.

The word *design* may mean either "a plan" or "a structure," and a lighting designer creates both, *planning* a *structure* of light by manipulating certain controllable properties of light to satisfy a specific set of functions. The designer must master not only instrumentation and control, but light itself and, finally, what and how the audience sees. The instrument plot is only the means to the end of designing the audience's visual experience.

To carry out this process of design in its broadest sense, the designer must command more than a knowledge of equipment. He or she must understand the process of seeing: the connections between what is lit, the properties of the lighting, and the eye and mind of the beholder. This book will concentrate on these links among subject matter, lighting, and audience response.

As stage lighting is an art form, it requires the designer to understand aesthetic principles in addition to technical skills. But lighting was not always considered an artistic enterprise. In the early years of this century lighting responsibilities fell to a master electrician who was viewed as a craftsman rather than an artist. Gradually the scenic designer became responsible for stage lighting and, in the 1930s, Jean Rosenthal was the first commercial designer to concentrate exclusively on lighting. Only in the 1960s did the professional designers' union, The

United Scenic Artists of America, recognize stage lighting as an independent design area.

Because stage lighting is an art, the lighting artist must deal with questions of creativity, beauty, and the power of light to evoke emotion. Any artistic endeavor involves a large element of intuition, but the word "art" has from ancient times implied order and systematic principles of approach which can be taught and learned. The study of art is called *aesthetics*.

The idea of "aesthetics" may be as intimidating to a new lighting designer as the bewildering array of available lighting equipment, but the word simply describes the idea that we can understand an art form, artistic creativity, and the response to art by isolating the principles which the artist uses to manipulate materials that produce predictable audience responses. In other words, aesthetics is the science of art.

This does not reduce the art of stage lighting to a set of rules. Inspiration remains important, but there are still basic principles to learn and master. Just as the painter must know the principles of color or the sculptor must understand the fracture characteristics of marble, so the lighting designer should understand the properties of light, aspects of psychophysics, stylistic conventions, and methods for analyzing the interdependence between lighting and a production concept.

In this chapter we will briefly examine the properties of light which the designer can vary and control, and we will survey the functions served by stage lighting. The next three chapters will discuss principles of psychophysics which help us understand how viewers respond to brightness, color, and the form-giving power of light. Chapters 5 through 7 investigate the compositional function of lighting, followed by two chapters on stylistic approaches to lighting design. The final three chapters discuss methods for analyzing a script and other production elements in order to develop a lighting design that fuses production concept with audience response.

THE CONTROLLABLE PROPERTIES OF STAGE LIGHTING

There are eight distinct properties of light which the designer controls.[1] These elements are analogous to the painter's concern for the hue, brightness, saturation, density, reflectance, and texture of pigment. The painter must also know the properties of different color vehicles for pigment, brushes, and painting surfaces, just as the lighting designer should understand the properties of different lighting instruments and the workings of lenses, reflectors, and dimmers, but in neither case does the mastery of the art consist primarily in the mastery of tools. The true medium of stage lighting design is light, and the art consists of the manipulation of the eight properties of light.

Intensity. The amount of light energy reflected from the stage. The designer controls intensity by the type, size, wattage, and number of lighting instruments used and by a variety of intensity control devices (dimmers). The reflective properties of surfaces on stage also influence intensity, but the scenic, costume, and makeup designers hold primary sway over this factor. The lighting designer must adjust the intensity to accommodate predetermined reflective surfaces. Brightness is the chief attribute of light intensity, and a variety of psychological factors influence the audience's perception of brightness, such as adaptation level, brightness contrast, glare, and irradiation.

Color. The hue, saturation, and brightness of objects as influenced by the spectral composition of the light striking and reflecting from their surface. This is primarily controlled by the use of colored filters, but is secondarily determined by the varying spectral profiles of different sources of illumination, by the red shift in incandescent lights as they are dimmed, by the cumulative reflection of light from colored surfaces, and by an array of perceptual variables.

Direction. The orientation of the apparent light source in relation to the lighted object and the viewer. The mounting positions of individual lighting instruments primarily determines direction, but the flow of intensity differences on stage and the organization of lighting color can also induce the audience's perception of directionality. The direction of light strongly influences space and form perception.

Form. The shape of individual pools of light, patterns of light and darkness created by either a number of instruments or various projection devices, and the play of light reflected from the surfaces of a complex solid. The selection of instrument types, mounting position, the use of shutters and gobos, and the arrangement of instruments are among the means of controlling form. The designer controls form to create visual composition with lighting.

Diffusion. The scattering of light through a translucent medium or the inherent "hardness" or "softness" of a beam. The quality of light reflected from a surface is partly the product of the apparent size of the light source. *Specular* (mirrorlike) reflection implies a small source, and *diffused* reflection, a large source. By using diffusion media or by throwing instruments out of focus we enlarge the apparent size of the source. The control of diffusion affects the perception of color, form, and composition.

Frequency. The intermittency of light through time. The frequency may be short, as with strobe lights, or long, as with the dimming rhythm established for an entire production. Frequency, which may be random or rhythmic, can influence the perception of brightness and color, and provides a time dimension to composition. The development of a lighting score, described in Chapter 12, depends on the control of lighting frequency over the length of a production.

Motion. Light changing place in space. This may be actual motion, as with follow spots, or apparent motion created by crossdimming or by using chasers. As with frequency, motion involves the manipulation of light over time.

Luminousness. The quality of light. This is properly a variable created by a combination of other factors, but in such subtle proportions as to almost defy analysis. The liveliness of a laser image, the glowing quality of a fluorescing color, the flatness of a carbon arc light, the radiance of an incandescent source are all recognizable examples of this property. It is usually a product of the type of illuminant or filter color.

THE FUNCTIONS OF STAGE LIGHTING

What are the objectives of the lighting designer? What does lighting accomplish? In the broadest sense, the designer must create the luminous world of the production. Just as a specific clearing in the forest or a specific cathedral has a unique quality of light on a given day at a certain time of year, so too should a stage production have its own characteristic light.

It is often said that the business of the theatrical lighting designer is "to light the play, not just the stage." Indeed, many theatrical performances are attempts to elucidate a script, and in these cases the lighting designer, like all other members of the production team, must labor to discover the visual reality demanded by those words.

A staged production, however, always provides more than words. Occasionally the additions are detrimental, but more often the production adds a richness of experience far beyond that provided by the script alone. This is the justification for theatrical performance: that it engages all of the senses to a greater extent than any other art form. Performed theatre is never just the enactment of scripts. It is a thing unto itself: the totality at that particular moment of actors, words, music, costume, properties, makeup, scenery, lighting, the performing space, and the audience. The script may be central to this effort, but it is the total event which must be lit. The lighting designer lights productions.

In practice, the theatre has rarely been dominated by the script. We tend to judge the theatrical activity of any period from the perspective of literary scholars, partly because they dominate our educational institutions, partly because the script is the most easily preserved part of a production. Yet theatre today, as it has always, appeals largely to the eye, and there the lighting designer has final control.

The lighting designer may be called on to light improvised works, happenings, spectacles, operas and musicals, dance concerts, actor vehicles, even productions without live performers. The source of artistic unity for these events is not scripts but rather the production concept. Thus it might better be said that the designer "lights the *production, not the stage.*"

Another troublesome adage that muddies an understanding of stage lighting is the notion that lighting must never call attention to itself. In part, this is a further legacy of literati, but it has been reinforced by exponents of extreme realism and by actors and scenic designers nervous about the potential competition of attention-grabbing light. There are always defenders of special interest theatre: Jerzi Grotowski wants to return theatre to the actors and has them perform under unchanging white light; Gordon Craig wants to eliminate the actors altogether; playwrights form their own theatres out of feelings of abuse and neglect.

All of these are legitimate points of view, but they represent only a selection from the total possibilities of the theatrical experience, which is capable of bringing all sensory resources to the stage.

The extent to which lighting justifiably calls attention to itself should be determined by the production concept, by the function designed for the light at that moment in the performance. Theatre at its best is a collective enterprise, a synthesis both of creative artists and of the parts of the total theatrical art. If the lighting best serves the style of the production by being unobtrusive, then unobtrusive it should be, but if a spectacular display of light best enhances a production, then let there be a spectacular display. The art consists in knowing when the lighting should be transparent—only revealing other production elements—and when the lighting should beckon for attention.

There are at least nine functions of stage lighting, all of which are in effect at any given moment.[2] The designer must manipulate the controllable properties of light in order to serve these functions, and any failure to consciously consider any of these uses of stage lighting represents a potential loss of control over the art form.

Selective Visibility. The control of what can and cannot be seen. This is largely a matter of manipulating lights and shadow. We often think of illumination as a matter of seeing, but what is not seen may also be of great importance. In *A Streetcar Named Desire*, Blanche Dubois puts a colored shade over a bare lightbulb because she wants to soften and conceal the harshness of her environment. The scenic designer wants his elaborately painted wallpaper to be visible, but *not* the hinges underneath the dutchman on the face of the flat.

Frequently, limiting or eliminating visibility can be far more difficult than enhancing visual acuity. The designer must consider reflective surfaces, beam angles, and brightness contrasts in order to make one area of the stage invisible while another area is well lit. This is not always a matter of withholding illumination. Sometimes glare or poor color enhancement can help limit visibility.

We tend to approach a lighting design in terms of areas of light, but it is often a useful approach to execute an "antilight" design. In other words, with sketches or on floor plans, indicate clearly what should not be seen or where shadows are desirable.

Improving visibility entails more than increasing illumination. As we shall see, above a fairly moderate level of illumination, increased acuity is obtained only with disproportionately large increases in intensity. Brightness adaptation constantly works to offset the potential gains of increased intensity, and in certain conditions a high level of intensity may produce eye fatigue. Visual acuity can often be better improved by closer attention to figure/ground contrast, selection of lighting angles to improve textual and spatial perception, and choices of lighting color which enhance form perception.

Establishing "Given Circumstances". Setting the time of day, season, historical period, location, and apparent lighting sources. Stage lighting may lack the specificity of scenic or costume design in establishing the reality of a setting, but light can contribute greatly to the believability of the stage illusion, particularly for a realistic play. Lighting designers must carefully study the rich variety of lighting in the real world or envision the ambience of light in a past age, an unfamiliar setting, or an imaginary place in order to recreate with stage lighting instruments the particular effects of sun, moon, or firelight, of candle, gas, or electric light, of light filtered through trees, stained glass, or fog, of light reflected from water, sand, or polished floors, or light produced from any of thousands of other sources. The lighting not only confirms the reality provided by other elements of production, but it implies the reality that extends beyond the stage space, and for less literal styles of realism, suggests things not otherwise shown on stage. Thus the clearing under a canopy of trees, or the moonlit lakeside, or the deck of a ship in a squall comes to life more vividly and believably with lighting than by any other means. In a sense, we recognize all objects by the light they reflect. If the designer recreates the reflected light the audience may still sense the presence of that object.

Coloring the Stage Picture. The regulation of apparent colors within the visual field by controlling the color of the light. Except for psychoperceptual factors (to be considered in Chapter 3), the color of anything depends upon its selective reflection of light. If a given wavelength is not present in a light, the surface will not reflect that color. If an object lacks a pigment or a surface that reflects the color in the light, the lighting color will disappear or modify. The perceived color of anything changes by changing the color of the light on it. Color influences our perception of form, our ability to distinguish detail, mood, style, characterization, and most of the design elements of makeup, scenery, and costume. When we consider the variety of filter colors available from different manufacturers and the possibilities of combining and altering these colors, the range available to the designer and the potential number of permutations of color from multiple instruments is in the order of millions. It is understandable why so many otherwise well-plotted designs go astray at the color-selection stage.

Shaping Space and Form. The arrangement of light to give size and shape to the performance area and to enhance or alter the apparent form of scenery, objects, and actors. A major cue to our perception of three-dimensional form is the play of light and shadow over surfaces. Texture is basically a question of three-dimensionality on a small scale and is similarly dependent on lighting angle and degree of diffusion. Our judgment of the size or extent of a space depends on how much of it is lit, and without other visual cues we tend to interpret darkness as a void without spatial limitation. Emphasizing different surfaces with light can change the apparent ratio of height to depth to width, and the stage can appear deeper or more shallow by changing gradations of color and intensity.

The great contribution of Adolph Appia to the aesthetics of lighting design was his articulation of the principle that changing lights on three-dimensional forms altered the appearance of those forms. This idea transformed scenic design from a two-dimensional painter's art into a sculptural time art where the form of the stage space could change through time just as the play or opera develops in time. *Mise-en-scène* could no longer be satisfied with mere illumination to reveal the painted light on a flat surface. The New Stagecraft was born and with it, the art of lighting design. The stage was conceived not just as a painted background or a realistic environment but as a form in space to be brought to life with changing light.

Focusing Attention. Determining the relative attention-getting value of elements in the visual field. This is often considered a matter of brightness, but other factors may have equal or greater power to attract attention. As we shall see, certain colors draw attention more readily than others. Specular rather than diffused lighting, areas of high light-dark contrast, lighting angles which produce abnormal shadows, moving lights, unusually large or small areas of light, and repeated patterns of light are among the many ways of creating focus.

A visual field without focus is anathema to any art form and produces boredom. The need for focus is so strong that in a generally amorphous composition, the eye will seize upon the slightest variation or cue for attention. The challenge, therefore, is always to be in control of the focus, to be sure

that it is placed where it best serves the purposes of the production at that moment.

Obviously stage blocking, the flow of dialogue, costumes, scenic design, and many other factors contribute to the organization of the audience's attention. The lighting design must work in harmony with these other elements. If the focus created by light is not synchronized with the area where the audience feels the need to focus, the lighting will be distracting. Even the various senses may be in conflict. An extremely rich visual stimulus can compete with a strong need to hear. It is the ultimate responsibility of the director or choreographer to orchestrate all elements controlling focus.

Composition of the Stage Picture. The arrangement of light to create an overall visual design. Light must strike some object in order to be seen. Even though the lighting designer occasionally works on a plane surface—a projection screen or flat stage floor—or may sometimes encounter air with enough dust or moisture in it for a beam of light to be seen, in most cases composition begins with elements provided by other members of the production team. Because of this, the idea prevails that composition is not a primary concern of the lighting designer. Writings on scenic design will usually devote considerable attention to matters of composition, but the subject receives only passing mention in lighting books. And yet, the lighting designer is the ultimate determiner of the stage composition. No other visual element will work without light and all elements can be changed, enhanced, disrupted, or harmonized by light.

The moving performer is at once the greatest compositional asset and the most uncontrollable compositional element. Numerous scenic designers, including Gordon Craig and Robert Edmond Jones, have rendered very effective designs based primarily upon light striking human figures. But what if the figures move? The composition changes. Dancers provide a higher degree of predictability in movement during performance, but actors are notoriously prone to change blocking. The lighting designer may be tempted to support Craig's cry to remove actors from the stage so they don't interfere with the design. But there are alternatives.

The lighting designer simply does not have absolute control over all compositional elements in the way that a painter does. Onstage, light uses static or predictable elements to create a compositional context in which the moving human figure may play a part. The analogous artistic medium is perhaps the mobile, a composition in which all parts may change within limitations.

On an even more practical level, the lighting designer who is aware of compositional objectives and can communicate these to the director and actors, is likely to receive a good deal of cooperation in accomplishing the desired effect if it serves the production.

Elements of composition are variously classified and will be considered in more detail in Chapters 5, 6, and 7. In a sense, all controllable properties of light can be taken as the elements of composition; but more specifically, composition deals principally with light in a spatial context and includes considerations of size and proportion, line and axial direction, shape and pattern, gradation and tonal value, harmony and contrast, and texture, focus, balance, rhythm, and dynamics.

All elements of composition influence one another. It is almost impossible to perceive any one aspect of a visual field without being influenced by its context. Isolation of components is for the convenience of analysis and control, but composition is essentially a synthetic act. It is the putting together of all visual aspects of a production to create a unified whole.

Establishing Rhythm. The structure of lighting changes through time. A static composition establishes rhythm by movement of the eye over space or by the order in which we view parts of the visual field; but with theatre, the entire composition changes in time. Rhythm may be created by movement of the performers, by changes in the scenery, by the sound of music or the cadences of spoken language, by the rise and fall of dramatic tension, and by light. Here again, the lighting designer must work in cooperation with other production components, but factors as simple as the speed with which lighting cues are executed can enhance or destroy the overall rhythm of a production.

Establishing Style. The reinforcement with light of the distinctive or unique mode of presentation of a production. To some extent every production has its characteristic style, and the lighting should be adapted to that particular production. But we can also group many productions which share stylistic features. These major styles are frequently described in terms of "isms": classicism, realism, expressionism, surrealism, cubism, and so forth. Directors, actors, and scene designers are more comfortable with these designations than are lighting designers, and many lighting designs fail because they clash with the overall style of production. The lighting may be limited to realistic effects in a performance which has otherwise moved beyond realism, or unmotivated lighting may destroy the illusion of an otherwise naturalistic production.

Naturalism or the establishment of realistic effects is often considered a major function of stage lighting, but this is true only if the production aims for realism. The art of modern stage lighting developed in a period when realism dominated the theatre, and we still too often limit ourselves to realistic approaches when they are unjustified by the overall production concept.

Lighting can make as clear a stylistic statement as any other production concept, and Chapters 8 and 9 will explore in detail the lighting approaches suitable for the major theatrical styles.

Setting a Mood. Using light to stimulate a specific emotional response by the viewer. Lighting for mood is frequently described as "atmosphere" and discussed in terms of "lightness" and "seriousness" or of "comic" and "tragic," but a whole range of possible responses lie between or outside of these extremes. Our language shows the extent to which light influences our moods. Consider the number of words we use interchangeably to describe both states of mind and qualities of visual experience: light, bright, somber, gloomy, dull, shadowy, lurid, dreary, bleak, drab, brilliant, radiant, lustrous, beaming, and so forth.

Because of the subjectivity of these responses and the difficulty of measuring or predicting them, we must approach the entire question of the emotional responses to light with considerable chariness, but this does not justify passing easily over these effects. Audiences will respond emotionally to light—any light; the only question is the degree to which we can control these responses.

The "theatricality" of light is also an important consideration here, or to state it in another way, no matter what the mood created in the theatre, it must be a theatrical mood. In *The Dramatic Imagination,* Robert Edmond Jones declared, "Our purpose must be to give by means of light an impression of something out of the ordinary, away from the mediocre, to make the performance exist in an ideal world of wisdom and understanding."[3] He further described this light as "lucid," "penetrating," and "aware."

Creating the theatrical mood, however, does not translate to the designer asking, "Should I use a fresnel or an ellipsoidal spotlight for penetrating light?" There is no simple equation between lighting hardware and lighting design. One has only to look at Jones' renderings to see that he could transform his metaphors into practical lighting. But he began with a vision, with a visual image, a design, and worked back to the means of accomplishing it.

We must begin by understanding light, vision, and design. Only then can we select our instruments, color media, and level settings.

Psychophysical Considerations: Light, the Eye, the Brain, and Brightness

Stage lighting might better be called "stage seeing." The designer controls what the audience sees. The uninformed observer accepts seeing as a simple response to an objective reality. He believes that what he sees is a blue sofa and would not find it helpful if we hastened to correct this mistaken impression, pointing out that what he is really experiencing is a cerebral response to nerve impulses triggered by the photoelectric sensitivity of his retina to an inverted image refracted by his pupil from electromagnetic waves selectively reflected by a sofa.

What an audience sees as a homogenous experience actually has multiple components, each of which influences the nature of that experience: light is reflected from an object, received by the eye, and converted into impulses which the brain registers. The emission and reflection of light might be considered the domain of physics; the action of the eye, a question of physiology; and the response of the brain, a matter for psychology.

The lighting designer is interested in the physical and physiological aspects of seeing only as they lead to an understanding of the mental responses. The word "psychophysics" describes this subject.

We will touch briefly on the nature of light and the eye, then investigate in some detail how the complex process of seeing influences the designer's use of intensity, color, and space.

THE NATURE OF LIGHT

Wave Length

In spite of its importance to our lives, scientists disagree as to whether light should be considered simply a form of energy or a substance composed of infinitesimal particles. This is a minor issue for our purposes. All visual phenomena of importance to a lighting designer can be explained if we consider light to be energy emitted by a radiant body.

The important point for us is that this radiant energy pulsates or travels in waves with crests of high intensity and troughs of low intensity. This pulsation could be expressed in terms of time: so many pulses per second; but radiant energy travels at about 186,000 miles per second. The time measures are so extremely small that it is more convenient to speak of wavelength: the distance energy travels between pulses.

Radiating bodies may emit energy in wavelengths ranging from smaller than .000000001 of a millimeter to thousands of kilometers. This full range of energy is called the electromagnetic spectrum and includes cosmic, gamma, and X-rays; ultraviolet and infra-red light; radar; television and radio waves; and electricity. What we normally call light is the visible portion of this spectrum, which includes waves ranging in length from about 4/10,000 to 7/10,000 of a millimeter (Plate I). In ideal viewing conditions, some individuals may see light from 3/10,000 to 1/1,000 of a millimeter in wavelength, but the shorter range covers the full sensitivity of the normal eye.

For ease of notation, these wavelengths are usually expressed in millimicrons (mμ), which are 1/1,000,000,000 of a meter, or in Angstrom units (Å), which are 1/10 of a millimicron. The visible spectrum ranges from 400 to 700 mμ or from 4000 to 7000 Å.

Isaac Newton discovered that a narrow beam of white light passing through a prism spread over a full spectrum of color, and subsequent studies found that specific colors were produced by particular wavelengths. However, as we shall discover, the relationship between wavelength and perceived color is not a simple one-to-one correspondence. The wavelength of light is related to perceived color but not in a simple fashion.

Measures of Intensity

Light of any given wavelength may occur with different degrees of intensity. From a perceptual perspective, we describe this as brightness. In physical terms, this may be thought of as the amplitude of the waves, the quantity of energy, or the amount of luminous flux. Again, the physical phenomenon correlates with the visual perception but in a complex relationship. A given amount of light energy does not always appear to be the same brightness; however, studies of light perception usually require some constant measure of objective illumination, using one of the following units of measure:

UNITS FOR MEASURING ILLUMINATION

Foot-candle—the direct illumination on a surface everywhere one foot from a special candle of carefully controlled dimensions.

Candela or *candle*—a more modern unit of luminous intensity equal to 1/60 of the luminous intensity of a black body heated to 1773.5°C (the temperature at which platinum solidifies).

Lumen (lm)—the quantity of light falling on one square foot of a screen at a distance of one foot from a candela.

Lux or *meter candle*—one lumen per square meter or .0929 (1/10.764) foot-candles. A lux is a lumen converted to a metric scale.

Milliphot—ten lux.

Phot—10,000 lux.

Apostilb(asb)—.00003183 candela per square centimeter.

Stilb—one candela per square centimeter.

Nit—one candela per square meter.

Lambert—one lumen per square centimeter or 2.054 candelas per square inch.

Footlambert—one lumen per square foot or .00221 candelas per square inch, i.e. the luminance of a perfectly reflecting surface receiving an illumination of one foot-candle.

merous examples of good lighting in the theatre and a few bad examples; to scenic designers with an eye for light; and to illumination engineers and psychologists who conducted basic research in lighting. My specific indebtedness is indicated in acknowledgments accompanying figures and illustrations, footnotes, and the bibliography.

I particularly appreciate a sabbatical leave given by Washington University, which allowed me to begin work on this book, and the support of my colleagues at the College of William and Mary: Christopher J. Boll, Louis Catron, Jerry Bledsoe, and Bruce McConachie. Professor Cameron Harvey, the School of Fine Arts at the University of California-Irvine; Professor John Williams, the Theatre Department at Northwestern University; Professor Robert Shakespeare, the Department of Theatre/Fine Arts Center at the University of Massachusetts; and the Theatrical Lighting consultant Geo Ulnic all reviewed the book while it was still in manuscript form, and I'd like to thank each and every one of them for their suggestions and criticisms. My wife, Rebecca Palmer, provided encouragement, editorial assistance, and a layman's eye. My children, Virginia, Zachary, and Katherine, have had to tiptoe at appropriate times for years and surely deserve mention.

Richard H. Palmer
College of William and Mary

The normal range of intensity with which the lighting designer deals is from approximately 10,000 foot-candles, the brightness of snow or white clouds on a bright day, to 0.000001 foot-candles, the least perceptible brightness that can be seen in optimum conditions. A bright level of artificial illumination is 100 foot-candles, but it is possible to read with less than one foot-candle of light. The average stage illumination is about 50 foot-candles.

Because the eye responds to relative rather than absolute brightness, these measurements are more important to an understanding of the principles of lighting than they are to the practical design of stage lighting for an audience.

The Inverse Square Law

The intensity of light varies in inverse proportion to the square of the distance from its source. In other words, a spotlight 100 feet from a stage will create a beam one-fourth the intensity of the same spotlight 50 feet away. However, the size of the area lit by the more distant light will be four times as large; so energy is not lost, just spread over a larger space. The inverse square law predicts the diminishing intensity for a fixed area of illumination, not the total light output of the instrument.

We must further qualify this law when the intensity is measured on a surface which is not perpendicular to an axis drawn between the light source and the surface. Most stage lights strike surfaces at an angle, which results in further loss of intensity at any point. This illumination is proportional to the cosine of the angle made between the axis of the beam and a line perpendicular to the surface, divided by the square of the distance ($\cos O/D^2$).

The appearance of a pool of light striking a surface at an angle is further complicated by the fact that all points within the pool are not equidistant from the light source and those further away are therefore less bright.

Indeed, even if the axis of the beam were at right angles to the surface and the beam were of uniform intensity, it would lose some brightness at the edges of the pool on a flat surface because those edges are slightly further from the light source than the center of the pool. Only a spherically concave surface with the light source at the focus of the sphere would produce a uniformly lit surface.

Under normal circumstances, the eye is not sensitive enough to these gradual changes of intensity within a pool of light for them to be noticeable, and the unevenness caused by poor focus or the poor optics of the instruments is likely to be more bothersome.

The inverse square law is an important measure of the loss of brightness as the distance increases between the light source and the object being illuminated, but what about the distance between that object and the eye of the observer? Even though the intensity of light reaching the eyes decreases with the square of the distance, the area of the image on the retina becomes proportionately smaller. Although more light reflected from the object reaches the eye when we are closer to the object, that light is spread over a larger retinal image. As long as the lit object is more than 7 inches away, its perceived intensity will not vary significantly as the observer becomes more distant. When we talk about lighting for the back row of seats, we are therefore correcting for loss of visual acuity, not for diminishing brightness.

THE EYE

A person with normal vision can see the light from a standard candle 27km away, can detect differences in color produced by variations in wave length of 0.0000014 cm, and can distinguish a line of less than 1/8 in. width from a distance of sixty feet. At the same time the eye cannot focus simultaneously presented areas of intense red and blue, cannot accurately differentiate the components of a color mixture, and persists in seeing a variety of visual phenomena for which there is no direct external stimulus.

What characteristics of the eye account for this marvelous mixture of acuity and inaccuracy?

Useful comparisons are frequently made between the eye and a camera. Both have a lens to gather light and refocus it as an inverted image on a light sensitive area: the film of the camera, the retina of the eye. Just as the shutter of a camera may be adjusted to control the amount of light entering the camera by adjusting the size of the aperture, the eye's iris opens and closes according to the intensity of the light. The distance between the camera lens and the film is adjusted to focus objects at various distances, and in an analogous way the ciliary muscles change the shape of the crystalline lens and cornea to focus objects at different distances.

The retina contains photosensitive chemicals (rhodopsin) as does the film, and in both cases the amount of resolution possible is partly a product of the physical size of the receptors. The retina is covered with 75 to 150 million "rods," which are sensitive to small amounts of light but make practically no color discrimination, and 6 or 7 million "cones," which are principally responsible for color vision. The cones are more densely packed in the central area of the retina (the fovea) and as a consequence, day vision is much more acute in the center of the eye, night vision at the perimeter. However, because the eye is almost constantly moving, this difference has little practical effect outside of the laboratory or a nighttime foxhole.

The lens of the eye produces chromatic aberration just like an uncorrected camera lens. The varying thickness of a lens and the varying relationship between the angles of its two surfaces result in light of different wavelengths being bent to different degrees, particularly at the edge of the lens.

Short wavelengths are bent more than long; so blue light will focus nearer the lens than red light. As a consequence the eye cannot focus simultaneously on the elements of a sharply defined pattern of intense red and blue, a phenomenon used by many modern artists to create disturbingly pulsating paintings.

A designer recently used interestingly composed projections to introduce the titles of mime pieces. The titles were in red and blue lettering against blocks of the opposite color. When the projections first appeared, they seemed out of focus for a few seconds while the eye tried to decide which color should be focused on. Because the letters contained the important information, the color of the lettering was eventually selected (e.g., red letters against a blue block), but in the meantime everyone assumed something was wrong with the projection equipment that took so long to focus the image. The blurring was in the eyes of the audience, not the projectors.

Chromatic aberration also accounts for the frequent fuzziness of purple objects. As we shall see, certain purples and magentas do not exist in the natural spectrum and can be created only by combining red and blue lights from the two ends of the spectrum. If these two wavelengths are pure enough, the lens of the eye focuses them at different points, resulting in an indistinct image. If you want to blur the world, try magenta lights.

The pupil, as we all know, dilates when illumination suddenly falls and contracts when we encounter sudden brightness. However, unlike the iris diaphragm of a camera, there is no ideal or fixed relationship in the eye between pupil size and brightness. The ratio of the area of the pupil opening from its maximum dilation to its maximum contraction is about sixteen to one, but the range of intensity of illumination in which the eye can comfortably see is in excess of one-million to one; so the variation in pupil size can account for only a portion of our adaptation to varying brightness.

The pupil, in fact, functions like an over-load buffer to only temporarily offset the effects of sudden intensity changes. After several minutes of exposure to a given level of illumination, the pupil returns nearly to its "normal" diameter. It also contracts much faster than it dilates, and its diameter can be influenced by many things other than light level: drugs, emotion, and age, for example. The principal means of adaptation to brightness occurs in the retina and, as we shall see, in the brain.

THE BRAIN

If the photography metaphor is pursued, the brain is the darkroom of the eye. Just as the darkroom technician can interpret, correct, and distort the data collected on film in all sorts of ways, our brains take the impulses generated by the retina and translate them into visual experience. When we consider the quantity and complexity of information we must assimilate, interpret, and act upon for even the simplest visual tasks, the capacity of the brain is awe inspiring. Most of the basic research in perceptual psychology has attempted to unravel the mechanisms for rudimentary perceptual processes: depth perception, the constancy of the visual field, and the ability to distinguish between a surface and its illuminant, for example. We will concentrate only on aspects which involve variables important to the lighting designer: intensity, color of the illuminant, and the use of light to enhance spatial perception.

The brain is not a neutral responder to information conveyed by the eye. The brain imposes what has been called an "experience filter" on this raw data so it can impose order on the multiplicity of sensations and make new encounters conform to previous experience. For example, if we expect a banana to be yellow, we will persist in seeing it as yellow even though it reflects no physical light which would normally be described as yellow.

There is also a "need filter" that selects information required to satisfy our immediate physical and emotional demands. For instance, even though attention is fundamentally phototropic (drawn to light), if we are threatened by something in shadow, that is where the focus of our attention will be. A single level of illumination around us may appear bright or dim, depending on whether we want to be seen or how much we need to see.

There is even subjective seeing: vision without external stimuli. Some of this, such as afterimages, subjective colors, and autokinetic perception of moving light can be easily explained, but what is the external stimulus for dreams or visions?

Even though the reactions of the mind to our experience of light are extremely complex and may vary from individual to individual or from situation to situation, there are predictable, and in some cases, measurable factors which influence the manner in which we respond to light. These are obviously important elements in the lighting designer's art and will occupy much of our further discussion.

BRIGHTNESS

Effect of Brightness on Visual Acuity

Much of the research on the influence of light on vision deals with thresholds, the minimum amount of light that can be seen or the minimum light required for specified visual tasks. Numerous variables influence the threshold point: the length of adaptation to darkness, the duration of the light, the size of the lit object, the color of the light, and the type of background contrast. We see better at lower levels of illumination when our eyes have had time to adjust to darkness, when the light is sustained and either full spectrum white or a hue near the middle of the spectrum, and when the object viewed is large and in high contrast with its background.

A lighting designer is usually concerned with thresholds of intensity only in order to stay below them for true blackouts or to keep portions of the stage unseen when other areas are lit. Movements of actors or stagehands during blackouts, for example, are less likely to be seen if they occur immediately after a bright level of illumination, if exit lights in the auditorium or offstage trouble lights are colors at the end of the spectrum, and if there is little contrast between the human figures and the background. With the normal amount of ambient light in an auditorium during a blackout, stagehands setting props in front of an unlit white cyclorama may be less noticeable dressed in light colors rather than black.

Once we are above the threshold of vision, the next question is how much can visual acuity be improved with increased illumination—or how much light is enough? Studies have found direct relationships between the level of illumination and the effi-

ciency of workers or children in the classroom, yet there is a law of diminishing returns that influences these results. The graph in Figure 2-1 shows acuity for this specific task to be 57 percent at 1 footlambert, 78 percent at 10, and 81 percent at 20, but the difference between 100 and 110 footlamberts increases acuity only by 0.1 percent. Above about 10 footlamberts the amount of illumination must be almost doubled for each step of significant improvement in acuity. In addition, a fair degree of brightness, around 100 footlamberts, may produce fatigue, and many of the effects of brightness, as we shall later see, are offset by the adaptation of the eye.

The question of the maximum desired level of brightness has serious economic implications both in and out of the theatre. The difference between industrial standards that require 100 lumens and standards that require 50 lumens of light amounts to billions of dollars in lighting fixtures, lamps, and energy consumption. Doubling the intensity of stage lighting for one production may require the rental or purchase of a large number of additional in-

FIGURE 2-1 The relationship between brightness and task efficiency. The horizontal scale is logarithmic. Efficiency improves very little above 10 footlamberts and virtually not at all above 100. [From William M. Lam, *Perception and Light as Formgivers* (New York: McGraw Hill Book Co., 1977), p. 62. Used by permission of the publisher.]

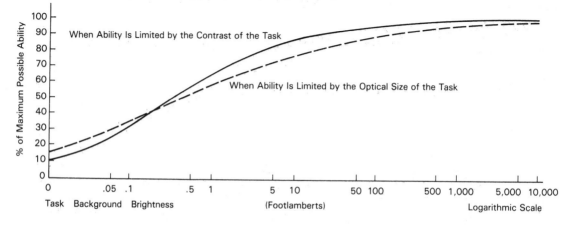

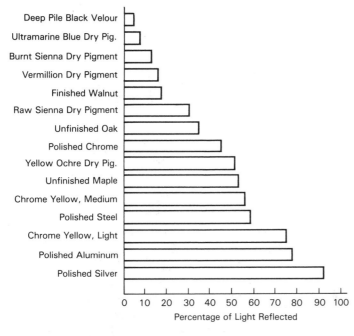

FIGURE 2-2 The percentage of light reflected by different surfaces. Percentages vary considerably according to the color of the light source and the angle of incidence. These figures assume sunlight perpendicular to the surface.

struments with corollary consumption of lamps and electricity.

If adequate time is allowed for adaptation, a candlelit production can be quite satisfactory for even a modern audience accustomed to high levels of artificial light. There may be some loss of detail, but in certain conditions this can be offset by the mood created by low level illumination. I have seen a candlelit performance of *The Second Shepherd's Play* in which the light was not only adequate, but the shimmering quality of candlelight gave a certain vibrancy that helped compensate for static moments in the script.

Visual acuity is, of course, not the only objective of bright lighting. The so-called "jewel lighting" of many Broadway productions uses bright lights far in excess of what is needed to assure good visibility. The objective is to enhance the theatricalism or create a vibrant mood, and the appeal is the same as the glitter of crystal, which will be discussed later.

The designer must also be wary of equating brightness with the light that strikes the stage. Since the perception of brightness is the product of light reflected from stage surfaces, the percentage of reflection may vary from almost zero for a dark velour curtain to 90 percent for a highly reflective white surface. The chart in Figure 2-2 gives a sampling of reflection factors for various materials, but a quick reading with a light meter of light reflected from various objects onstage will show how wide this range is. This is why it is so risky to set stage light levels without a fully painted and dressed stage or even without costumed performers in makeup.

Designers encounter questions of acuity and brightness again when they seem to have too few instruments to light the stage brightly enough for the audience to see well. The ideal lighting plots provided in many texts ignore the limited resources of many community, college, and small commercial theatres; nor do they mention the constant tradeoff between the need for brightness and the desire to use what instruments are on hand in selective groupings at various times during a performance to gain as much flexibility as possible in the control of color, area, or direction of light.

In general, the best way to achieve the highest level of visibility with the least amount of light, or a limited inventory of instruments, is to minimize brightness adaptation and to maximize other aids for acuity such as high figure-ground contrast, concentration of the light source, color contrast, and form-revealing beam directions. These features will be discussed in more detail later.

Brightness and Darkness Adaptation

We can see comfortably in both moonlight and sunlight, although the relative brightness of the two is of the order of one to one million. Thus we see in a tremendous range of brightness levels—but not all at once: at any given moment we have a much narrower compass of sensitivity. After exposure to a given level of illumination for a sufficient period of time, the eye accepts that level as normal and all other intensities are seen relative to that norm, which is called the *brightness adaptation level*. At a certain point below this level, called the *black point*, all stimuli will be seen as black. This level rises as the brightness adaptation level rises, or to state it in other terms, our sensitivity to low levels of illumination decreases as the overall level of brightness increases (see Figure 2-3). However, we see a wider range of brightness as the adaptation level rises. The range of intensity the eye can appreciate is about one thousand to one in full daylight, but only of the order of ten to one at the lowest levels of intensity.

Our perception of white and gray is also relative to the adaptation level. In a field of vision, the brightest nonselective reflecting surface that is not a light source will appear white. A nonselective surface is one which reflects light of the same color that strikes it, regardless of the color. Any nonselective surface that is not the brightest in the field will appear gray, or if there is no other nonselective surface of lower intensity, it

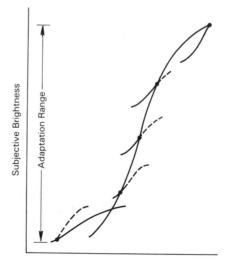

Logarithm of Intensity

FIGURE 2-3 Changes in the adaptation level of the eye. A schematic diagram showing how the range of discernible intensities varies as the brightness adaption level changes. The short curved lines represent the range of brightness perceived at any given level of brightness adaptation. [W. H. Marshall and S. A. Talbot, *Biological Symposia* 7 (The Jacques Cattell Press), p. 130.]

will appear black even though its brightness is above the black point. In addition, a colored surface with a brightness lower than the white in a field will appear to contain gray.

The eye generally adapts to the average brightness of a field of vision, but if it concentrates on one part of that field it tends to adapt to the brightness of that part. If we wish to see something that is in shadow, for example, we see increasingly more detail in the shadowed area the longer we look at it. Inversely, concentration on a bright object will lower sensitivity to less well-illuminated areas.

Our perception of absolute brightness is a product of our adaptation level. An automobile headlight that is hardly noticeable in daylight can seem blindingly bright if our eyes are adapted to darkness. A level that seems bright at first will appear normal with the passage of time. Our judgment of brightness is therefore a product of the relative intensity of a stimulus in the visual field, or of our previous level of adaptation.

The eye may be considered a "null" instrument which makes poor judgments of the absolute quantity of illumination but perceives "more" and "less" brightness fairly accurately. However, even relative judgments are based on ratios and relationships rather than absolute differences in intensity. At levels of intensity less than one foot-candle, it requires a higher ratio of intensity between two levels of brightness for us to perceive the difference. Of course the absolute difference in terms of foot-candles is fairly small at these low levels. At normal intensity levels for vision, the eye indicates constant changes when the stimuli are changed at constant ratios. In other words, we see one object as twice as bright as another when it reflects twice as much light, regardless of the absolute difference in terms of foot-candles. A difference of 20 foot-candles will be twice as bright if the less intense object is reflecting 20 foot-candles but only half again as bright if the less intense object reflects 40 foot-candles (see Figure 2-4).

Time considerations are also important to brightness adaptation. The eye requires time to adjust to a major change in the level of illumination. The time required and the consequent loss of visual efficiency during the interval is greater going from bright to dark than the opposite, but there is no discomfort. In going from dark to bright, the greater brightness increases visual efficiency, and adaptation is faster, but discomfort more often results from the excessive innervation of the iris muscle.

With darkness adaptation, sensitivity increases significantly within the first 30 seconds, but maximum sensitivity does not come for 45 minutes to an hour. Cone function adapts more quickly, reaching maximum within 10 minutes, but rod sensitivity

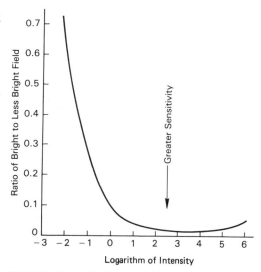

FIGURE 2-4 Brightness differentiation at different brightness levels. A greater ratio of brightness difference is required for the brightness difference to be noticeable at lower levels of intensity. However, the difference in absolute brightness is smaller at the lower intensity. [Leonard T. Troland, *The Principles of Psychophysiology,* vol. II (New York: D. Van Nostrand Co., 1930), p. 78.]

requires more time (Figure 2-5). After half an hour, sensitivity is 1,000 to 100,000 times greater than it was at the beginning of the adaptation period.

Dark adaptation is fairly persistent, and moderate increases in intensity produce only a slow destruction of dark adaptation. If we cover one eye for half an hour while the other is exposed to light, then uncover that eye, it will remain more sensitive for nearly an hour. There is a direct relationship between the slowness with which we recover dark adaptation and the length of time we are exposed to a brighter light (see Figure 2-6). Prolonged exposure to a high level of brightness also retards subsequent dark adaptation.

The rate of dark adaptation is also influenced by the color of the light to which the eye has been previously adapted. For

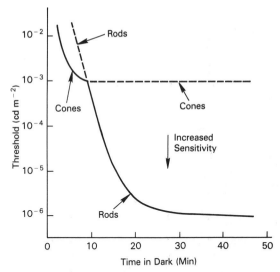

FIGURE 2-5   The increase of dark adaptation with time. Maximum sensitivity is almost reached within 25 minutes. The broken lines are hypothetical continuations of rod and cone function. [From C. A. Padgham and J. E. Saunders, *The Perception of Light and Colour* (New York: Academic Press, 1975), p. 41.]

wavelengths longer than 650 mμ (red), the longer the wavelength to which the eye adapts, the faster the rate of subsequent adaptation. This is why the so-called "battle lights" used by the Navy for night combat are red. They interfere less with subsequent night vision than other light colors or white light.

The practical effects of brightness adaptation for the stage lighting designer are numerous. The maximum contrast between highlights and darkness is attained at high levels of adaptation; however, more light will be required to create a sense of the relative brightness of one area at higher levels of adaptation.

Concentration on objects or persons in a bright pool of light will decrease sensitivity to other areas of the stage less brightly lit and will make low-intensity areas appear black. Visibility in a low-illumination area will be enhanced when the eye is adapted to

an overall low level of brightness. The effect of a bright pool of light is further enhanced if the eye is adapted to a lower level of illumination.

The effect of brightness for a constant level of light diminishes with time; therefore, the effect of constant brightness requires a regular increase in the level of illumination and the effect of increased brightness requires either a disproportionate increase in illumination or an intervening period of lower illumination. The maximum effect of brightness is obtained the longer the audience has had to adapt to a lower intensity level and the darker that previous level has been. A bright preset or bright house lights, for example, will diminish the impact of an opening scene which is intended to be bright. The brightness could be enhanced by adapting the audience to red light, but this may have limited application outside of nightclub entertainment.

A dark scene following a bright one or a shift in visual focus from a bright to a darker area will make the dark scene at first appear disproportionately dim with an ac-

FIGURE 2-6   The recovery of darkness adaption after a period of intervening brightness. Line *A* represents a low-level sensitivity to brightness. Line *B* represents the sensitivity immediately after viewing a bright source. The time above each curved line indicates the duration of the bright interval. Recovery comes faster for a shorter interval of brightness. [From Ralph M. Evans, *An Introduction to Color* (New York: John Wiley & Sons, 1948), p. 126.]

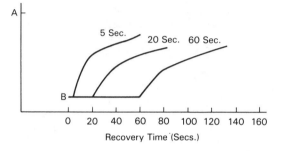

companying loss of visual acuity. If bright scenes or effects intrude into lower-intensity lighting, the shorter their duration, the less will be their subsequent effect on visibility. Also, rapid progression from dark to bright scenes may produce eye fatigue.

Because of the progressive desensitizing of the eye to brightness, a lighting design should progress from darker to increasingly brighter scenes unless some special effect of gloom or poor visibility is desired.

Brightness Contrast

Because the eye adapts to the overall level of brightness, a bright object in a dark field will appear disproportionately brighter than it would in a bright field. Over 450 years ago, Leonardo da Vinci observed, "If you mean to represent great darkness, it must be done by contrasting it with great light; on the contrary, if you want to produce great brightness, you must oppose to it a very dark shade." The smaller the area of brightness is or the larger the ratio between darkness and brightness, the greater will be the enhancement. However, the contrast of an excessively small, bright area may produce glare fatigue as we will discuss later. There is evidence that excessive contrasts will reduce visual efficiency when the bright field is smaller than 30° (e.g., a pool of light 15 feet in diameter from a viewing distance of 60 feet).[1] Visual efficiency is at a maximum when the brightness of the central field is equal to that of the surroundings, but maximum acuity is not necessarily the goal of the stage lighting designer.

The difference in the apparent brightness of any two surfaces is exaggerated if they are adjacent, and the effect is maximized if a relatively small area of one is surrounded by the other. This is known as *brightness contrast.*

The discrepancy between adaptation level and the brightness of a small field is not the sole explanation for brightness contrast. Apparent brightness is also enhanced by surrounding the bright surface with a thin, dark line that could not significantly influence the adaptation level. Shadow lines on moldings, for example, exaggerate highlights in this way.

With a sharp boundary between two areas of uniform but noticeably different brightness, luminosity appears higher within the brighter area where it is adjacent to the darker area. For example, when there are two adjacent squares of light at different intensity levels, the brighter of the two appears even brighter still near the edge of the less intense area.

The important factor here is a sharp boundary. The eye is fairly insensitive to changes in stimuli in which no parts of the retina undergo rapid changes in illumination; therefore, a gradual transition from high to low luminousness appears indistinguishable from a uniform field, but a sharp boundary between two fields aids in distinguishing them. A more uniform wash of light is therefore produced by spotlights with soft edges, either fresnels or ellipsoidals with diffusion gel. No matter how carefully ellipsoidals are shuttered, the sharp edges exaggerate any intensity differences.

Brightness as a Factor in Focus and Distraction

Because we are phototropic, the eye tends to concentrate attention or focus on the brightest object in a field of vision. Experience, however, conditions this focus. For example, the sun outside or a light indoors may not attract particular attention because we expect it to be where it is and discount its presence. However, we judge a source of brightness which has no perceivable reason for being where it is as "too bright."

Brightness distracts when it is not consistent with other incentives for visual attention. The only difference between focus and distraction is that the latter term describes a stimulus for attention that draws the viewer somewhere other than where he or she wants to look.

A large distracting area of low brightness draws steady attention more readily than a small source of high brightness. Eye movements in the presence of a distraction of relatively low brightness covering a large area consist of a series of fairly slow traverses toward the distracting source where the gaze stays for several seconds at a time. Eye movements toward a small source of high brightness (a glaring spotlight) consist of jerky darts with the gaze never fixed for more than a fraction of a second at a time.[2]

Distraction may generate tension and, as a consequence, may be a valuable theatrical tool when used carefully. An illumination engineer struggles to eliminate distracting sources of brightness in order to create a visual environment in harmony with the needs of the viewer, but the stage lighting designer may not want visual harmony. The use of brightness or any other source of distraction for dramatic purposes must be justified by the dramatic context of the production. Attention called to the distracting light per se may intrude technique into substance.

A good example of the use of distracting brightness to create dramatic tension is with foreshadowing, or we might say "fore-brightening." A person, object, or area of the stage involved indirectly or ironically in the action or about to play a more prominent place in the action is gradually brightened. Such "distracting brightness" could be used for Banquo's empty chair at the beginning of the banquet scene in *Macbeth* or for the dueling pistols with which Hedda will kill herself.

A shift of focus in a dramatic production is really a progression from distraction to split focus to a new focus. In concrete terms, rather than use a cross fade to shift the focus, the brightness of the new focus or source of distraction is increased until it becomes primary, and the old focus decreases in brightness.

Glare

Glare is a distracting source of brightness interfering with our need to see: too much light in our eyes. In general it comes either as a result of brightness raising our adaptation level so that objects we need to see are near or below the black point, as an overall level of brightness that obscures fine gradations of contrast which we need to see, or as brightness occurring so rapidly that we do not have time to adapt to the higher level.

"Blinding glare" is so intense that for a significant length of time no object can be seen. "Direct glare" is produced by unshielded light sources in the field of vision. "Reflected glare" results from specular reflections of high brightness in polished or glossy surfaces. "Veiling glare" results from reflections which partially or totally obscure the details of an object by reducing necessary contrast.

A frequent source of glare in the theatre comes from lighting instruments facing the audience. This is a particular problem in arena or three-quarter staging where front lights for one part of the audience are back lights for another part.

Glare can be reduced by increasing the angle between the glare source and the object being viewed, by increasing the brightness of the general background, by lowering the intensity of the glare source, by changing the size or diffusion of the glare source, and by concentrating the glare source in a horizontal rather than a vertical axis. We will discuss each of these methods in more detail.

Increased Angle. The further the glare is from our point of visual concentration, the less distracting it is. If we were to draw a line from our eyes to the object we wish to view and a second line from the glare source to our eyes, the angle of intersection between these two lines where they meet at our eyes is known as the glare angle. As Fig-

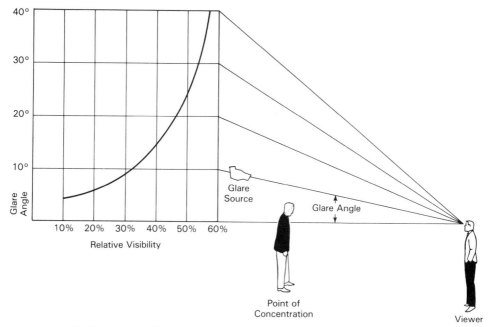

FIGURE 2-7 Relationship of relative visibility to glare angle. As the glare angle increases, a greater percentage of visual acuity results.

ure 2-7 shows, relative visibility increases significantly as the glare angle increases. This effect is even more accentuated for light bouncing off of a highly reflective horizontal surface when the glare is a result of both the source and the surface. Because the angle of reflection equals the angle of incidence, more light bounces over the head of the viewer for the higher angle at which the light strikes the surface. If the surface is mirrorlike or specular, the gain is even greater than for a diffuse surface, but virtually all surfaces reflect a greater percentage of light at the angle of reflection.

Background Lighting. Regular back lighting for a proscenium production is usually sufficiently masked and at a high enough angle to prevent serious glare problems. Increasing the vertical angle of lights for arena staging is more difficult because the back light for one side of the audience is front light for the other, and the higher angled front light may produce objectionable shadows under the brow and nose. A more-reflective-than-average floor compensates somewhat for these shadows and allows the instruments to be placed in higher positions, but the reflection may also disturb the audience.

If more light is placed in the background, the glare from a small source is reduced. A higher general surrounding brightness, that is less brightness contrast between the glare source and the surrounding area, raises the adaptation level and reduces glare discomfort.

Lowered Intensity. Lowering the intensity of a glare source also improves visibility, but the important consideration is the ratio between the glaring light and other forms of illumination. In other words, increasing the level of front illumination decreases the effect of glare. The problem in arena staging is that increased front illumination for one part of the audience may mean an increase in the intensity of the offending source of glare for another part of the audience.

In the theatre, the most effective way to reduce glare intensity is by carefully focusing instruments. Even though lenses and color media radiate some light, looking at most spotlights is like looking down the mouth of a tube. Intensity drops rapidly as one moves away from the central axis of the instrument. Instruments with short focal lengths, floodlights, and spotlights with diffusion filters are more likely to create glare problems outside of their central axes. Recessed lenses, top hats, and barn doors on instruments help to focus the beam and eliminate glare from peripheral light.

Size and Diffusion. The effects of glare also relate to the size of the glare source. Glare increases directly in relation to the apparent size of the source, and the effect of a number of sources equals that of one large source of the same brightness and total area. An attempt to reduce glare by spreading out instruments visible to the audience may only increase visual fatigue by enlarging the size of the glare source. However, the larger the size of the source, the less the reduction in brightness necessary to reduce comfort by the same amount.[3]

Horizontal Axis. Long sources of glare give more discomfort if mounted vertically than if mounted horizontally.[4] It would seem that vertical mounting would place more of the source at a higher angle and reduce glare proportionately, but in fact horizontal mounting produces less glare, perhaps because habitual eye movement is sideways. Lights mounted vertically on stands are more prone to create glare than lights on horizontal battens.

Glare from specularly reflected images of light sources such as produced by polished metal, mylar, plexiglass, or glass, may be eliminated by adding diffuse illumination or by diffusing the offending light source. This glare is less easily suppressed when the brightness or angle of incidence of the light source increases. If adjustments cannot be made in the lighting, some manner of dulling the offending surface to reduce its reflectance may be the only recourse.

Even though glare is usually a problem to be eliminated or minimized, if carefully controlled it can be used for positive effects in the theatre. A so-called "light-curtain" works by illuminating moisture particles, dust, or artificial fog in the air to a sufficiently high level that anything upstage of it cannot be seen. Bright floodlights thrown directly into the eyes of the audience have the same effect. Glare can create tension or a sense of mystery by concealing what the audience wants to see. Supernatural or superterrestrial beings are often represented by a strong glare source. The persistent religious or mystical associations with a "blinding light" may be some vestige of the awe with which man has always viewed the sun. It is a great irony that our lives depend on the sun, a potential glare source so great that it can blind us.

Sparkle

High brightness ratios in the field of vision are not inherently undesirable if the viewer can justify the cause. Glitter and sparkle are forms of "attractive brightness"; they may limit visual acuity but are not objectionable unless a need to make fine visual discriminations outweighs aesthetic values. Light from reflective surfaces such as glass or mylar and the light from exposed lamps can create visual interest on stage. Sparkle always strongly draws attention and must be carefully controlled to avoid creating an unwanted focus.

Afterimages

One of the effects of an extreme source of brightness viewed for a period of time is to produce an afterimage, a continuation of sensation even after the stimulus has gone. Positive afterimages have the same appearance as the original stimulus and are brighter than a subsequent lower-intensity stimulus. Negative afterimages are either darker than the subsequent field of view or have colors complementary to the original stimulus (to be discussed in Chapter 3).

As shown in Figure 2-8, the persistence of an afterimage is longer in proportion to the intensity and duration of the source of stimulating brightness. For example, the afterimage of a stimulus of 100 C.P. (candlepower) exposed for one second, endures for about 8 seconds, but the afterimage of a stimulus of 1080 C.P. exposed for one second will endure for 45 seconds. In addition, the positive afterimage will remain brighter if the subsequent illumination level is bright, but it will disappear or "decay" faster than if the subsequent visual field is

dark. During decay, the afterimages for a white stimulus pass through a series of hues: blue-green, indigo, violet-pink, and dark orange. Then the afterimage will appear darker than the surroundings.

The most common occurrence of positive afterimages in theatre follows the rapid blackout of a bright scene. The sensation of lingering light is further accentuated by the overcompensation of the opening iris responding to the loss of illumination and the afterglow of incandescent lamps. It is much more difficult to achieve a sharp blackout of a brightly lit stage than with a lower illumination level.

Emphasizing the important prop or character with a lingering afterimage provides an interesting conclusion to a scene, particularly when a "lag fade" leaves just the object in a bright light for a moment, "setting" the afterimage. Alwin Nikolais used afterimages in combination with colored shadows as an arresting device in one of his dance pieces. There seems to be considerable variation from individual to individual in the perception and durability of afterimages, which limits their use on stage, and the presence of an uncontrolled afterimage can be a source of distraction in a subsequent scene, but afterimages represent one more possibility in the designer's arsenal of special effects.

FIGURE 2-8 The effect of brightness on the duration of an afterimage. A greater length of exposure and a brighter image produce a significant increase in the duration of the afterimage. [Adapted from Matthew Luckiesh, *Color and Its Application* (New York: D. Van Nostrand, 1915), p. 171.]

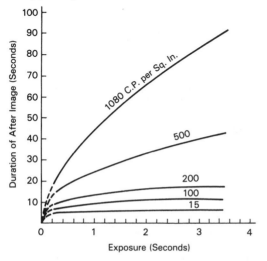

Irradiation and Autokinetic Effects

A small bright object will appear larger than the same-sized object at a lower illumination. Different colored objects of the same size and under the same illumination will appear to be different sizes. Yellow will be seen as largest, followed by white, red, green, blue, and black. Pastels will appear larger than shades. Brightness, when it strikes the nerves on the retina, tends to spread, forming a larger image than anything dark.[5] This apparent increase in size with an increase in illumination is called irradiation.

In a related phenomenon, a bright white light source frequently appears surrounded by a halo with an angular diameter of seven or eight degrees in size. On a dark stage, the light source may be seen surrounded by a dark ring and beyond this a colored ring in which various colors appear, violet being nearest the light source. This effect is caused by diffraction in the lens of the eye.[6]

A small, fixed, bright light viewed in darkness or in a visual field with no frames for reference or stability, will be seen as moving in an erratic, unpredictable fashion. The larger the light, the less the apparent movement. This is known as the "autokinetic effect" and may account for some of the bizarre movements attributed to UFOs. Similarly, points of steady brightness will appear to fade in and out. These effects may result from the compulsion of the mind to search for a frame of reference for a visual experience, but humans are so accustomed to a state of flux that even when a stimulus is constant, we physiologically and psychologically experience fluctuation.

In 1974, Hume Cronyn and Jessica Tandy toured the United States with a production of Ionesco's *Not I*, during long portions of which the only light on stage was a pin spot sharply focused on Ms. Tandy's mouth. The autokinetic effect was so strong for so many members of the audience that they either closed their eyes or complained of headaches. This may be an extreme case, but it is a vivid example of the way perceptual limitations must be taken into account by a lighting designer.

Flashing Lights

Designers of display advertisements and safety engineers have known for a long time that flashing lights attract more attention than a stationary light source, but the ability of the strobe light to transform movement into a series of still action pictures resulted in a plethora of special effects on stage using flashing lights. However, the eye and mind take a length of time to adjust to a scene, so momentary flashes of light can cause fatigue. Clinical studies have shown that flashing lights can induce seizures of epilepsy, and pulsating, stroboscopic flashes may be hypnotic and result in headaches and nausea.[7]

The fact that the eye may perceive a flashing light as a continuous source of illumination makes possible the illusion of motion picture projection. The fusion point, the frequency at which separate flashes are seen as a constant source, varies with the intensity and color of the source. At very low light levels where night vision is in use, 4 flashes a second may fuse, while at very high brightness levels, 100 flashes a second may not fuse. Modern film operates at the rate of 24 frames or flashes per second. Blue lights require a significantly slower blinking rate than red lights if the blinking is to be seen.[8]

A flashing light seems brighter than the same light shown continuously. The intermittent periods of lower illumination probably result in a lower adaptation level.

A flash of light, as long as it is above the perceptual threshold, no matter how brief, seems to last for an appreciable time of about 15 to 18 one-hundredths of a second, increasing a little in duration with increased luminance. This lingering effect is why a moving point of light appears to form a line and is the basis for image fusion.[9] There is also a short delay of about two-tenths of a second between the introduction of a flash and its perception.

Some years ago interest developed in subliminal suggestion, using images flashed slightly below the temporal threshold to condition responses. This caused considerable alarm among those concerned about possible brainwashing. Assuming that it works, such a device could have considerable application in the theatre. But how brief must the flash be in order to be below the limits of perception? The relationship between duration and brightness is shown in Figure 2-9, but the time is also influenced by figure-ground contrast, the size of the im-

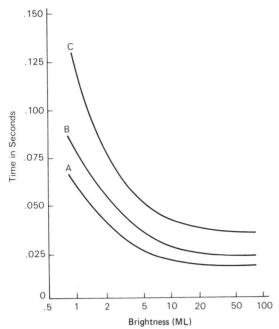

FIGURE 2-9 Relationship between visual threshold and the duration and brightness of a flash of light. The brighter the flash, the shorter duration necessary for us to discern an object. Curve *C* represents the relationship when the object is seen correctly practically every time. Curves *B* and *A* represent 80% and 50% correct identifications. [Adapted from Matthew Luckiesh and Frank K. Moss. *The Science of Seeing* (New York: D. Van Nostrand, 1937), p. 157.]

age, and the position of the image in the field of vision. The simplest approach to apply here is trial and error at around two one-hundredths of a second.

Effect of Brightness on Color

Colors seem to shift hue under brighter light, which is known as the Berzold-Brucke Effect. Increased luminance makes red more yellow and violet appear bluer. Colors above 577 mµ (green) tend to shift away from the red end of the spectrum, and below 577 mµ they shift towards the red end. With decreased illumination, they move in the opposite direction. These hue shifts may be as great as 40 mµ. Some hues do not ap-

pear to change with increased brightness, and these are located at approximately 571, 506, and 474 mµ in the spectrum (green, blue-green, and blue).[10] Furthermore, an intense orange light (c. 620 mµ) will appear yellow after ten seconds, green after a minute, and finally settle down to a yellow.[11] When an intense light of any wavelength shorter than 560 mµ is steadily viewed, it will appear colored when first turned on, but will desaturate, and if it is intense enough, will soon appear to be white.[12] Apart from these hue shifts, colors in general appear more saturated at low than at high levels of illumination and colors viewed under a flash of light will appear more intense than under a steady light.

Our ability to make differentiations in color value or color brightness is also influenced by the level of illumination. If we create a "gray scale" for any hue showing a range of values from white to black, the relationship of steps will remain normal for all illumination levels above 30 foot-candles. However, as the light grows dim, the gray scale becomes shorter from the bottom up and all dark tones below any judged midstep tend to blend together and appear alike in value or brightness. At 30 foot-candles, the midpoint on the gray scale will be judged as a shade having a reflectance of about 20 percent. Under 20 foot-candles, 25 percent reflectance is required to appear halfway between white and black. At 10 foot-candles, 30 percent is required. At 5 foot-candles, 40 percent. At one foot-candle 45 or 50 percent.[13]

White alone maintains its constancy in decreasing illumination. In fact, we perceive white as white even in shadow, a response known as *brightness constancy*. Within any level of illumination, we always perceive white as the brightest color. If another color appears brighter than white, we assume that it is separately illuminated.

Our expectation of the color of white light, however, is influenced by the intensity level. Called the *Kriuthof Effect*, we judge a redder or warmer white light to be normal at low illumination levels and perceive a bluer or cooler white light to be normal at daylight levels. Low-intensity illumination with the same color temperature as daylight creates an eerie pallor. This should make us cautious of heavy reliance on cool color media when a "normal" interior lighting effect is desired.

With respect to stage lighting, levels of illumination below 30 foot-candles will result in loss of contrast in color brightness, but, as the brightness level increases, colors will lose some of their hue saturation and may even be seen as radically different hues at much brighter levels. These changes in the color of scenery or costume can be as extreme as the color toning produced by many of the color filters available for the theatre.

Emotional Responses to Brightness

That moderately bright light, under normal circumstances, produces a positive emotional response is obvious. Studies have shown that heart rate is higher for subjects reading in bright as opposed to dim lighting. This simple equation between brightness and elation has led to the often repeated axiom that comedy requires bright lights and, by implication, that tragedy or serious drama is better lit at low levels. However, even if we assume a direct relationship between brightness and mood, we would also have to assume a simple relationship between mood and dramatic form for this principle of comic lighting to be valid. Indeed, tragedy may contain moments that cry out for bright lighting and comedy may touch the bass strings of very somber moods.

Emotional responses to bright light are difficult to measure because all emotion can only be subjectively quantified, and furthermore other variables condition the value we place on brightness. As a general rule, we want to see, and the better the visibility, the more comfortable we are. However, if bright light reveals something unpleasant, our response will be negative, though perhaps not as negative as the anticipation of something unpleasant that we cannot see well.

Being in bright light may also produce mixed responses. Experienced actors will find the bright center of a spotlight beam, but others may be nervous about being seen and seek shadows. The cat burglar caught in a searchlight hardly has positive emotional responses to brightness. Some members of a modern audience accustomed to a darkened auditorium will feel very inhibited if the house lights are left up during a performance.

We have also seen that our judgments of brightness are relative to the environment and our level of adaptation. The proverbial little candle does indeed shine a great distance in darkness. How do we measure the relative pleasantness of a candlelit banquet table and of spring sunlight streaming through a window?

We also know that glare, sudden brightness, or too much brightness contrast can produce eye strain and fatigue, which will certainly result in other unpleasant responses by the viewer.

One of the emotionally colored words often applied to brightness levels is "gloom," which, simply stated, is the sensation that our luminous environment is not bright enough. This judgment frequently requires time orientation. A level of outside brightness that seems satisfactory at dawn or dusk, seems insufficient in the middle of the day. An audience must know what time of day it is meant to be onstage before judging a low lighting level to be gloomy.

The absence of brightness contrast is an additional cue for gloom. If an uninteresting sky is brighter than the ground or if the landscape lacks the highlights and shadow which create visual interest, the result is gloom. Similarly, an interior may be adequately lit for visibility, but the lack of directional light, shadowless light, or too-even distribution in the lighting may seem gloomy.

Other variations in brightness contrast may, under normal circumstances, produce different responses. A scene in which the brightness contrasts are slight but sufficiently varied to avoid gloom, will produce a somewhat somber and romantic feeling, regardless of whether the overall visual field is bright or dim (see Figure 2-10). As the contrast increases, we receive more detailed visual data and rational responses tend to replace emotion, but if the brightness contrast becomes extreme, the tensions created between brightness and shadow may again arouse emotion.

The size and distribution of brightness contrast also invoke different reactions. Large, massive areas of different brightness are more calming and restful than a scene with a more active chopped pattern or contrast, which seems more lively. Here, however, we are considering brightness as an aspect of composition, and emotional responses are being made more properly to elements of line, mass, and balance rather than brightness per se. These compositional aspects will be discussed in more detail later.

To the extent that instrument selection and placement and dimmer control setting are methods for manipulating brightness levels, a large portion of the stage lighting designer's time is spent managing the intensity and distribution of brightness. These decisions must take into account not only the play and the production, but the psychoperceptual variables we have discussed here. In other words, the eye and brain of the viewer are instruments of even greater importance than those listed in the catalogs of stage lighting suppliers.

EXERCISES

General Note. The exercises below—and those following Chapters 3 and 4—may be set up on a stage, in a lighting laboratory, or even at home. A lighting laboratory can be improvised in a fairly small room, preferably with dark walls, with several rolling pipe stands on which small stage lighting instruments are mounted. Permanently mounted overhead pipes add useful flexibil-

FIGURE 2-10 Lee Simonson's setting for *The Rise of Silas Lapham* (1919). [From Lee Simonson, *Part of a Lifetime* (New York: Duell, Sloan, and Pearce, 1943). Copyright © 1943 by Lee Simonson. Copyright renewed 1971 by Lee Simonson. Reprinted by permission of the publisher, E. P. Dutton, Inc.]

ity, but any arrangement should allow instruments to be quickly and easily moved. A small, portable dimmer system will provide needed control. Even at home, a slide projector and a PAR lamp in a clip-on fixture plugged into a circuit controlled by a wall dimmer provides enough equipment to carry out most of these exercises. (Don't try to dim the slide projector without special equipment or without putting the fan motor on a nondim circuit.) In addition to a collection of filter colors for your lighting sources, other materials may be purchased very inexpensively. Be willing to try different things. You may discover a more graphic way to demonstrate these lighting phenomena!

1. *The Effect of Contrast on Visual Thresholds* (p. 14)—Cut two silhouettes, one black and one white, from construction paper and mount them on a white surface. Beginning in darkness, gradually increase light intensity until one of the silhouettes can be distinguished against the background. Which is seen first? Try the same thing with a black background. What does this tell you about clothing colors for stagehands shifting props during a near blackout against a white cyc background or against a background of stage blacks?

2. *Perception of Brightness Differences* (p. 17)—Place two matched lighting instruments side by side, and, at low-intensity levels, project two separate but matched pools of light onto a white surface. Measure the intensity of each light at the surface with a light meter. Raise or lower the intensity of one of the lights until the viewers can see the brightness difference. Measure the change in brightness of that light. Now match the brightness of the two beams at their full intensity. Dim one of the lights until the viewers can see the brightness difference and again measure the change. Compare this with the difference at the lower intensity level. Is the same amount of brightness change required at both high and low levels

for the viewer to observe the brightness difference? Make the same comparisons at bright and dim levels, asking viewers to indicate when one pool is "twice as bright" as the other. Record all dimmer settings and then try to duplicate the results after allowing time for viewers to adapt to various brightness levels. How does brightness or darkness adaptation influence the perception of brightness differences?

3. *Darkness Adaptation* (p. 17)—Make several signs with lettering just large enough to be readable in normal room light. Use a different message on each sign. Place the signs on top of one another on a stand in a strong spotlight circuited to a dimmer. Leave the viewers in darkness for several minutes and change to a new sign. Gradually increase the lighting intensity until the viewers can just read this new sign. Note the dimmer setting at this threshold. Now bring the lights to full intensity. What do the viewers experience? After the viewers become comfortable with the brighter level, quickly return to black, change to the next sign, and raise the brightness until a new threshold is discovered. Note the dimmer setting. Is this the same threshold that occurred after darkness adaptation? Try the same procedures using different levels and lengths of brightness adaptation. Try the experiment with different colored lights. Keep a careful record of all of the threshold changes in response to different conditions. (Note that thresholds will be lowered if viewers know the content of the signs. In a small space, a large type book saves time from having to make signs.)

4. *Brightness Adaptation* (p. 17)—Wear an opaque eye patch on one eye for half an hour. Remove the eye patch and carefully record the time required for the brightness sensitivity of both eyes to match. You can test this by looking at objects with first one eye closed and then the other. Try wearing the eye patch for shorter periods of time and record the varying time required for the sensitivity of the masked eye to match the unmasked eye. Test the different sensi-

tivity of each eye to different lighting levels. With a mirror, observe the different pupil diameters immediately after removing the eye patch. How much time is required for pupil size to match?

5. *Influence of Color on Brightness Adaptation* (p. 18)—Make a patch for one eye using a deep red filtering material that does not easily tear. Fit the patch as closely as possible to the eye while still allowing the lid to open. Wear the patch for at least 20 minutes; after removing it, immediately test for the different sensitivity of each eye and test for the brightness sensitivity of each eye using the methods in Exercise 3 above. Try the same procedures using different colored eye patches and different colored signs or lights for the threshold test.

6. *Brightness Adaptation* (p. 18)—In a normally lit room, set a projected pool of light at the midpoint on a dimmer scale. Ask viewers to carefully note the brightness of the pool. Darken the room for several minutes and then bring the pool of light up until the viewers judge it to be the same brightness as the original pool. Is the dimmer setting the same? Now bring the light to full intensity for a few moments and then dim it until the viewers indicate that it matches the original pool. What does the dimmer setting indicate?

7. *Brightness Contrast* (p. 19)—Cut a circle in the middle of a large piece of black fabric or a large sheet of black construction paper. Tack this black frame to a light-colored wall and focus a spot light sharply to the circle. Immediately next to this black frame focus an identical spot light so the two beams do not overlap. Set the intensity of the second beam so viewers indicate that it matches the first. Now remove the black frame. Do the intensities still match? Try the same comparison showing first the framed light and then the unframed light. Try the comparison with a grey frame.

8. *Brightness Contrast* (p. 19)—Take two squares of the same gray construction pa-

per, place one on a white background, and place the other on a black background. Put them in the same beam of light and ask viewers to tell which square is the brightest.

9. *Influence of Surface Reflection on Glare* (p. 20)—Place a transparent but highly reflective piece of plastic over one of the signs used in Exercise 3. Light it with a spotlight from the front. What happens? Will dimming the light improve visibility? Place a diffusion filter in the spotlight. Does visibility improve? Place a diffusion filter on top of the sign. Does this reduce glare? With the original reflective plastic over the sign, move the lighting source to a position which lights the sign but reduces glare. Try different positions. Where does the light produce the least glare?

10. *Influence of Surround Light on Glare* (p. 21)—Predetermine the threshold level required to read one of the signs with a front light. Place a second spotlight behind and slightly above the sign so that it lights the viewers. With this backlight at full, bring the front light to the threshold level. Can the viewers read the sign? Try lowering the intensity of the backlight to make the sign readable. With the back light at various levels, try to find the ratio of front light which enables viewers to read the sign. Vary the mounting position of the backlight and find what effect different backlighting angles have on glare. Increase the illumination of the space behind the sign surrounding the backlight to see if this changes the level of discomfort glare.

11. *Autokinetic Effects and Afterimages* (p. 24)—In a completely darkened room, tightly focus a pinspot on a small round object so that no light spills around the object. After watching the object for some time, do viewers see any movement in the object? After a minimum of five minutes viewing time, completely darken the room and ask viewers to describe the appearance of afterimages. Try the same arrangements with different colored lights and see how these influence autokinetic effects and the ap-

pearance of afterimages. Keep track of how long it takes different colored afterimages to decay.

12. *Influence of Brightness on Hue* (p. 25)—In separate pools of light created by a low- and a high-wattage instrument, place identical sheets of colored material, particularly red and violet. Do the colors match in the different illuminants? Why would simply dimming one of two instruments of the same wattage not produce identical results?

13. *Influence of Brightness on Value* (p. 25)—Using watercolors, create a nine step "gray scale" for any hue with values ranging from white to black. Place this scale in a spotlight and gradually lower the intensity, paying particular attention to the differences in value on the darker end of the scale. Ask viewers to judge the midpoint on the scale as the lighting reaches low intensity.

Psychophysical Considerations: Color

Our perception of color depends upon three variables: the spectral composition of the light source, the chromatic selectivity of the object reflecting the light, and the complex eye and brain response of the viewer. Of these three variables, the lighting designer controls the source. Scenic, costume, and makeup designers largely decide the characteristics of reflective surfaces, but because light is not seen unless it strikes some object, the lighting designer depends upon the chromatic characteristics of these surfaces and must fully understand how they behave under different lights. How color ultimately is interpreted naturally rests with the eye and mind of the beholder. Discounting the approximately 8 percent of all males and 0.4 percent of all females who have some form of abnormal color vision, normal human color perception is very complicated and must be well understood in order to predict with any certainty the effects of variations in light source.

The Color of Light Sources

The bulk of human experience with color is in sunlight, and so-called "normal" color is produced by full sunlight at noon. Even under these conditions, however, the sun does not produce equal energy in all parts of the spectrum. Figure 3-1, which gives the spectral distribution of sunlight, shows a fairly flat response from 480 to 700 mμ, but the relative energy tapers off very rapidly below 480 mμ (blues).

Sunlight has different spectral properties according to variations in the time of day, atmospheric conditions, latitude, and altitude. Figure 3-2 shows some of these differences. As one part or another of the solar spectrum is emphasized by these changes,

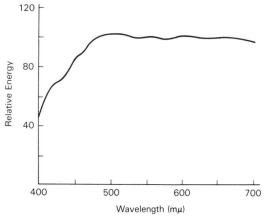

FIGURE 3-1 The spectral distribution of sunlight. Except at the blue end of the spectrum, distribution of energy is relatively constant across the range of hues. [Ralph M. Evans, *An Introduction to Color* (New York: John Wiley & Sons, 1948), p. 15.]

FIGURE 3-2 Spectral properties of skylight under different conditions in Cleveland, Ohio: (c) Zenith skylight, (d) North skylight, (e) entire overcast sky, and (f) sun plus clear sky. [A. H. Taylor and G. P. Kerr, *Journal of the Optical Society of America* 31 (1941), p. 7..]

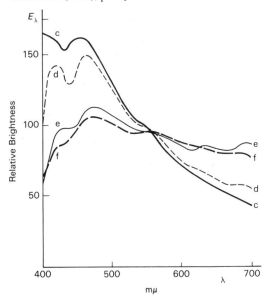

those colors will become relatively more prominent. A lighting designer trying to duplicate with artificial light the realistic effect of sunlight under some of these specific conditions would recreate light with a similar spectral emphasis.

Even though a detailed spectral analysis is the most precise way to describe the spectral profile of sunlight under any given condition, a single number known as the *Kelvin temperature* is frequently used. Certain substances, when heated, emit light, and the color of the light progresses from red to an increasingly bluish white as the temperature increases. Tungsten is used as the standard radiator, and it begins to emit visible energy at 873° Kelvin (K), which is the bottom point on the Kelvin scale. Figure 3-3 shows the color temperatures for various radiant bodies commonly found as apparent light sources in a stage scene. Photographers are quite familiar with the Kelvin scale: color film is usually adjusted to give optimum color fidelity at 3200°K, and deviations from this in light on a photographic subject require color correction.

Most stage lighting instruments will accommodate lamps manufactured to produce light of different color temperatures, but most commonly used lamps are designed to radiate light at 3200°K when operating at full wattage. This temperature lowers, however—resulting in a shift to red—when the lamp burns at less than full capacity or as the lamp ages. And even 3200°K is less than sunlight under almost all conditions and will require color correction to duplicate sunlight. Furthermore, the profile of relative spectral energy for an incandescent stage light is significantly different from that of sunlight (see Figure 3-4), with a resulting difference in the apparent color of objects illuminated by each. The practical effects of this are not as extreme as it may seem, because, as we have seen, the Kriuthoff Effect leads us to expect a lower color temperature at a lower brightness level and to judge this warmer or more red light as "normal."

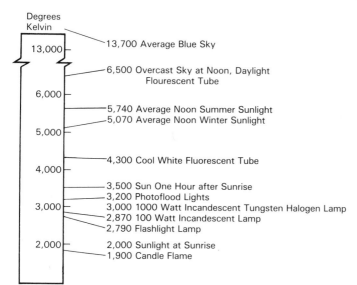

FIGURE 3-3   The color temperature in degrees Kelvin of various radiant bodies and lighting environments.

Most stage lighting is done with tungsten or quartz-iodine lamps, which have basically the same spectral profile, but other light sources produce quite different profiles (see Figure 3-4). Selectivity is most apparent with fluorescent lamps, which may appear to the eye to produce full spectrum light but in fact produce peaks of light in narrow sections of the spectrum and little light at all in other portions. An object which reflects light only in a narrow portion of the spectrum where a fluorescent tube generates little energy appears to gray. More commonly, an object's color depends on a mixture of reflected wavelengths, some of which are absent under fluorescent lighting, with the result that the object appears an entirely different color than under sunlight or incandescent light. Even though two illuminants appear to match each other in color, the color of objects lit by each may be different depending on the spectral profile of each light.

Filtration of the Source

The color of sunlight can be naturally altered by a variety of conditions. Light filtering through leaves reflects off the surface of the foliage, which absorbs colors at the red end of the spectrum and casts a decidedly greenish tint on objects below. A cloud cover filters out red light and produces a blue tint. Sunlight reflected from the moon

FIGURE 3-4   The spectral profile of sunlight (top curve), a typical incandescent light (broken line), and a cool white fluorescent lamp (bottom curve). The narrow lines of radiation are produced by the mercury-arc discharge in the fluorescent tube; the continuous spectrum is produced by the phosphor coating of the lamp.

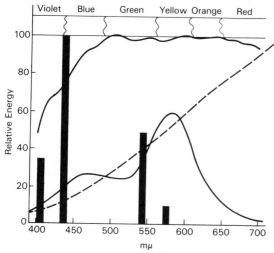

is almost as rich in red as violet light and has a color temperature of only 4100°K.

The most common natural alteration of sunlight comes from an effect known as "scattering," in which light passing through extremely fine particles bends or diffracts around these particles. This scattering follows what is known as *Rayleigh's Law,* which states that more short wavelengths are scattered than long ones. Such a medium therefore transmits red light, and the scattered light seen from the side appears quite blue. This accounts for the blueness of the sky and of distant haze and the comparative redness of bright objects seen through haze or fog. Red clouds in a sunset are similarly the result of the scattering out of blue light when the sun's rays pass obliquely through the atmosphere. Rayleigh's scattering also explains why red lights transmit a great distance through fog or haze when blue lights cannot be seen at all.

Most color filtering in the theatre is done with glass, gel, or plastic color media which absorb wavelengths in certain portions of the spectrum and pass or transmit the remainder. The absorbed light is converted into heat, and the less light transmitted by the filtering medium, the greater the heat stress. Some of the more intense blue filters pass less than 2 percent of the light entering them, while light tints of amber and yellow may transmit 90 percent of the light. Manufacturers of color media have spectral profiles (Figure 3-5) that show the percentage of any given wavelength transmitted by each filter.

The process by which colored media work is known as *subtractive filtration* because unwanted colors are subtracted from the beam of light. The narrower the spectral profile of the transmitted light, the fewer the colors that will be reflected from stage surfaces. For example, a purple filter that transmits virtually no light between 500 and 650 mμ will provide no illumination for objects which reflect only green or amber and absorb all other wavelengths. These objects, which appear green or amber under white light, appear black or grey when lit with purple light.

If subtractive filters are placed on top of one another, the effect of the second is multiplied on the first, not just added to it. For example, if a light salmon filter transmits only 40 percent of the light at 500 mμ (blue), an added second filter will pass only 40 percent of the original 40 percent, or a total of 16 percent. This same principle would apply if we simply doubled the thickness of the original filter. This is known as *Bouger's Law* and states that if the transmission at any wavelength is T and the thickness is n times that of a single layer, the transmission at that wavelength equals T multiplied by itself n times or T^n. Therefore, a light salmon filter three times as thick as the original filter that passed 40 percent of the light at 500 mμ would transmit only 6.4 percent of the light at that wavelength or 40 percent × 40 percent × 40 percent. Some modern color media are made from multiple layers of colored and transparent materials, so the actual thickness of the colorant is not always apparent; but a disproportionately higher efficiency is obtained from a colored filter when it is kept as thin as possible.

When two different colored media are placed on top of one another, the second can transmit only that percentage of light passed by the first. Therefore a primary green filter placed over a purple filter will transmit virtually no light because the green filter can pass only those wavelengths already absorbed by the purple filter. An amber filter placed over a magenta filter will pass only red light because the amber filter absorbs blue and transmits only green and red while the magenta filter absorbs green and passes only red and blue.

Colors can also be subtracted from white light by destructive interference where light waves come together in different phases of their vibration, amplifying some frequencies and canceling others. These filters are made by sandwiching a thin layer of cryolite between thin films of silver. They pass a

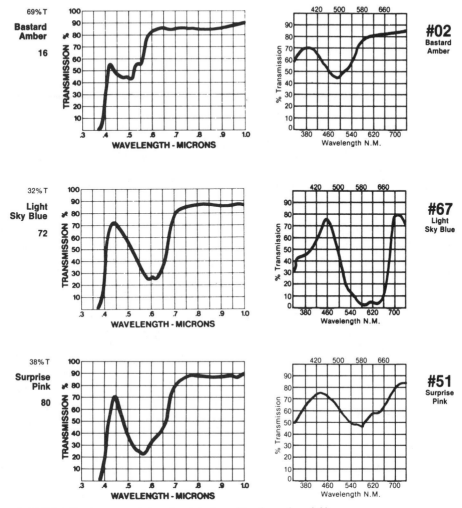

FIGURE 3-5 A comparison of spectral profiles for colored filters manufactured by Berkey Colortran (Geltran on the left) and by Rosco (Roscolux on the right). Color names are obviously an unreliable indicator of the actual properties of the filter hue as indicated by the different profiles for colors of the same name.

very narrow band of wavelengths, determined by the thickness of the cryolite, and have high light transmission at these wavelengths, but at present their production is too expensive for general stage use.

One type of interference filter more widely useful on stage is the polarizing filter. Light from most natural and artificial sources vibrates in all directions, but a polarizing filter screens out all light except that vibrating along a given plane. Light reflected from certain surfaces, particularly metal and glass, tends to vibrate along a limited number of planes, which accounts for the efficiency of polarizing sunglasses in cutting glare from these surfaces. In addition, many crystals and some artificial materials such as cellophane tape, transmit light at different wavelengths along different planes, a phenomenon known as *birefringence*. If thin sections of crystalline minerals or slides of cellophane tape are attached to a polarizing sheet and placed in a projector with a second, revolving polarizing disc placed in front of the projector, the projector image will show changing patterns of color, a striking effect suitable for some dance lighting, dream sequences, and underwater effects.

Diffraction gratings can also change the color of light. *Diffraction* is the bending of waves around the edge of an obstacle. Very fine lines etched on a transparent medium result in wavelength separation caused by interference patterns. Diffraction gratings are most frequently used over reflective surfaces or over low-illumination sources rather than over major transmission sources. They may cast spectral colors or cause the apparent color of an object to change as the viewer moves.

Reflective Surfaces

The color of objects largely results from their selective reflectance of specific wavelengths of light. A red object absorbs and converts to heat energy all wavelengths except those which create the impression of red in the eye. If the light contains none of the wavelengths needed to create the sensation of redness, the object will appear black or gray. Unless the object fluoresces, it cannot add wavelengths that are not originally present in the light striking it.

Different surfaces have different reflective properties that influence the apparent color of a surface under various colored lights. A specular or highly reflective surface may have only a small amount of selectivity, meaning it will reflect a large percentage of the light striking it without significantly absorbing specific wavelengths. The apparent color of such an object may

closely approximate the color of the light illuminating it. For example, leaves in a lily pond may appear quite blue because they are reflecting a large portion of the light from a blue sky. If there is detail on a specular surface that must be seen, this nonselective reflection may become veiling glare.

Polished metals reflect light selectivity so that highlights take on the color of the metal. Nonmetallic, highly reflective surfaces such as porcelain, glazed ceramics, and shiny plastic reflect light nonselectively, so that highlights are always the color of the light.

Many objects have more than one reflective surface. A darkly stained oak panel gives a diffused reflection of brown colors, but if it is varnished, a specular surface is added that nonselectively reflects a portion of whatever colored light strikes it. Some of the light passes through the varnished surface and is reflected by the stained wood, but a percentage of the light reflects directly from the varnished surface. The proportion of specularly reflected light will depend on the angle of reflection in relation to the viewer and on the degree of diffusion of the light source.

The apparent color of an object may be deepened by the addition of a thin coat of wax or flat varnish. Part of the light bouncing from the diffused surface under the coating is reflected from the underside of the surface finish. This light is again selectively absorbed and diffusely reflected. This process of multiple reflection enhances the selective action of the colored material.

The deepening of colors due to multiple reflections also operates in larger spaces. One of the reasons why colors on a paint chip frequently seem to intensify when painted on the walls of a room is that a portion of the light striking any wall bounces from other walls which selectively reflect the color of the paint. A large number of nonselective reflective surfaces in a space will have the same cumulative effect for colored light so that the coloration may seem to be greater than the sum of the component parts. This piling on of bounce light can obviously have important consequences for stage lighting.

The colors of surfaces in a space are the result of the total action of the color of direct and reflected light. The effect of reflected light is most noticeable in shadows, areas which receive no direct light. For example, outside, on a clear day, shadows have a decidedly blue tint because they are lit by diffused light from the blue sky at about one-fourth the intensity of sunlight. If there are scattered clouds, the intensity of the shadows increases and the blueness decreases. Indoors, shadow color is influenced by the color of bounce light from walls and other surfaces.

Some surfaces reflect one color of light in one direction and another in other directions. The striking effects of satins or opals are examples of this. There are also fluorescent pigments used in fabric dyes which give off colored light when struck by certain wavelengths whether within or beyond the visible spectrum. If the stimulating light is within the visible spectrum, the fluorescent color is generally of a longer wavelength than that of the stimulating light (Stoke's Law). Blues take a greenish tint; greens appear yellowish; and yellows have an orange cast. The light reflected from the surface is actually a combination of the color of the illuminating light and the fluorescent color.

Two surfaces with the same apparent color under a given light source may not continue to appear the same color when the color of the light changes. This is called *metamerism,* a term also applied to our perception of the color of light sources. Even if two sources match in apparent color, they may not have identical spectral distributions; so identical objects seen under two metameric lights may not reflect the same colors.

The color and brightness of an object are influenced by the color and intensity of the illuminant, the reflective efficiency of the object, the direction of the light with respect to the object and the viewer, and the degree of diffusion of the illuminant. When a colored object with a relatively glossy surface is lit by a small, concentrated source, the object appears more specular and the colors deeper than when the same object is lit by a diffused source. The concentrated, directional light source produces more clarity in the reflected light, while the diffused source results in more diffusion of the light reflected from the surface.

Surfaces may be selective or nonselective, the latter usually described as white, gray, or black. It would seem that reflective white or gray surfaces would always appear to be the color of the illuminating light, but as we shall see in a later discussion of color adaptation, this is not the case. Also for perceptual reasons, which we will discuss in a later section on color constancy, if a viewer knows that an object is supposed to be white or gray, the viewer will see the object as white or gray regardless of the color of the illuminant.

A stage lighting designer confronts a vast array of surfaces with different reflective properties that, in the course of a production, may be subjected to extreme variations in the color, direction, and diffusion of light. Each production presents a new set of problems, making it difficult to impose any one system that will work in all cases. Even though the complexity of the problems necessitates some willingness to proceed by trial and error through technical rehearsals, the behavior of these surfaces does follow fixed principles which have been described. The designer should diligently seek information about the scenery, furniture, floor coverings, properties, costumes, and makeup in advance of the actual design of the lighting. If there are new surfaces with which the designer has had no experience, they should be tested beforehand under different lighting conditions. Two slide projectors filled with stage color filters projected onto sample boards of costume fabric and paint colors can save expensive hours of time (which otherwise would be required to rehang or regel a lighting plot when the dyes in costumes or scenic drops behave in unanticipated ways under colored lights).

Color Sensitivity of the Eye

Colors are generally perceived to have three attributes: hue, saturation, and brightness. *Hue* is the main qualitative factor that leads us to describe a color as green or red. *Saturation* is the percentage of hue in a color or the degree of whiteness. *Brightness* is the perception of intensity or the apparent difference from black. All three factors combined are called *chroma*. If we consider hue alone, the eye can differentiate about 175 colors. However, some researchers have estimated that a person with normal vision can distinguish 17,000 different chromaticities.

Even though the normal eye responds to all wavelengths between approximately 400 and 700 mμ, it is much more sensitive to color in the middle than on the ends of the spectrum. As shown in Figure 3-6, two separate curves have to be plotted according to the intensity of the light. Scotopic or twilight vision, which depends primarily on the sensitivity of rods, has a curve shifted about 40 mμ further toward the lower end of the spectrum than photopic or daylight vision, which depends more on cone sensitivity. If green and yellow are seen as the same brightness in daylight, at very low levels of illumination the green will appear brighter. This is known as the *Purkinje Phenomenon* and accounts for extreme green hues that may predominate at twilight on a spring or summer day. The apparent shift in relative brightness of various colors in a stained glass window can be attributed to this phenomenon. If we chart the sensitivity of the eye to specific colors as intensity decreases, as shown in Figure 3-7, it is apparent that blue-green and violet dominate at low brightness levels while orange-yellow and red, which are relatively brighter at daylight levels, move rapidly toward gray as intensity

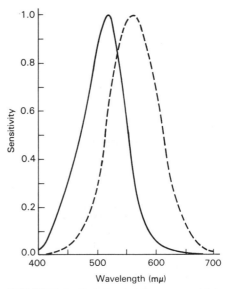

FIGURE 3-6 Relative brightness sensitivity of the eye for night (scotopic) vision (solid line) and day (photopic) vision (dotted line). With night vision the eye is more sensitive to blue. [From K. S. Weaver, *Journal of the Optical Society of America* 27 (1937), p. 39.]

falls. Of course atmospheric conditions, such as a sunset, would change the spectral profile of the light passing through stained glass and influence the relative brightness of the colors.

FIGURE 3-7 Variations in visual sensitivity to color at different brightnesses. At low levels of brightness the eye is very sensitive to blue-green and relatively insensitive to other colors. [From Louis Erhardt, *Radiation, Light, and Illumination* (Camarillo, Calif.: Camarillo Reproduction Center, 1977), p. 83.]

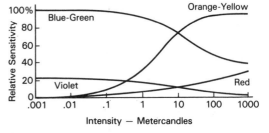

Another measure of the sensitivity of the eye to color is the amount of spectral separation between two wavelengths necessary for them to be perceived as different colors. As shown in Figure 3-8, the eye can differentiate colors in the middle of the spectrum with a separation of between one and two millimicrons, but at the ends of the spectrum four to six millimicrons are required. However, when the color of lights is near white, sensitivity to change of color is greatest near the end of the spectrum, particularly for blues. When yellow light is added to white light, the change is first perceived as an increase in intensity rather than a change of hue. Yellow, therefore, has a weak coloring power.

Even though the three attributes of color, hue, saturation, and brightness, usually have external stimuli that can be manipulated with a considerable degree of predictability, all three are ultimately based on subjective perception and are interdependent. We have seen, for example, that changes in light intensity can cause major shifts in apparent hue and that the apparent relative brightness of different colors changes as the illumination level changes. In addition, some colors appear much brighter at higher saturations even though luminance is kept constant. This effect is most

pronounced at the ends of the spectrum. We will find numerous perceptual factors which change the colors we see.

Color Fatigue

As with brightness, the sensitivity of the eye to color diminishes with time, a characteristic known as "color fatigue." The effect is less noticeable when viewing under a constant colored illuminant than it is when the color of the light subsequently changes. For example, if white light follows a scene lit with blue light, the blue hues on stage will noticeably diminish in intensity for a few moments.

The red and blue ends of the spectrum produce more color fatigue than the middle, and fatigue is faster for red than blue light. Fatigue occurs more rapidly with yellow and orange light than with white light, but at high intensities white light produces a decrease in color sensitivity across the spectrum. If after exposure to an intense white light, the level of illumination is significantly lowered, all colors disappear for a few seconds and then gradually the warmer tints reappear, the blue tints coming back last. Generally color fatigue induced by light of longer wavelength appears more quickly but also disappears sooner than fatigue induced by light of shorter wavelength. The higher the intensity of the fatiguing light and the longer the exposure time, up to about three minutes, the slower the recovery of color sensitivity.[1]

The apparent shift in hue of colors under bright light (the previously discussed Berzold-Brucke Effect) and the appearance of colored afterimages (to be discussed later) are both products of color fatigue. If we assume that the eye contains sensors for each of the primary colors, red, green, and blue, and that stimulation of any of the sensors produces bleaching of the receptor photopigment and an accompanying loss of sensitivity, the cause for color shifts becomes apparent. For example, an intense yellow light will appear green after about a minute

FIGURE 3-8 Ability of the eye to discriminate hue differences at different wavelengths. The eye is much more sensitive to small differences in hue at the middle of the spectrum. [From W. D. Wright and F. H. G. Pitt, *Proc. Phys. Soc.* 46 (1934), p. 459.]

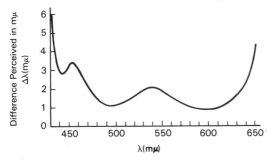

and then will gradually return to yellow. A yellow light stimulates both red and green receptors, but the red fatigue more rapidly than the green with the result that the light appears more green as the red sensitivity fades. After a time, the green receptors also become bleached and a fairly equal response from red and green receptors is restored, making the light appear yellow again.

When using saturated colored lights or progressing from high- to low-level illumination, the lighting designer must beware of color fatigue. Even though its effects are moderated by color adaptation, which will be discussed later, gradual shifts in apparent color can be distracting for an audience. Contrarily, special effects where colors gradually emerge from a painted drop as the eye recovers from color fatigue, or where costumes mysteriously deepen in hue, can be very effective in the proper circumstances.

Small-Field Tritanopia

Some colors that remain relatively constant in hue when moderately illuminated in large fields may lose their chromaticity in small areas. To predict this effect, we must be able to calculate the angle made at the eye by the edges of field of color. This is stated in terms of degrees, minutes, and seconds of an arc. A full circle has 360 degrees; each degree has 60 minutes; and each minute has 60 seconds. For small objects which subtend an angle of less than 20 minutes of arc at the eye, the perception of blue disappears. To determine the size of a field represented by this angle for a viewer 60 feet away, we determine the dimensions of the full circle (2×60 ft $\times 3.14 = 376.8$ ft) and divide by 1080 (1/3 of a degree or $1/3 \times 1/360$) to obtain a result of about .35 ft or about 4 in. (see Figure 3-9). Light greenish-yellow objects with a small visual field usually appear light gray or white. Dark reddish-blue objects will appear dark gray or black. Objects that are blue, blue-green, or green appear green when their angular size is sufficiently reduced and gray when further reduced. Yellow-red, blue-red, and pink will usually appear pink when the visual angle is small and gray when it is further reduced.[2]

Even though this effect, known as *small-field tritanopia,* is primarily important to the costume and scenic designer, the lighting designer may modify its influence by careful selection of lighting color. Where it is im-

FIGURE 3-9   Method of obtaining the visual angle created by an object at the eye. The angle can be determined by applying the simple formula:

$$\frac{\text{height of object} \times 360}{\text{distance of eye from object} \times 6.28} = \text{visual angle in degrees}$$

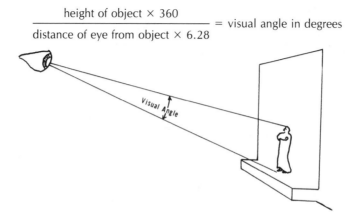

portant for the audience to see the chroma of fine details, lighting can emphasize the hues less affected by small-field tritanopia, stressing, for example, the green rather than the blue portions of cyan, a combination color.

Color Mixing

Our perception of any given color may be stimulated in a variety of ways, and the eye cannot differentiate between them. With the exception of purple, light of a single wavelength can stimulate our perception of most hues; these are known as spectral colors or spectral hues. However, a spectral color of a single wavelength can be matched by combining two other lights of entirely different wavelength. For example, the sensation of a green color may be produced by light of the wavelength 550 mμ or by a combination of lights with wavelengths of 480 mμ (blue) and 620 mμ (yellow), and the eye will not be able to tell the difference between the two colors.

The mixing of spectral colors to form a third color follows certain basic principles:

1. Any two wavelengths of light will combine to create a color falling between the two in the spectrum, except that components with wavelengths near the end of the spectrum will combine to create a series of purples. The exact wavelength matched varies according to the relative intensity of the components, being continuous from one to the other as the percentage of each varies from zero to one hundred.

2. There are a series of pairs of monochromatic lights which produce white light when combined. These pairs are called *complementary colors.* Every radiation of shorter wavelength than 492 mμ has a complementary greater than 567 mμ.

3. Green light (492–567 mμ) has no monochromatic complement but will produce white light when combined with purple light, which in turn is a combination of red and blue at the extreme ends of the visible spectrum.

4. When spectral lights are mixed to match a specific color, there is a general loss of purity so that white light needs to be added to produce an exact match.

A mixture of no more than three principal or "primary" colors will produce most hues, and the widest range of colors is provided by primaries of red, green, and blue (615, 520, and 447 mμ, respectively). Pairs of these primaries combine to create "secondaries": red and green create yellow, red and blue make magenta, and blue and green produce cyan. A combination of all three primaries produces white, as does a combination of any one primary and its "complementary" secondary, which in turn is a combination of the remaining two primaries. Plate II shows the traditional arrangement of these colors as overlapping circles.

The International Commission on Illumination (*Commission Internationale de l'Eclairge*) has devised a method known as a *Chromaticity Diagram* for schematically representing the relationship between any hue and its color components in a conventional three-color mixing system (Plate II). The position of any color on this diagram indicates its hue and degree of saturation. The degree of saturation increases as the position of the hue moves closer to the outer perimeter of the diagram. The outside curved line represents pure spectral colors; the bottom straight line represents purple. A line drawn between any two points on this diagram shows the range of hue produced by adjusting the relative brightness of the two hues at those two points. A triangle formed by connecting lines from three color points encloses an area of color within which any hue may be produced by adjusting the intensities of the three colors.

It is extremely useful to be able to produce a range of colors from only three sources of colored light, but it is important to remember the limitations of this system. A few colors simply cannot be produced by a combination of these particular primaries.

For example, they cannot combine to match a bright spectral yellow.[3] Also remember that the secondaries do not represent the full range of colors possible by combining primaries. These three secondaries result when the primaries are at equal intensity, but variations in intensity result in a range of colors on the spectrum between the two primaries.

There is nothing unique about red, green, and blue as primary colors except that, on a practical level, they produce the widest range of colors when combined. Numerous sets of three monochromatic colors will match almost all colors, and the lighting designer may obtain more intense production of specific hues by using a different set of primary colors.

Primaries are frequently described as colors which themselves cannot be made from other colors, but this is true in only a limited sense. For example, primary red results from combining wavelengths above and below 615 mμ, but, to the extent that we describe all light above 615 mμ as "red," we do not produce primary red by combining totally different hues. A combination of spectral yellow and blue will make a primary green, but this combination has such a strong tendency to create white that the green tint is of very low saturation.

The mixing of colored lights is known as the *additive color system*, but what of the primaries, red, blue, and yellow, used by painters and learned by children in their early years of school? These may be thought of as primaries in a *subtractive color system*. If we place a cyan filter over a yellow filter, only green light will be transmitted because the yellow filters out the blue in the cyan and the cyan filters out the red in the yellow. The artist's "blue" is really the lighting designer's "cyan" and the artist's "red" is "magenta" on the lighting wheel, or to state it in another way, the additive secondaries are the primaries of the subtractive system. Because colors are being selectively filtered out, the combination of primaries in the subtractive system produces black or the absence of light. In the additive system, a mixture of primaries produces white, which is the aggregate of all colors.

The operation of the three-color additive system leads to the hypothesis that the eye actually has a different set of responders with primary sensitivity in the region of each of the primary colors. The range of response for each type of receptor is shown in Figure 3-10. According to this idea, known as the *Young-Helmholtz Theory,* our perception of yellow results from the simultaneous stimulation of red and green receptors. The tendency of a yellow light to appear green for a time before returning to a constant yellow state results from the faster fatigue of the red receptor with a correlative increase in the relative sensitivity of the green sensor. Because the receptors are sensitive to a range of wavelengths and because their ranges overlap, the fatigue of any one receptor does not necessarily produce a total loss of sensitivity to all hues within its range.

Unfortunately, the Young-Helmholtz Theory fails to explain forms of color blindness wherein an individual can perceive yellow but not red or can perceive cyan but not blue. If the perception of yellow results

FIGURE 3-10 Spectral responses for each of the three color mechanisms of the eye. Note that there is considerable overlap, particularly between red and green. [From L. C. Thompson and W. D. Wright, *Journal of the Optical Society of America* 43 (1953), p. 890.]

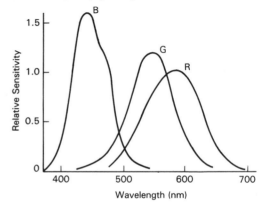

from the combined sensitivity of the red and green sensors, the insensitivity of the red sensor should affect the perception of yellow as well. In general, yellow seems to be the sticking point in the Young-Helmholtz Theory because all untrained observers tend to see yellow as a "pure" color along with red, green, and blue. That is, they do not see yellow as a mixture of other colors.

An alternate color theory, developed by Ewald Hering in 1870 and now known as the *opponent-process theory,* proposed different functions for the three receptors: one for degree of brightness, one for red-green perception, and one for blue-yellow perception. Each color receptor theoretically has a building-up phase (anabolic) responsible for one of each linked pairs of color and a tearing-down phase (catabolic) responsible for the opposite paired color. The receptor cannot react both ways simultaneously, and when a stimulus is withdrawn an afterimage of the contrasting color appears as a result of the reversal of the anabolic/catabolic process.

The mechanisms for color perception are still much debated, but most modern theories combine these two earlier approaches and posit three color receptors at the level of retinal reception and some type of opponent process for the linkage between the eye and the brain.[4] Virtually all of the color phenomena of importance to the lighting designer can be explained in terms of a trichromatic system such as the Young-Helmholtz Theory.

The mixing of colored light is extremely important to the lighting designer; it provides a range of colored light from a limited number of instruments and creates colored highlights and shadows that have a different hue from the overall illumination. Because each colored filter used in the theatre tends to transmit light over a fairly broad portion of the spectrum, the effects of combining lights transmitted through different filters is not always easy to predict. Here again, experimentation with different colored media projected from two or three slide projectors onto a screen or onto colored samples will lead to practical knowledge of the effect of color combinations.

Color Adaptation

Just as the eye adapts to the intensity of illumination, it also adjusts to the presence of a dominant-colored illuminant or object, which is known as *color* or *chromatic adaptation.* In general, because of color fatigue, the sensitivity of the eye decreases in time to the dominant color. This tends to minimize the coloring effect of any illuminant. However, this decrease in sensitivity to one color influences our perception of other colors or subsequent stimuli.

Shifts in hue under colored light relate to the reflectance of surfaces with respect to the general luminance of the space (adaptation level). Surfaces, both chromatic and achromatic, whose reflectances are above the adaptation level tend to take on the hue of the illuminant. Surfaces having reflectances below that level increasingly take on the hue of the complementary color of the illuminant, and surfaces at the adaptation level appear achromatic. This is known as the *Helson-Judd Effect.*[5]

The apparent color of a surface under colored light therefore depends on the reflectance of that surface in relation to other surfaces in the visual field. For example, a medium gray surface with a white surround, illuminated by red light, will take on a complementary blue-green tint. With a gray surround the same surface will appear achromatic, and with a black surround it will have a red tint.

Because shadows, by definition, have a lower reflectance than the adaptation level, they will assume the tint of the complementary color. For instance, in extreme red light, shadows have a green tint. The complementary colors involved are not necessarily identical to the complementary colors in the conventional red/green/blue color triangle but are the complementary colors of afterimages, produced by the increased relative sensitivity of the remaining visual receptors when color fatigue reduces the sensitivity of others.

Color adaptation works most effectively for "tints" of white, particularly when the viewer is not aware that the illuminant is tinted. The eye does not adapt as easily to extreme hues of colored light or when it is obvious that the light is tinted, but will rather persist in seeing the objects as "colored" by the light. Chromatic adaptation is affected by time. As it progresses, surfaces progressively change hue, rapidly at first, then more slowly until an almost steady state is reached. Gradually surfaces with a low hue purity and small stimuli in the periphery of vision will lose their color saturation.

Once our eyes adapt to a particular color, our perception of subsequent colors may be distorted if we shift our visual focus to a contrasting hue or if the illuminating light changes color to a contrasting hue. In general, chromatic adaptation alters spectral sensitivity, suppressing the adaptation hue and accentuating the hue of its complementary afterimage in subsequent viewing. If white light appears after a colored light to which the eye has adapted, a normally neutral surface takes a hue complementary to the adaptation color, a stimulus normally complementary to the adaptation color increases its saturation, and a hue near the adaptation stimulus appears less saturated. A hue of the same color as the adaptation hue, but less saturated, will usually appear gray. If a scene with white light immediately follows a fairly long scene using blue tints for a nighttime effect, grays in this subsequent scene will take an amber cast; ambers, reds, and greens will seem more saturated; and blues, particularly of low saturation, will appear more gray. This effect will diminish fairly rapidly as the blue receptors in the retina regain sensitivity.

Color Contrast

The appearance of any color is influenced by the color previously stimulating the retina, whether we are talking about the eye roving over a field of vision or a succession of colored illuminants. The influence of colors juxtaposed in time or space is known as *color contrast*.

When different colors are in close proximity, the eye tends to subtract one from the other and intensify the remaining components, a result of the reduced sensitivity of the eye to any hue shared by two stimuli and the relatively greater sensitivity of the eye to any remaining hues not shared by the stimuli. For example, if we crosslight an object with red and yellow light, the shadow that we might expect to be yellow will appear blue-green and the shadow that should be red will be tinged with blue. The red light suppresses the red receptors, making the yellow shadow appear more green. The yellow light suppresses the red and green receptors, resulting in a blue tinge in both shadow areas. When two colored lights throw a shadow of the same object onto a white surface, the two colored shadows always have tints roughly complementary to each other regardless of the hue of the two lights, although closely related hues produce very low saturations of the complementary tints.

A stage lit by two colored light sources may, under ideal circumstances, produce a wide range of hues rather than the three which we might expect from the two colorants and their simple mixture. For example, if we use green and orange crosslights (550 and 600 mμ), surfaces of high reflectance lit by only one light will take on that hue, but the two hues will appear to have an exaggerated difference, the orange shifting to red and the green to blue. The surfaces lit by a mixture of the two illuminants will appear yellow, but shadows will appear bluish, the complement of yellow. Therefore, red, green, blue, and yellow hues, plus their mixtures, will be seen by a viewer.[6]

Juxtaposition of similar hues also influences their appearance. If colors of the same hue but with high and low saturations are placed in proximity, they appear respectively even more and less saturated in hue. The stimulus with the lower saturation may appear either achromatic or tinted with a color complementary to the dominant hue. For example, a faint blue wash used for acting areas appears white or even slightly amber in front of a deep-blue sky cyc. Also, a colored surface, particularly of a hue on the blue end of the spectrum, appears less bright when seen in close spatial or temporal juxtaposition with a matching field. Inversely, a dark surround or the isolation of a hue increases its luminosity but decreases saturation. Therefore the blue tints in a costume would be suppressed in front of a blue cyc or when used in a scene which follows the heavy use of blues in the visual field, but a tightly focused light on the costumed actor with a surrounding area of darkness would compensate somewhat for the loss of brightness resulting from the blue background.

To use color contrast to emphasize the color of any surface, utilize complementary colors in the background but not on the surface itself. If possible, precede the appearance of an object with an illuminant complementary in color to the color of the object. To emphasize the difference between two related hues, light with a color complementary to the shared hue or with a tint present in one hue but not shared by the other. For example, the blue in a costume is emphasized if the preceding scene has been predominantly amber or if the background light is amber. To emphasize the differences between a blue and a blue-green costume, use blue and amber crosslights. The blue will prevent suppression of the blue in the costumes, and the amber will stress the complementary hue and the green, the hue differentiating the two costumes.

Color Constancy

In spite of hue shifts resulting from color fatigue, adaptation, and contrast, an observer has a strong compulsion to see the colors expected. This is partly caused by the progressive insensitivity of the eye to a colored illuminant, which tends to subtract the effect of the illuminant and restore all hues to "normal." For example, incandescent light is richer in red than sunlight, but our red sensitivity decreases under incandescent lighting to the point that colors have much the same appearance that they do in daylight.

Past experience also exerts a strong influence on our perception of color. Particularly if we know that the illuminant is colored, we continue to ascribe the predetermined hue to the object, regardless of the data the eye receives. The persistence of expected daylight colors is known as *color constancy.*

A stage lighting designer may either call attention to the color of the light itself or handle colored light with such subtlety that the audience is unaware of the illuminant and assumes that the color is inherent in the surface. If the effect of a sunset is being created, the audience should sense that the light is red, but if we are trying to change the apparent color of a wall painted with pointillism, the shift in lighting hue should be concealed from the audience. If the illumination has a highly saturated hue or changes color rapidly or drastically, the audience will judge the scene to be tinted by the lights and hold on to their conceptions of "normal" colors. If different parts of a continuous planar surface are lit by different colored lights, the audience will be aware of the differences. However, if variations in the color of light are subtle and if they are consistently coordinated with changes in the surfaces of objects on stage, the audience is more likely to perceive the color as residing in the objects themselves.

Color constancy, fatigue, adaptation, and contrast are all factors influencing the use of colored light in both a spatial and temporal context. The designer must not only consider the effect of colored light on a specific surface, but also take account of the influence of various colors on one another within the total stage space and the sequence of lighting colors as the production progresses.

A college production of Eugene O'Neill's *Ah, Wilderness!* lit the principal acting areas with a predominantly amber tint and a large backing cyclorama with a fairly intense blue. Throughout the production, the audience was aware of the unnaturalness of the amber tint because the blue cyc counteracted any adaptation which might have suppressed the sensitivity of the eye to amber. The combined blue and amber light used all three primary color sensors in the eye; so color fatigue occurred equally in all three, maintaining the relative hue intensity of the blue and amber. In another production, the actors in a musical love scene took on an unflattering green tint because the amber toning of the scene followed rapidly after a scene which used deeply saturated magenta lights. The magenta depressed the sensitivity of the audience's eyes to red and blue, but increased the relative sensitivity to the green component of the following amber light.

Lighting cues are frequently set at technical rehearsals where the normal time line of a production is not followed. The adaptation of the designer's eye during the time it takes to set the cue may not be identical to the audience's adaptation time, and the apparent color of the lights may consequently appear quite different in the final production. Particularly when saturated color filters are used, the designer must be aware of the influence of color adaptation on audience perception for the finished production.

The Effect of Color on Attention

Do certain colors have inherently more visual interest than others? The answer to this question is important to the lighting designer using color to create focus on stage, but as can be imagined, it is also of great importance to designers of advertising, manufacturers of safety signals, and a host of others. The problem is complex.

With respect to the chromatic response of the eye, our vision is much more sensitive in the middle of the spectrum than at the ends. If we are dealing with colored light at threshold levels or the perception of distant lights in a clear atmosphere, we see white, yellow, or green light much more readily than red or blue. The scattering of light by fog or haze makes red more easily visible but this is a special case.

As far as visibility is concerned, we see better with white light or hues in the middle of the spectrum; however, there seems to be a difference between visibility and focus. Tests show that white light holds little visual interest because of its lack of "chromaticity." It does not have the dynamic qualities of spectral hues. Studies of light signals conclude that red draws the most attention, followed by green, yellow, and then white and blue.[7]

The precedence of red is further enhanced by its tendency to advance in the visual field. Because blue light is of shorter wavelength and focuses within the eye nearer to the lens in the same manner as light from more distant objects, we tend to see a blue light or object as more distant than red even though both in fact are on the same plane.

Even though purely empirical considerations give blue very little chance of competing for attention with other colors, subjective preference studies complicate the issue. Tests of color preference yield highly variable results depending on cultural background, visual sophistication, sex, and age, but the combined results of 26 investigations, in which there was considerable variations, yield the following order of color preference: blue, red, green, violet, orange, and yellow.[8] If we assume that a preferred or favorite color is more likely than another to attract the eye, blue is back in contention.

In final assessment, hue taken by itself probably has limited use as a reliable stimulus for determining the general focus of audience attention. However, if we disregard hue and talk about the other attributes of color, we are on much safer ground.

The brighter or more saturated a color,

the more attention it demands. When comparing two areas of the same color, the larger area draws more attention, but there is a point where decreased area results in an apparent increase in the saturation and brightness of a color, which may compensate in attention-getting power for its diminished size. The point at which this occurs varies with the characteristics of the color and the relative size of the two areas. In general, a bright or highly saturated color of small area has greater or equal attention-drawing capacity than a larger area of less bright or less saturated color. Changing or moving colors, hues which contrast with the general chroma of the visual field, fluorescent colors, and unexpected colors are all able to draw focus.

Even though the isolation of a single attribute of color in the laboratory is an interesting way of confirming which variables govern focus, the stage lighting designer would rarely have such limited resources. All of the attributes of color are simultaneously at work in a production, and the designer must be able to orchestrate their dynamic interplay to control the attention of the audience.

Emotional Responses to Color

Do specific colors arouse specific emotional responses? Here again the testimony is complex and often contradictory. There are three general approaches to the problem: measurements of physiological response to color, studies of attributes that test subjects ascribe to various colors, and the affective attributes assigned to colors by artists and writers over a considerable span of time.

Colored lights are clearly able to influence blood pressure, heart beat rate, respiration, skin response (perspiration), brain waves, frequency of eye blinks, and muscular tension. One study found that red raised all of these functions, blue depressed them, green was more or less neutral, orange and yellow were akin to red but with less extreme responses, and purple and violet produced less extreme suppression than blue.[9]

Apparently the physiological responses to color are usually temporary. There is an immediate reaction but after a short time responses return to normal or may in fact swing somewhat in the opposite direction.[10] Also, repeated exposure to the same color does not produce a repeated response. Familiarity reduces response towards indifference.

Furthermore, the emotional effect of a specific color is raised when viewed after a less pleasing color or lowered when viewed after a more pleasing color, a reaction that could be described as "affective contrast enhancement."[11] These factors suggest that frequent changes in the color of lights are necessary to maintain any significant response.

The physiological response to color varies considerably according to the personality of the viewer. One study found that red was more disturbing to viewers with an already high level of anxiety. These same subjects were more noticeably calmed by blue.[12] Other studies conclude that no one color produces a specific response, but that preferences for specific colors or prior associations with colors result in variations from individual to individual.[13]

Even if we grant physiological reactions to color, how do we equate these responses with specific emotions? An acceleration of heart beat may, among other things, indicate both anxiety and exhilaration. If a lighting design were to produce one of these when the other was desired, the effect on a play could be quite damaging. We need more specific indicators of the emotional responses to color.

Another way to discover responses to color is to measure patterns of word associations applied to colors. This may be done either by free association, selection from a list of adjectives, or more commonly by using Semantic Differential scales which require a subject to choose between pairs of words that express opposite values. This approach's principal limitation is that it forces the subject to assign emotional value to a color when in fact there may be no natural tendency to do so. As might be expected these word associations vary considerably from person to person and are strongly influenced by personality, culture, symbolic associations, degree of visual training, and contemporary vogue. Much effort has been exerted to isolate these various influencing factors and to find an innate or natural basis of response. From the perspective of the lighting designer, however, this question is largely moot. The designer works for a given audience, usually with a fairly wide range of personality types and a relatively narrow range of cultural conditioning. The problem is to discover any pattern of emotional response this particular audience may have to specific colored lights, regardless of what conditioned that response.

In spite of individual variations, traditional patterns have emerged. Red, yellow, and orange are associated with excitement, stimulation, and aggression. More specifically, yellow is associated with gaiety, cheerfulness, and fun; red with passion. Blue and green are associated with calm and security, blue encouraging more introspection. Purple is associated with dignity and sadness; black, brown, and gray with melancholy, sadness, and depression.

A most consistent association is with the adjectives "warm" and "cool." The short end of the spectrum (violet, blue, and green) is consistently described as "cool" and associated with calming or restful responses. The long end (red, orange, and yellow) is described as "warm" and its colors associated with excitement and stimulation. Warm lights do seem to make people more outgoing: when used instead of cool colors to light stores, warm lights can produce measurable increases in sales. Positive responses to warm tints are accentuated when flesh tones are involved: not only do cool lights make skin tones appear unnatural, but people actually prefer complexion tints that are redder than the actual tone of their own skin.[14]

The perception of warmth or coolness is not limited to full spectrum comparisons. If two lights of closely related hue are compared, the one closest to the long end of the spectrum or with the greatest percentage of longwave light will always be perceived as the warmer. As we shall see later, this perceptual factor greatly increases the combinations of colored light that can be used while maintaining the warm/cool cross lighting prescribed by the so-called McCandless System of stage lighting.

We must consider colored light in its context when we discuss our response to it. A color quite pleasing in one situation may be disturbing in another. The greenish tint of light filtered through leaves may be very pretty in the summer woods, but skin colors seem weird under the same tinted light. A flashing red light on the track ahead obviously evokes a very specific and special emotional response for the engineer of a fast moving train.

The extent to which we place emotional values on colors is indicated by how we use color terminology in the English language to express moods. We talk about "seeing red," "feeling blue," "being green with envy," and a "purple passion," to name only a few. Granted these may be linguistic vestiges of a time when our culture had a detailed color symbology, but those symbols in turn were rooted at least partly in emotional associations.

One fairly controversial manifestation of belief in the emotional effects of light is so-called "color therapy" in which colored lights are used to treat various emotional and sometimes physical ailments. The most spectacular example is the use of blue light to lower the bilirubin level and correct jaundice in newborn infants. Most of the effects for which there is some scientific evidence deal with the negative effects of prolonged exposure to limited spectrum light, particularly fluorescent lighting. The lighting environment in a theatre is not of sufficient duration to have any comparable influence, but some color therapists claim significant responses from brief exposure to colored light. For example, violet supposedly slows the activity of the pancreas. Orange stimulates the thyroid, and indigo suppresses it.[15] There is presently inadequate scientific evidence to support conclusively the effects of colored light, but we do know that light stimulates the pituitary and pineal glands and possibly other regions of the brain controlling the production of hormones influencing the way we feel; so there is a basis to justify further investigations of the measurable physiological responses to colored light, which in turn may lead to a better understanding of emotional responses to color.

At least from the time of Leonardo da Vinci, artists and writers have developed the idea that specific colors evoke specific emotions. In 1810, Goethe published an extensive investigation of color which included a list of emotions produced by colors.[16] Similar lists can be found in modern times in any number of method books designed for artists. The most prolific recent exponent of this approach is Faber Birren, who has written a number of books espousing the power of color to evoke specific emotions.[17] These approaches are synthesized from studies of color symbolism, reflections of contemporary taste, practical experience, and the subjective sensibility of the writer. The lack of objective scientific support does not mean that these systems are wrong, only that it is difficult to test their reliability.

The following list of emotional responses to colored light draws on the little reliable scientific data available, a survey of similar lists compiled by other writers, and the experience of this writer. It is intended as a rough guide, subject to revision whenever more reliable or better evidence becomes available. In no case should it be viewed as a set of rules.

The subject here is response to colored light, not to color per se. Of course, in a technical sense, most color perception results from light striking the eye. The color of objects is really our perception of light re-flected by these objects. However, when we are aware that the illuminant is tinted, we make a distinction between the color of the light and the color of the lit object. Because of the effect of colored light on some colored surfaces, particularly the skin, our response to the color of an illuminant may be very different from our response to the same color ascribed to an object.

Because many audience members may be visually unsophisticated, it is quite possible that their emotional responses to colored light are minimal. Fortunately, light alone rarely carries the total burden of evoking emotion in the theatre. There are also numerous personal responses to specific colors which will deviate from any generally ascribed responses, and a specific production can endow a given colored light with emotional overtones by conditioning the audience to respond in a given way through repeated associations between the light hue and emotion-producing events occurring onstage.

There are dozens of distinguishable hues and thousands of combinations of different hues with various degrees of brightness and saturation. Given the uncertainty of ascribing any emotional response to any one hue, it seems pointless to attempt more refined distinctions among more subtle differences in lighting color. We will therefore concentrate on major hues and principal variables.

Violet and Purple. These two colors are often confused or related. Technically, purple does not exist on the spectrum but is a secondary color produced by the mixture of red and blue light. A true violet is the shortest wavelength light on the visible spectrum and contains no red. Most theatrical color filters, even those named "violet," contain some red light. Because both visibility and color-filter efficiency are low in the violet area of the spectrum, because violet is the "coldest" of the colors, and because violet light supresses all warm tints, it is usually viewed as a melancholy color.

The introduction of red light, changing the violet to purple, considerably alleviates the heavy mood. Purple light seldom occurs in nature, so it is likely to be seen as a highly artificial color. We often perceive purple as a rich color, probably because colors at the ends of the spectrum appear more saturated in hue than colors in the center, when all are at one brightness level.

Blue. A clear sky gives daylight a blue tint. In this case our psychological and physical response to the warmth of the sun balances the normally perceived coolness of blue light. The slightly more extreme blueness of an overcast day usually seems drab. Because distant objects often undergo a blue shift and because blue focuses short of the retina in a full spectrum field of view, we tend to be somewhat more detached from objects in blue light than in warmer tints.

Blue light emphasizes the veins rather than the arteries in human skin and suppresses natural skin tones; so in blue illumination the skin appears lifeless. Blue is a popular color, particularly among men, but not as an illuminant for human activity. Manufacturers of fluorescent and mercury lights have gone to considerable trouble to add warm tints to these light sources because so many people find that the normal blue cast of these lights creates an unpleasant working environment. The tendency of blue light to orient a person inward, found in some studies, may result from a psychological rejection of a blue-tinted environment.

Even though moonlight and most other nighttime illuminants are considerably richer in warm tones than daylight, the convention of using blue light for night scenes strongly persists. This may partly result from the fact that the eye is more sensitive to the short end of the spectrum than the long end at very low levels of illumination. However, by this line of reasoning, blue-green is the last color seen before the shift to achromatic night vision and would be a more logical color to use rather than purer

tints of blue. Daylight shadows have a more blue tint than direct sunlight; so there may be some learned association between shadow and blueness. We also perceive some analogous relationship between the limited spectral response of objects under blue light and the absence of hue perception in night vision, even though this spectral suppression is no greater than it would be for any narrow spectrum illuminant. Regardless of the cause, the compulsion of an audience to equate deep blue light with night is strong, and the designer who chooses to substitute red or green should beware.

Green. The least popular of the three primaries, green is also the least flattering to human skin tones. People in green light seem macabre. In nature, green light tints are usually reflected from vegetation and carry that association. As an illuminant for anything other than people, green light is very efficient with a high degree of visual sensitivity in that portion of the spectrum, particularly at low levels of illumination. Most studies of emotional response find green to be the most neutral of the major hues.

Yellow. Because untrained observers perceive yellow as a "pure" hue rather than a mixture of any other colors, it is often classified as one of the "psychological primaries," and some theories of color vision have attempted to include yellow receptors among the principal mechanisms of the eye.

With the use of daylight vision, the eye is more sensitive to yellow than any other hue. Slight shifts of wavelength are more readily perceived in the yellow part of the spectrum than any other portion. However, yellow has a relatively weak coloring power. When yellow is added to white light, we at first interpret the addition as an increase in the brightness of the white light rather than a hue change.

There is a strong tendency to equate the lighter tints of yellow with white light. The traditional depiction of the sun as yellow is an example of this. At a given percentage of saturation, yellow seems brighter than other hues, and an increase in saturation is more likely to be interpreted as increased brightness than is the case with other colors. The low place usually occupied by yellow in color preference tests may be the result of its perceived low chromaticity. Yellow is more frequently associated with brightness than chroma.

Yellow is perhaps the most easily corrupted of the hues. In its purest form it evokes feelings of cheer, but if it is darkened, neutralized, or muddied it is the most unpopular of all colors. On stage, yellows or ambers emphasizing green rather than red are unflattering to skin colors and produce negative responses. Because yellow or amber in combination with its complementary blue creates a white light, these colors are frequently used as cross lights on stage. The capacity of yellow to provoke such a range of response makes it a valuable lighting color but one to be used carefully.

Orange. As the red component in yellow increases, the light becomes more amber and then orange. We also move more clearly into the region of "warm" colors. Orange carries most of the associations of red light but to a lesser extreme. It depresses the blue and green portion of the spectrum, but green retains more of its hue under orange than red light. Orange is not an unflattering light color for most skin tones. Its most frequent realistic occurrence is in association with fire and candlelight, and most responses to it are positive.

Red. The most popular color among women and traditionally the most stimulating color, red produces measurable quickening of body functions. Responses to it are generally positive, but it is still a color to which the eye is relatively insensitive and deep tints of red suppress other hues; so it can be used to provoke a feeling of threat and anxiety. There is no concrete evidence that red light is specifically a sexual stimulant even though popular support abounds

for this idea. A red lighting environment does seem to make people more outgoing than white light or other hues, which may be a related response.

The most common natural occurrence of red light is in sunsets. Of the primary colors, red is the most flattering to all skin colors, but in saturated form it is still seen as an unnatural lighting color.

For the stage lighting designer, the ultimate test of the ability of light of a certain color to stimulate a mood or emotional response is in the actual response of the audience. Unfortunately, it is difficult at best to gauge audience response, particularly in an area where there is not much refinement of sensitivity and where responses are likely to be largely subconscious. One helpful consideration is that when a concensus exists that a given color has a certain meaning, that concensus in itself is sufficient to assure that the meaning is conveyed. In practice, the lighting designer and the director serve as a microcosmic audience, deciding what colors have an emotional effect on themselves and trusting that the same effect will be produced for the audience.

Colored Afterimages and Subjective Colors

Afterimages are visual sensations persisting after the original stimulus is removed. Positive afterimages result from the continued excitation of receptors after the stimulus ceases, a time lag in the termination of a response. Positive afterimages are usually of short duration. Negative afterimages result from the fatigue of the receptors in the eye. For bright white light, the negative afterimage is black or darker than the surrounding field. If the eye is fixed for a time on a color, the negative afterimage seen on any achromatic field is the complement of the color producing the fatigue. We have discussed the manner in which this color fatigue influences color contrast and causes shifts in the apparent hue of subsequently viewed colors.

If the colored area is sharply defined and

either very bright or viewed for a period of time, the afterimage keeps the silhouette of the original object. This is usually a source of distraction for subsequent viewing, but in rare instances afterimages can make a dramatic point by emphasizing the lingering influence of an object or person.

Afterimages persist even when the eyes are closed. Even though they are outside the domain of the lighting designer, other "subjective colors" are noted here in passing. Many persons dream in color; colors may be induced by pressure on the eyeball; and displays of color can be produced by drugs, electrical stimulation of areas of the brain controlling visual functions, and other means.

Synesthesia

Through mechanisms not fully understood, for some individuals there seems to be a degree of crossover between different senses. A person can feel an odor or hear a color. This may result from interaction between nerves or portions of the brain controlling different senses, which influence one another by some interchange of bioelectrical impulse, or it may result from a trained habit of analogy-making so strongly conditioned that it actually stimulates the analogous sense.

Even though experimental data is limited, there is convincing evidence for the interaction of sound and color. It has been found that loud noises, as well as strong odors and tastes, tend to raise the sensitivity of the eye to green and decrease sensitivity to red.[18] Low-pitched sounds tend to make colors appear to deepen: red shifts somewhat toward blue, orange appears more red. High-pitched sounds make colors seem lighter. Also, a loud sound seems to decrease the sensitivity of rods and increase the sensitivity of cones.[19]

The analogy between color and musical harmony has intrigued observers at least since Aristotle discussed the matter in his *De Sensu*. Attempts to design an instrument combining color and music date from the eighteenth century, and a variety of such "color organs" are commercially available today. Light shows—which often are no more than visual interpretations of music, using a variety of projection devices—are now fairly commonplace.

There seems to be a fairly consistent tendency for observer-listeners to equate pitch with brightness or the lightness of a color. The more saturated a color, the more likely it is to be associated with low notes on the musical scale. Colors in the middle of the spectrum—which give the impression of greater brightness for a given degree of saturation than do colors on the end of the spectrum—are likely to be equated with higher musical notes. However, no consistent correspondence between a specific sound and a specific color has been experimentally confirmed and all systems that artificially establish analogues between the musical scale and the spectral continuum break down when they attempt to find similar correspondences between chords and color combinations. There seems to be no psychologically "natural" or physically inherent connection between specific colors and sounds.

There are alternative approaches. A lighting designer may create an internally consistent correspondence between light and sound which gains compelling force for an audience by repetition throughout a musical work. The designer has spatial and compositional elements in addition to color that can be manipulated to establish a relationship between light and sound.

An even more familiar approach, used whenever a lighting designer allows musical considerations to influence lighting changes, is to "interpret" or "translate" musical elements into a lighting design. Here, the lighting designer either expresses with light the mood evoked by the music or constructs with light a composition in which changes and relationships are analogous to those in the music. This method, though admittedly subjective, provides a more flexible and varied expression of the music with light than systems which attempt to establish rigid correspondences between musical and visual elements. In the absence of compelling objective reasons for associating specific colors with specific musical notes, this approach is as valid as any.

In considering the relationship between sound and light, we do not have to limit our attention to analogy or parallel structure. Light or color may function in contrast or counterpoint to sound. Light and sound together may be thought of as the warp and woof of a complex tapestry of sensory experience.

In summary, even white light is composed of colored light; so in one sense, the designer uses color whenever light is used. The range of tints available in filters, the millions of combinations possible using these filters, the often extraordinary reflective properties of objects and surfaces onstage, and the complexities of human color vision make the manipulation of color in lighting design an extremely complicated thing. The designer must not only consider the color of the light source when dimmed, the properties of the filter and the surface being lit, but also the relationship between the color and the demands of the text, music, other colors visible, and how the eyes of the audience condition to some previous color.

Certainly there are basic principles of color control and composition to be mastered, but the effects of light on color and the color of light should be as much an object for lifetime study for the lighting artist as they are for the landscape painter.

EXERCISES

1. *Polarized Light* (p. 36)—Obtain sheets of transparent polarizing material from a scientific supply house. Mount small pieces of the polarizer in slide mounts along with small pieces of cellophane tape arranged in random order and overlapping. Make a polarizing wheel attached to a small motor or turn a second piece of the polarizing material by hand in front of the lens of a slide projector into which the prepared slide has been placed. If a changing display of colors does not result, reverse the slide so the polarizing material faces the lamp. Try preparing slides from thin sections of rock obtained from a geology department, from mica crystals, or from aspirin crystals.

2. *Influence of Reflective Surfaces on Color Selection* (p. 36)—(a) Try to find a multicolored porcelain object with a mixture of glazed and unglazed surfaces. If that cannot be found, dull the glaze on portions of a glazed object by sanding lightly with fine grained emery cloth. Try not to remove color. Place this under a small spotlight and note any differences in the quality of the color between glazed and unglazed surfaces. Place a diffusion medium on the spotlight and see if the quality of the colors remains the same. (b) Take a piece of stained wood, varnish one third of the surface, and wax another third. Test under light to see if the surface treatment darkens the color. Try different colors and different diffusion in the lighting instrument.

3. *Piling on Bounce Light* (p. 36)— Construct two open-ended boxes, one with black walls, the other with red walls. Place the boxes side by side and place identical objects in each box. Light them with a single beam of light from the front. See how the color of the objects varies as a result of the bounce light. Notice particularly the color of the shadows. See what effect a red and then a blue light has on the appearance of the objects.

4. *The Coloring Power of Different Hues* (p. 39)—To a pool of white light projected onto a screen, add a blue light, then a red light, and finally a yellow light. Which color has the least influence on the combined hues?

5. *Influence of Brightness on Color* (p. 39)—Place identical color filters in a

250-watt and a 2000-watt instrument. Project the two instruments side by side onto a white screen. Do the hues match? What would influence this comparison if instruments of identical wattage were used and one instrument merely dimmed? Try this experiment with different matching colors. See if the same principle works when matching color samples are compared in the light of each unfiltered instrument.

6. *The Recovery of Color Sensitivity After Brightness Fatigue* (p. 39)—Project an intense bright white light onto a white screen for a few moments. Lower the lighting to a very low intensity and immediately view a multicolored picture. Note how colors become more saturated over time. Do different colors emerge at the same rate?

7. *Color Fatigue* (p. 39)—(a) Project an intense yellow light onto a screen. After a minute, the light should take a greenish tinge and then gradually return to yellow. (b) Project a primary red onto a screen for a few moments. Follow this immediately with a yellow. Does the yellow have a green tint?

How long does this tint persist? (c) Project a saturated color onto a screen for a few moments then immediately follow this with a white light on a fabric or wallpaper pattern that relies heavily on the same color originally projected. Does the hue gray?

8. *Color Adaptation* (p. 43)—Take three squares of the same medium gray construction paper. Place one on a white background, one on a gray background, and one on a black background. View them in sequence under a red tinted light, asking viewers to describe the tint of the gray square in each case.

9. *Color Contrast in Shadows* (p. 44)—(a) Cross light an opaque, free-standing object with red and white light so that each light casts a distinct shadow. What colors are the shadows? Cross light with red and yellow and observe shadow colors. (b) Cross light a white object which has a variety of surface reflectances, using green and orange lights. What colors are seen in the shadows, from the combination of the two hues, and from surface reflectance?

Psychophysical Considerations: Space and Form Perception

We assume that our perception of three-dimensional reality results from the place objects and surfaces actually occupy in space. In fact, this three-dimensional perception depends on a wide array of visual cues, many of which can be "faked." The ability of paintings, photographs, moving pictures, and television to create an impression of tridimensionality on a flat surface depends on this "trickery." A variety of optical illusions further emphasizes our dependence upon manipulatable cues for spatial perception.

The theatre, to the extent that it deals with illusions, is particularly a place where we want things to appear different from the way they are. Depending on the style of production, we may wish flat surfaces to appear three-dimensional, shallow stages to seem deep, small objects to look large, or enclosed spaces to appear open.

In other respects, theatre is a sculptural art form; so rather than tricking the eye, we wish to enhance the textures, forms, and structural relationships that actually exist on stage by reinforcing natural visual cues.

In practice, most theatrical production mixes these two objectives: the creation of illusion and the enhancement of reality. The balance between the two varies with the style of production and involves selective control: knowing when to emphasize reality and when to disguise it.

Theatre is also a time art; so the perception of the stage space changes over time. This can be done by actually moving scenery, but we can often change the appearance of a stationary scenic structure by altering only its lighting.

The scene designer controls many of the cues for the perception of form and space on stage: superposition, scale, lines of perspective, relative sharpness of outline, texture, and relative surface color, for example. However, the lighting influences all of these as well as other perceptual cues under the principal control of the lighting designer: the direction of shadows and the relationship between form and light, for instance.

We will discuss here how lighting influences the perception of depth, texture, shape, flow, and pattern. A later section will explore in more detail the total compositional aspects of lighting design.

Depth Perception

A lifetime of visual experience leads us to assume that, with no other visual cues to the contrary, the bluer of any two objects is the furthest away. Distant objects do appear more blue than near objects because of the scattering of blue light by the atmosphere. We also know that distant objects blur slightly, and in a full spectrum field of vision, chromatic aberration of the eye's lens focuses blue just short of the retina, causing it to be ever so slightly blurred. The mind equates this blurring with greater distance. Therefore when a bluish and a reddish light separately illuminate two objects the same distance from a viewer, the viewer sees the bluer of the two as the more distant. Consequently, we can accentuate stage depth by using blue or cool lights upstage and warm or red tints downstage with a graded shift in color from one to the other in between. Landscape painters have long practiced this technique known as *aerial perspective.*

Distant objects also appear less sharply focused and show less surface detail. Diffused front lighting reduces surface texture and softens the separation of colors, in contrast to sharply focused angular lighting which emphasizes texture and accentuates color differences. Therefore using diffused front lighting upstage and angular, specular lighting downstage, accentuates depth by the approximation of the progression from sharply focused to unfocused detail.

Because of the inverse square law, it might seem that decreased brightness would act as a cue for distance. This, however, is not always the case. In a relatively shallow

visual field such as an auditorium, the more distant object subtends a proportionately smaller visual angle at the eye, compensating for the loss of intensity over greater distance. Our perception of brightness remains relatively constant over distance. There are also too many instances in our experience where illumination is brighter at a distance than nearby.

Brightness differences can, however, help to accentuate the sense of depth. The important factor is the contrast in brightness that defines spatial planes receding from the viewer. Whether the foreground is bright and the background dark or the reverse is less important than differences in brightness related to the apparent distance of a surface or object from the viewer. A space with an apparently random arrangement of bright and dark objects creates much less of an impression of depth than a space with an orderly correlation between distance and brightness (see Figure 4-1).

In general, high contrast, whether in brightness or color, tends to enhance depth perception, and loss of contrast tends to "flatten" a visual field. If the contrast emphasizes the idea of receding planes, the sense of three-dimensionality will be even greater. As a result, high-contrast side lighting—as opposed to diffuse front lighting—produces a much greater perception of depth, particularly if there are alternating bands of light and shadow to accentuate receding planes (see Plate III).

To demonstrate vividly the effect of contrast on depth perception, take a slide of a painted landscape drop or flat and project it back onto the painting in perfect registration. The range between black and white available in scenic paints is usually limited to a relative-brightness ratio of about one to thirty, but the projection considerably increases this range. The result is often a striking enhancement of the three-dimensionality of the painted unit. Scrim drops painted with combinations of transparent dyes and opaque paints similarly increase the brightness ratio when lit both from the

FIGURE 4-1 Josef Svoboda, Lighting for *Svatopluk*. [From Jarka Burian, *The Sceneography of Josef Svoboda* (Middletown, Conn.: Wesleyan University Press, 1971), p. 76. Copyright © 1971 by Jarka Burian. Reprinted by permission of Wesleyan University Press and KaiDib Films International, Glendale, California.]

front and from behind by an illuminated backing drop. Properly painted and lit, they create a much greater sense of depth than a painted opaque drop.

Given a proper atmospheric condition in which beams of light can be seen passing through the air or with beams visible on the stage floor or on drops, the linear characteristics of a light beam strengthen the illusion of depth just like lines in a drawing. Shafts of light converging diagonally on or diverging diagonally from a small upstage area, for example, will make that area seem more distant. The principal is the same as the convergence of lines onto a vanishing point in a perspective drawing.

Thus far we have dealt with the use of light to increase the apparent depth of the stage, add an impression of depth to a flat painted surface, or increase the apparent distance of an object. On a smaller scale, light gradients and shadows define the form and volume of any three-dimensional object, including the actor. Our experience, primarily conditioned by the combination of directional sunlight and diffuse sky light, which we encounter outdoors, creates a definite expectation of how most objects should look when lit. We must have a sufficient interplay of light and shadow to give us needed data to judge volume. One of the problems with flat front lighting, not just on

the human face and body but on any object, is that it deprives us of shadows that cue us as to the tridimensionality of the object.

Shadow by itself is an insufficient guide to form. Unless we can correlate shadow with its light source, we are liable to misinterpret the form. Previous experience is very compelling; so even when we know that the light is coming from an unusual angle, the effect can be disorienting. We expect dents or concave surfaces to have shadows in their upper portions and bumps or convex surfaces to have shadows at the bottom. This is because we usually see them lit from above. If we see a bump with a shadow on top we are more likely to see it as a dent than as a bump lit from below (see Figure 4-2). Similarly, when we can see the lower surface of an object, we usually expect it to be darker than the upper surface. If there is little or no modulation in light and shade from upper to lower surfaces, there is less modeling.

We are not irrevocably locked into overhead lighting sources. If we can clearly perceive that the light is coming from another direction, we will adjust our interpretations of the interrelation between light and shadow to derive a perception of form consistent with the direction of the light, but objects may still appear unusual to us. Presumably only a small child is genuinely

FIGURE 4-2 Shadow as a cue to whether a surface is convex or concave. The photograph on the left shows lighting from above. The photograph on the right shows the same surface with lighting from below.

frightened when the human face is unaccountably lit from below, but the rest of us may still find it a bit strange. Well designed interior moldings and other architectural features above windows or above the usual source of artificial illumination may look very unattractive if lit from above (see Figure 11-2).

Of course in the theatre, the unusual, the unattractive, the macabre, or the disorienting lighting angle may be exactly the thing needed. Skillfully used, light can be a form giver and a form changer. The important thing is for the designer to be in control of the effect created.

Texture

The perception of surface texture is a matter of three-dimensional perception of small detail. Sharply focused light striking the surface at a high angle will accentuate rough texture, and diffused front light will flatten texture. If there are color differences between raised and recessed portions of a textured surface, any lighting color that accentuates the difference in surface colors will increase the texturing, and a light color that depresses the difference in surface colors will make the surface appear flatter. We also see fine detail better with increased brightness; so as long as we avoid glare and stay below the brightness fatigue level, we see texture better at higher levels of illumination.

All surfaces have some roughness, if only of microscopic scale. The difference between a glossy and a matte finish results from a difference of surface roughness which produces variations in the diffusion of scattered light. If the light striking a smooth surface is diffuse, the reflected light will be more diffuse and the surface will appear less glossy.

The problem for the lighting designer is to know when it is desirable to emphasize surface texture and when not. High-angle lighting on a scenic flat may only reveal patches and the hinges under dutchmen to the detriment of details painted on the surface. However, a scenic designer who has gone to the trouble of using textured paints or plastic appliques to enhance the realistic appearance of a flat representing a brick wall will be rightly upset with front light that fails to accentuate the detail. In general, painted detail, particularly with painted shadows, should be lit with shadowless light, but designed three-dimensional detail should be accentuated with highlights and shadows. Similarly, a costumer may wish to call attention to the texture of an expensive velvet and conceal the lack of texture of a cheap substitute. The lighting designer must approach the problem analytically and determine what textures to emphasize.

Shape

Our ability to perceive shape, the spatial form of an object or surface, depends on our interpretation of a multitude of visual cues with respect to previous experience. For example, unless we view a square table from directly above, its image which strikes our eye is not a square, but we still see the table as being square. The entire principal behind forced perspective and other spatial illusions is to provide false visual cues that the viewer interprets to make a distorted reality consistent with prior experience of an undistorted reality. One of the chief cues for shape is light, and *chiaroscuro* is a major artistic technique which creates the illusion of spatial form by manipulating the appearance of light and shadow.

Of course the function of light is not just to create the illusion of shape but also to strengthen the appearance of forms that do exist on stage and to exploit the variety of appearances these forms can take under different lighting conditions.

Light can define the extent of a surface or how far it seems to reach into space. It does this by either accentuating or deemphasizing boundaries and edges. Abrupt changes in brightness or in the color of light imply an end or change of direction in a surface. Constant illumination or gradual gradients suggest surface continuity. If we wish to conceal the sharp top edge of a scenic wall, we back it with a black masking piece and use a combination of spattered black paint and soft edged light to create a gradual progression from full illumination to blackness. If a cyclorama is as brightly lit at the edges where it disappears behind side masking as it is in the center, we assume a much larger expanse of light than we actually see. If the light gradually diminishes toward the edges, we assume a smaller expanse, but we perceive no sharp end to the lit surface. Scenic elements which suggest a large surface or object by showing only a portion of it on stage must be lit evenly or with constant gradients as far as the eye can see. A sharp edge to the lighting will help to destroy the illusion that the surface continues out of sight.

Light emphasizes shape by calling attention to the silhouette of an object or surface. This can be done by heightening the contrast in brightness or color against the background or by creating a dark or bright rim around the shape. The form, brightness, and color saturation of an object increase to a maximum when there is a dark border, a feature known as *border contrast*. The enhancement is less extreme and colors tend to lose some saturation with a bright rim, but the silhouette is still emphasized. A dark rim can be created for a rounded three-dimensional object on stage only by keeping the object at the edge of a very sharply focused high-angled light which picks up portions of the object extending toward the audience and leaves the receding surfaces in darkness. It is much easier to highlight silhouette with a bright border by placing instruments diagonally behind the object so that light strikes the edges but not the front surface. The maximum emphasis of the silhouette is obtained by the maximum contrast of brightness and dark still within the viewers' brightness adaptation range, but the need to see surface detail on the front of the object often requires the use of fill light from the front. The brightness ratio (perceived brightness, not simply foot-candles) needs to be at least two to one in order for the back and side lights to have any noticeable effect in emphasizing the silhouette.

The perception of three-dimensional relief is also an important part of our perception of shape and is, as we have discussed, influenced by lighting. Any variation in the intensity or color of light on a surface likely implies a change of shape to the mind's eye unless we can clearly perceive that the lighting itself has changed. Sharp shifts in illumination imply an edge and a change in plane. Gradual changes in illumination suggest a curved surface. Low relief is obscured if lit from the front or from multiple angles which confuse the shadow cues.

In some instances light can also change the apparent size of an object or the apparent ratio between height, width, and depth. For example, bright objects surrounded by darkness usually appear larger than a similar dark object against a bright background. The columns shown in Figure 4-3 appear thinner when they are silhouetted against a light background than when they are lit against a dark background.

The manipulation of brightness gradients can emphasize a particular axis of a surface and change its apparent shape. A wall lit uniformly from top to bottom but gradually becoming less bright on its side edges will seem taller than if lit at the same level overall. Similarly, darkening the top or the top and bottom but not the sides will increase its apparent width. Brightness at the top but not the bottom sustains the sense of height because it draws the eye up and the dark bottom is consistent with our expectation of the appearance of tall objects in nature.

Light striking a three-dimensional object from below or at a low angle also increases its appearance of height. Overhead illumination is so much the norm in our everyday experience that we seem to subconsciously look for a change in our external environment to explain low-angled lighting. When we do encounter objects lit from below, we are usually looking up at high surfaces lit by artificial illumination, which may account for this perceived relationship between height and bottom light.

A commonplace in dance lighting is that top light shortens the appearance of the human figure, which indeed it does. This, however, does not result from any inherent power of top light to depress apparent height, but rather from the relationship of surfaces on the human body. Top lighting tends to emphasize horizontal surfaces on the body, particularly the shoulders, which decrease the illusion of verticality. An object without large horizontal planes would gain rather than lose apparent height under top light.

Any complexly shaped object will change its appearance somewhat according to which surfaces or linear characteristics are emphasized by light. In general, it will appear to increase in size along the axis being emphasized.

Flow

Even apart from linear characteristics contributed by the object being illuminated, light seems to have its own inherent directionality, described as its "illumination vector" or more simply as its *flow*. Our per-

 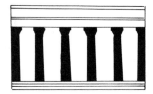

FIGURE 4-3 The relationship between brightness and the perception of size. Which columns seem thicker? They are both the same width. In one case the background is black; in the other, it is white.

ception of flow comes from visual cues which result from the simple fact that light loses intensity as it moves away from its source. If the source is unrestricted, the light flows spherically in all directions, but if the light comes into our visual field after passing through an aperture—a window or the shutter and lens of a lighting instrument—it will have an even more pronounced unidirectional axis. With sufficient particles in the air to allow us to see the actual beam of light, this sense of directionality will increase.

The flow of light is important because we are conditioned to expect it, because it enhances our perception of space, because its direction changes the apparent shape of object, and because it contributes to compositional unity in our field of vision.

Our sense of the directionality of daylight is, of course, most extreme under clear skies, but even in twilight or with overcast skies, some light still flows from overhead. Any lighting plot attempting realistic duplication of clear sunlight onstage can maintain the illusion only by consistently keeping all of the brighter light flowing in one direction or by providing a very clear motivation for the extraordinary exceptions where a bright light may be reflected in a direction inconsistent with the general flow.

Even at night, we are most accustomed to light emitted from a few strong sources that maintain a cohesive flow. There are certainly occasions when light at night comes from a variety of directions, as at the center of big city night life, but even though the effect may be visually stimulating, it can also be disorienting. If we desire to make a "splash" with lights, confusion may be in order, but if we want the audience to clearly see and understand what is being lit, a clear sense of the direction of the light flow will help.

Directional light facilitates our ability to interpret highlight and shadow and thereby improves our perception of form and space. When light flows in multiple directions, we must interpret anew the light and shadow configuration for each object with respect to the specific direction of light striking it. When there is an overall flow, we can use the same standards for the entire visual field.

Most persons seem to prefer a diagonal rather than a vertical or horizontal flow of light. The diagonal flow may provide better and more familiar shadow patterns to reveal form. The direction of the flow is also a visual cue for the apparent time of day, with lower angles as we move away from noon. For night lighting, a horizontal flow gives a strong impression of a distant light source and an upward flow seems to elevate the floor.

Lighting vectors also influence our perception of the linear aspects of form. Just as parallel lines can appear to bend or concentric circles to spiral when they are intersected by lines with a strong sense of directionality (see Figure 4-4), so lighting vectors exaggerate and modify the dimensions and lineation of forms. However, we must consider flow in the context of the surfaces being lit. For example, when beams of light are visible and strike dominant surfaces at an angle near to parallel, the flow of light accentuates the linear direction of those surfaces. As a contrasting example, a strong diagonal light may illuminate a horizontal surface, emphasizing the horizontal rather than the diagonal line. A vertical unit lit directly from overhead may receive very little illumination on its long sides thereby lessening the sense of height. Particularly in an air-conditioned theatre with little airborne moisture or dust to reveal the characteristics of the light beam, the direction of the light is less important than the surface lit. However, even an observer who cannot clearly discern the beam or source can deduce the flow from the overall pattern of highlight and shadow.

One aspect of light flow which influences our response is its ability to encourage eye movement in specific directions. Eye move-

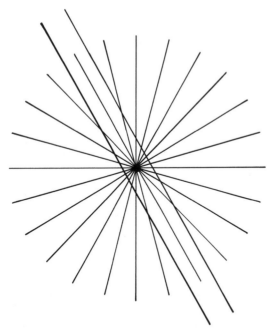

FIGURE 4-4 Influence of line on our perception of form. The two heavy lines are actually parallel but appear to bow out because of the influence of the other lines.

ment partly induces our perception of the horizontal or vertical aspects of a space. Books on directing advise that a character moving from audience-left to audience-right creates less tension than a movement in the opposite direction; for the same reason, the flow of light left to right in our visual field stimulates a greater sense of harmony than the opposite. Perhaps this is so because European languages read from left to right; but regardless of the cause, this preference for left-to-right movement persists enough to be a major compositional factor in Western art.

We usually look up at tall objects and down at short ones; so lighting that draws the eye upward cues height and that which draws downward suggests smallness. Incidentally, related to this is the influence of sustained eye position on fatigue. Investigation has shown that a television set placed near the floor produces less viewing fatigue than when positioned higher. One frequent argument made against luminous ceilings is that they draw the eyes upward to just that position the eyes occupy in sleep and produce an auto-hypnotic effect.[1] This may be another good reason for not designing theatres with the seats below the stage, but it also suggests a possible hazard for any lighting effect which draws the eyes upward for any long period of time.

Pattern

Lighting can call attention to patterns created by scenery, costumes, or performers; can change the appearance of those patterns; or can obstruct them by imposing a strong pattern within the lighting itself.

The perception of pattern is a fairly complicated process to explain. Efforts to do so have led to the creation of a separate branch of study called Gestalt psychology. Without exploring the complexities of the problem, we can define a visual pattern as *any perceived organization, design, or regular structure of visual components.* Controllable stimuli influence pattern perception, but the key to the recognition of pattern is in the perceptual process, a strategy for mental organization. The creation of pattern therefore depends both on the structuring of objects and forms, the stimuli, and on the control and manipulation of how they are seen. For example, an intricately designed Persian carpet may contain interlocking designs. Any given component may be part of more than one pattern and the perception of any one pattern may temporarily obscure others. A viewer may choose to see various patterns in sequence by self-consciously screening out others. The design of the carpet may emphasize certain patterns at the expense of others. We may also stress specific patterns by controlling the color of the illuminating light.

The subject of pattern is extremely important for the lighting designer because the creation of structure, of design, is a major enterprise for most arts. In general, the more complexity that can be organized and the more subtle and interrelated the patterns of organization, the greater the aesthetic value we place on a work of art.

The major methods of visual organization will be the principal topic of later chapters on composition with lighting, but at present, let us touch on a few of the elements of lighting which influence the way an audience sees patterns in scenic or costume design.

In general, the lighting designer may emphasize, neutralize, or obstruct patterns created by other designers. The most effective obstruction—a too frequent, inadvert error—is to impose a competing and unrelated pattern in the lighting itself. A structure of sharply defined pools of light or a conspicuous use of regularly patterned gobos can call inappropriate attention to the lighting and, in some circumstances, overpower the work of scenic or costume designers. A repetition of colored light, without regard for the forms being lit, or a superimposed pattern of color will similarly obscure other design features. This is a particular problem with the use of full-stage front projections. For example, a production which used brightly projected images of firework displays, presumably to emphasize climatic moments in a play, made it almost impossible to distinguish the actors from the scenery. Of course, in some cases such a sacrifice of other visual components to the lighting is a self-conscious directorial decision and presumably justifies the lighting design.

Patterns dependent on three-dimensional form are best emphasized by stressing those aspects of the structure which contribute to the overall design. If texture is the unifying feature, the lighting should reveal the texture. If scenic units are tied together by a common upper profile, the lighting should accent that silhouette. Not all form is justifiably revealed by light, only those forms which add to the total sense of design.

Many designs depend on the relationship between shape and background. Heightening the contrast between figure and ground usually helps the audience to discern any pattern. This can be done by using different colors, intensities, lighting angles, or degrees of diffusion to light separately the figure and the background or by highlighting the figure with back and side light. Occasionally the background should receive more emphasis than the figure. With some scenic designs, the space within openings may be a more important design feature than the structure around the openings. Shifting the emphasis from the background to the foreground figure can often drastically change the appearance of a unit setting (see Figure 4-5).

Lighting color primarily influences the appearance of two-dimensional painted designs, but sharp lighting angles can expose surface irregularities at the expense of the surface design. The most vivid example of the power of colored light to draw out design elements is the use of specially painted units where figures are made to appear and disappear by adding or removing the colored light which they selectively reflect, light which is necessary to make them visible against their background. Although a very limited pigment range must be employed and the lighting required may be of an unnaturally saturated color, the effect can be very striking in highly stylized productions, as is often the case with children's theatre. A somewhat more practical application of this technique can change the apparent pattern of wallpaper on multipurpose flats used for more than one interior in the same play. In general, colored light, correctly used, emphasizes the color of the desired pattern and heightens the contrast between the figure and the ground.

Another special use of lighting to control pattern on a two-dimensional surface involves a filled scrim painted with a combination of opaque, translucent, and transparent colors. Relatively high-angled front lighting emphasizes the opaque features. Flat front

FIGURE 4-5a Robert Edmond Jones' design for *Hamlet*, I, ii. [From Robert Edmond Jones, *Drawings for the Theatre* (New York: Theatre Arts, Inc., 1925). Copyright 1925 by Theatre Arts, Inc.; copyright © 1970 by Theatre Arts Books. Used with the permission of the publisher, Theatre Arts Books, 153 Waverly Place, New York, N.Y. 10014.]

FIGURE 4-5b Robert Edmond Jones' design for *Hamlet*, V, i.

lighting emphasizes opaque features plus any element upstage of the transparent sections. Scenic units upstage of the scrim have a foggy appearance under front light. Low lighting intensities from the front and bright light on elements upstage of the drop throw the opaque portions of the drop into relative silhouette and emphasize the shape of the transparent or translucent opening. Careful control of gradations between opaqueness and transparency and the bal-

ance between upstage and downstage light can result in a great sense of three-dimensionality from a flat drop and can provide a range of visual patterns as the lights shift.

Sometimes the lighting should neutralize a pattern in the scenery or visual background that is otherwise too strong. An extremely uniform pattern, particularly with high contrast, may cause visual fatigue because the eyes find it difficult to remain fixed on any definite part of the pattern. The brain requires a relatively steady, clear image, but the task of holding steady fixation on a repetitive pattern is too difficult and normal eye movements are greatly accelerated, resulting in fatigue. For example, a large scenic backing unit, consisting of vertical boards alternating their rough and sanded sides, was lit from sharp angles to emphasize the interesting texture. The effect on some audience members, particularly those with astigmatism, was positively nauseating. The lighting had to be changed to deemphasize the pattern of vertical striations.

Any strong pattern of visual information can dominate the visual field, much more so than when the same components are arranged in a random fashion. If this focus becomes a source of distraction, lighting may neutralize the pattern. This may entail more than keeping light away from the offending pattern. The light may emphasize structural components that do not contribute to the pattern, minimize figure-ground contrast, use uneven illumination that disrupts the units of the pattern, or impose a new, unrelated, but less distracting pattern. This is not just a matter of "doctoring" a poor scenic design. The production concept may require varying emphasis on the scenic pattern, and lighting may be the most efficient means for this change.

Light and the Human Form

In purely abstract terms, the human body is a three-dimensional form subject to the same principles of illumination as any other form. Some types of theatre—the Theatre of the Bauhaus being a notable historical example—and some modern dance keep their work on this abstract level; but the majority of theatrical productions do not. In most cases, a person on stage is emphasized more than any inanimate object. Much of the burden of communication and artistic statement likely rests on the human subject, and even though a good portion of this may be vocal, the visual experience is very important. Also, the audience probably has more refined visual expectations about the human body than any other form.

Our expectations as to the appearance of the human body are strongly conditioned by daylight experience with a strong overhead directional light (key light) from the sun and fill light reflected from the sky and other surfaces. On a cloudless, bright day, 90 percent of the light is directly from the sun, and on average sunny days, about 80 percent. Even though the angle of sunlight obviously varies according to the time of day, time of year, and latitude, most observers will judge an angle of between 30 and 60 degrees from the horizon to be "normal." An approximation of this lighting in the theatre, with diagonally mounted spotlights providing about 80 percent of the illumination and diffuse fill lights, the remainder, will nearly make the performers appear "normal." Of course some theatre has little concern for normality, and the lighting designer must consider other factors.

Everyone communicates with the entire body, whether consciously or not, as a recent surge of studies on body language have made us aware, but most people focus on the face as the primary communication tool, and actors particularly rely heavily on facial expression. Changes in facial muscles and lines around the mouth and eyes, which carry most of the communication burden, are extremely subtle and their perception requires a fair degree of visual acuity. Facial expression is easily obscured by too little illumination, front lighting which flattens facial contours, or by key lighting from extreme angles which casts heavy shadows from the nose and brow. The ideal condition is maximum intensity, within fatigue limits, and maximum modeling. However, these two factors, each taken by itself, work against one another. The most efficient light for brightness is from the front, but this obscures modeling. Lighting designs which use a large quantity of front light can restore modeling by using even more intense side lighting, but the resulting accumulation of brightness may be an inefficient and expensive way to maintain the desired balance. The compromise between brightness and modeling is most effectively done by emphasizing diagonal lighting, which has the added advantage of being the most familiar facial illumination.

The McCandless Lighting System, devised by Yale professor Stanley McCandless around 1930,[2] depends on the use of diagonal crosslight with instruments placed at an angle of 45° from both the vertical and horizontal axis. The use of two instruments compromises plasticity somewhat, but it eliminates shadows on the face when the actor turns away from one light. Furthermore one instrument provides a warm color and the other is filtered to produce a cool color, approximating the relationship between highlight and fill in daylight illumination and restoring some modeling by color contrast. Many college theatres with abundant front-of-house mounting positions used this approach. Broadway theatres usually lack the mounting positions to satisfy the angles specified by McCandless.

McCandless prescribed additional front flood or diffuse lighting, chiefly to help blend spotlit areas and provide general toning. To the extent that front blending lights illuminate both lit and shadowed areas equally, effective blending is possible only by raising the overall level of illumination to the point where the eye cannot differentiate disparities of intensity more apparent at lower levels. Unfortunately this destroys the modeling shadows for which the crosslighting was originally designed. The blending problem is most extreme with ellipsoidal spotlights, and recent developments in diffusion media and means of easily taking these spotlights out of focus provide better ways of blending than the wash recommended by McCandless.

The use of diffuse front light in combination with key light coming diagonally from only one direction more closely approximates daylighting than McCandless' system, and this is the basic lighting configuration used for television, film, photography, and much commercial stage lighting. Development of floodlights, which produce the most diffused lighting, has been mostly for media use rather than the live stage. But for these applications, light spill is much less of a problem. In the theatre, however, light is usually focused sharply within a proscenium or playing area. Consequently, stage lighting favors multiple spotlighting rather than floodlighting for front fill light.

The position of light sources in a naturalistic setting, design objectives, or the restrictions of available mounting positions, frequently necessitate situations where the key light strikes the face at an extreme side angle. When the direction of the key light is poor, the ratio between highlight and shadow or between maximum and minimum illumination should be low, ideally between two to one and five to one, to minimize the obscuring effect of undesirable shadows. When the direction of the key light is good, the ratio may be closer to ten to one, that found in bright sunlight, or even higher. Remember that these are ratios of apparent brightness and an increase in the overall level of illumination requires a greater difference in absolute foot-candles to produce a brightness differential. As long as other requirements for visibility and mood are met, modeling can be most easily attained by differences in an overall low level of brightness.

The distance of the spectator from the face of the performer also determines the extent to which light should emphasize modeling in the theatre. Actors in poorly lit early nineteenth century theatres used masklike makeup to emphasize a few prominent facial lines, visible from a distance. Lighting in large theatres today must also emphasize major expression lines in the face. In a more intimate theatre the same lighting might seem overstated, and softer modeling with less extreme light-shadow ratios is more appropriate. Even in large auditoriums, a significant percentage of the audience sits near the stage; so the designer must decide whether to design modeling light for the front, middle, or back of the audience. Just as perspective scenery in the seventeenth and eighteenth centuries was designed with the observation point in the royal box, so a democratic compromise on the modern lighting designer's part may not always be the correct answer. It may be wise, for example, to scale the lighting for the area of the auditorium with the highest-priced seats. The point is that the designer must make a conscious decision regarding the appropriate degree of modeling.

Good lighting for the face is usually good lighting for the actor's body. Unless the actor is nude or the costume particularly reveals the body, most of the actor's body language requires broad visual discriminations easily made with the same good modeling light used for the face. Where body movement requires particular emphasis, additional backlighting may help. Hair and rapidly receding side planes provide natural framing for the face, but body contours are more gradual and may require more modeling light for special emphasis.

Lighting for dance often introduces a different set of requirements. At one point, most forms of Western dance were totally uninterested in facial expression and the dancer performed with either a deadpan face or some frozen look of pleasantry. Some modern dancers have changed this, and the lighting designer must be sensitive to how much an individual dancer or choreographer uses the face as an expressive medium. If the face is unimportant, the lighting may aim at heavier modeling of the body or greater emphasis on silhouette at the expense of front illumination.

Generally speaking, ballet emphasizes silhouette and general body configuration more than surface musculature. In fact, with some ballerinas, the lighting must deemphasize surface contour in favor of a more romanticized general impression of body form.

The emphasis varies considerably among modern dance choreographers, but surface contour and musculature are likely to be important. Modeling, in these situations, is a higher priority than general illumination, or to state it in other terms, it is more important to see the shape of the body and surface contours than it is to provide realistic lighting or to reveal all the fine features of the face. Optimum modeling results when the flow of light is at right angles to the surface. The best modeling light for the human body is sharply focused top light, but as we have noted, this tends to shorten the appearance of the figure. Side light provides the next best modeling, but of course, light from just one side leaves the other in shadow. The common practice, therefore, is to light the dancer principally from both sides. Because the light from one side fills the shadows generated by the opposite light and thus eliminates some modeling, the use of different colors or different intensities helps to retain the effect of relief. In recent years, the side lights have moved from a high diagonal position and are now frequently mounted near the floor ("shinbusters"). This helps to accentuate the height of the human figure and keeps distracting pools of light off the stage floor.

Dancers usually like to stress the linear features of the body, but actors, particularly as an aid to characterization, may benefit from the shape-changing properties of lighting. Front light makes the figure appear more full. Side or diagonal lighting emphasizes angularity, particularly when it comes predominantly from one side. Top light shortens and makes the figure seem more massive. Low-angled light from the side heightens the body. Low-angled front light or footlights make the face appear flabby or puffy. High-angled front light creates a sense of gauntness. Backlight emphasizes body mass.

Frequently with dance and with theatre mounted on a bare stage, the lit performer is the entire visual show. It is certainly a challenge to build a lighting composition around a moving form, particularly with actors, who are uncomfortable maintaining exactly the same stage and body position performance after performance. However, if the actors and director have an appreciation of the visual effects possible with tight coordination between lighting and body position, they will usually cooperate with the lighting designer. In these situations, it is better to approach specific moments in the play with lighting in mind very early in the rehearsal process. The lighting designer should also provide as much physical latitude for the actor as possible. The more narrowly prescribed the body position and the more tightly focused the spot of light the actor must find, the greater the probability that the visual composition will go awry.

A striking series of designs by Robert Edmond Jones for *The Cenci* (see Figure 4-6) shows how much a designer can accomplish with light and actors alone. These designs indicate only brightness factors. Color would add an entirely new dimension. The very sketchiness of Jones's designs reinforces the extent to which brightness differences on very simple body, costume, and hand-prop forms can be a major design feature.

Jones was designing for a hypothetical production and could control actors and light on paper in a way rarely possible in production. Gordon Craig, another scenic designer acutely aware of the design potential of lit actors (see Figure 6-4), became so frustrated with the difficulties of controlling actors' placement within his designs that he contemplated ways of doing theatre without live performers. Many lighting designers do virtually the same thing by lighting primarily the setting without particular regard for the performer. Because lighting rehearsals with actors are expensive, because the actor is often impatient with technical demands, and because the director and actors often have little regard for spatial composition, the lighting designer may retreat to a concentration on lighting the scenery, which is static and predictable. As understandable as this temptation may be, it must be resisted.

FIGURE 4-6a Robert Edmond Jones' designs for *The Cenci*. This series of four sketches shows Jones' concern for the visual impact of lighting groups of actors. [Designs from Robert Edmond Jones, *Drawings for the Theatre* (New York: Theatre Arts, Inc., 1925). Copyright 1925 by Theatre Arts, Inc.; copyright © 1970 by Theatre Arts Books. Used with the permission of the publisher, Theatre Arts Books, 153 Waverly Place, New York, N.Y. 10014.]

FIGURE 4-6b

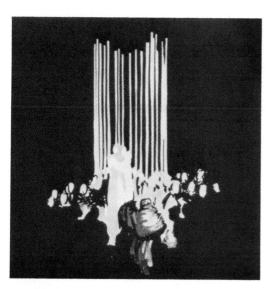

FIGURE 4-6c

FIGURE 4-6d

The performer is the soul of the production and special attention must be given to his light. His form is almost universally the most important for light, the form giver and form shaper.

EXERCISES

1. *Color as a Depth Cue* (p. 56)—Place identical objects side by side some distance from one another on a stage. Light one with a blue front light, the other with a warm front light. Try to keep light off of the floor and, if possible place observers so they cannot see the stage floor. Ask viewers to judge which object is the closest. Reverse the colors in the lighting and ask which object is now the closest.

2. *Tonal Variation as a Depth Cue* (p. 56)—Photograph a landscape painting in order to obtain a positive transparency (35mm slide) of the painting. Project the slide back onto the painting in perfect registration. What happens to the sense of depth? The same principle can be demonstrated by making a slide and a print from the same negative. Project the slide onto the print in perfect registration.

3. *Lighting Angle as a Depth Cue* (p. 56)—Hang moldings and any objects with an abstract three-dimensional pattern (such as "egg carton" packing) so they can be lit from both above and below at identical angles. With viewers at some distance, begin with bottom lighting and ask the viewers to tell which surfaces are convex and which concave. Shift to top lighting and ask the same question. This works most effectively when viewers cannot see the lighting sources.

4. *Emphasizing Surface Texture at the Expense of Surface Image* (p. 58)—Glue a completed jigsaw puzzle onto a rigid backing. With the puzzle in a vertical position, light it first from a high front angle and then from a flat front position. Which position emphasizes the texture and which emphasizes the surface image? With lights at 45°, see if diffusion filters make any difference in the appearance of the puzzle.

5. *Lighting Angle and Brightness as Revealers of Texture* (p. 58)—Collect a variety of black fabrics with different surface textures: velour, satin, burlap, canvas, leather, etc.

Make a collage by attaching all of the samples to a rigid surface. Light the fabric from a variety of angles, including front and high top. Which lighting position accentuates the surface textures? Do diffusion filters influence the perception of texture? What happens to the viewer's ability to differentiate textures when the lighting is very dim?

6. *Lighting Angle as a Cue to Form* (p. 59)—Obtain a large styrofoam ball. From a sheet of styrofoam cut a flat disc the same diameter as the ball. Without giving viewers an opportunity to see the two objects beforehand, place them side by side on pedestals with the disc standing on its edge. Bring up flat front lighting and ask viewers to describe what they see. Then shift to a high side-angled light and ask viewers to describe what they see.

7. *Lighting to Emphasize Shape by Accenting Silhouette* (p. 59)—From rigid styrofoam one or more inches thick, cut an interesting silhouette showing a village skyline. Place this silhouette against a backing sheet of the same material and light it from a flat front angle. Change to a top light so that the thickness of the cutout receives a highlight. What happens to the appearance of the silhouette? With the front light on, move the silhouette far enough in front of the background for it to cast a shadow larger than the cutout. Does this improve the appearance of the silhouette? With the cutout separated from the background, light each from a high angle with contrasting colors. Does this accentuate the silhouette?

8. *Backlighting* (pp. 59–60)—Light an object on stage with two identical highpowered spotlights at identical angles and distances from the object, one light in front and one in back. Gradually vary the ratio of intensity between the two instruments to discover the difference in brightness necessary to produce a clearly perceived bright edge around the object.

9. *Influence of Lighting on Pattern Perception* (p. 62)—Find a fabric or wallpaper sample with intricate interlocking patterns of different colors. Use different filter colors on lighting instruments or in a slide projector to emphasize one component in the pattern to the exclusion of other components. With gobos or patterned slides, project a strong lighting pattern on top of the surface pattern. What happens to the surface pattern?

10. *Effect of Lighting on a Variable Density Scrim* (pp. 63–64)—On a conveniently sized, framed scrim paint a landscape scene so that foreground features are opaque, middle distance objects translucent, and open sky and distant objects are painted with dyes. Opaque portions of the scrim may need filling before painting. Behind this scrim a few feet distant, place a second painted flat with distant mountain ranges against a blue sky. Using a combination of separate lighting on the scrim and on the background unit, try to produce as many different appearances to the units as possible. See if you can create different times of day or different weather conditions by changing light angles and colors.

11. *Pointillism* (p. 63)—Cut three distinct, fairly open stencils. Spatter a scenic flat or a piece of sign board lightly with red, blue, and green paint. Repeat the spattering, using a different color for each stencil so that the stencil patterns overlap. Light the flat with different colors so that first one and then another stenciled pattern emerges from the background.

12. *Influence of Lighting Angle on Body Form* (p. 65)—Find a statue, at least eight or nine inches high, of a standing human figure, the more realistic, the better. Place the statue on a small pedestal in a dark surrounding space and with a strong flashlight illuminate the statue from a variety of angles to discover ways of changing the apparent proportions of the figure. Use combina-

tions of lighting sources to obtain the best balance between visibility and modeling. Add back lighting. Go through the same process with a bust to determine how lighting angles change the appearance of a face. The same experiments may, of course, be done with a live actor.

Composition: The Visual Framework and Field of Light

If visibility were the sole concern of stage lighting, the lighting designer might be called simply a "lighter," or perhaps an "illuminator." The word "designer," however, implies more. Theatrical lighting involves design in the sense of advanced planning and of fitting something to a need; more importantly, stage lighting creates a design, a pattern of light, a composition, an arrangement of parts which are related to one another. Knowledge of the principles of composition is as important to the theatrical lighting designer as it is to any other visual artist.

It is true that the lighting design depends on many compositional elements over which the lighting designer has little or no control. The director, actors, and other designers often make decisions affecting composition prior to and often without regard for the introduction of lighting. Unlike the photographer who must also commonly work with predetermined features, the lighting designer cannot even choose a viewing angle. The only compositional element within the designer's absolute control is the lighting, but this alone provides much latitude for compositional choices and considerable power to enhance, or accidentally destroy, compositions created by others.

If for no other reason than the impact on other visual artists, the lighting designer must be able to recognize and deal with stage composition. Without an understanding of the visual statement made by a director's blocking or the scenic designer's treatment of space, a lighting design may inadvertently destroy the intended effect.

Moreover, lighting is a major aspect of almost all visual composition whether other artists realize it or not. Just the assumption of flat, even front lighting for a two-dimensional abstract painting represents some judgment concerning light. The substitution of high-angled lighting, which emphasizes the texture of the paint on the canvas rather than the pattern on the surface, would quickly stress this point.

Of course, the less conspicuous other visual forms are, the more important lighting is as a compositional device. Bare-stage productions or fairly abstract unit settings, in some respects, place more emphasis on the composition of the lighting than a more complex three-dimensional visual field which offers a greater range of opportunity for lighting design. The use of projections, particularly in dance lighting, often is the domain of the lighting designer, and here particularly, mastery of all aspects of visual composition is important.

The model assumed in the following discussion is the familiar one of the lighting designer working with other aspects of the production. In practice, the latitude available for lighting to make an important compositional statement will vary. In the best possible circumstances, lighting will be involved from the time the production is first conceptualized, and scenery, blocking, costuming, and makeup will evolve with particular reference to the lighting. In the worst conditions, which occur all too frequently, the lighting designer will, in effect, have to work alone, creating the most appropriate and interesting visual composition possible from predetermined features conceived without special attention to how they will be lit. In any event, the blindness of some theatre practitioners to the uses of lighting is no sign that the art of lighting itself lacks a compositional dimension.

Discussions of composition involve a considerable degree of abstraction. We will analyze what the audience sees in such terms as line, balance, focus, and tonal value, even though the audience member thinks of the scene as a living room or a clearing in the woods. This abstract analysis of composition seems more natural when the production itself uses an abstract approach. We easily conceive of light, like music, in abstract terms without reference to realistic, natural sources. However, even when the context is realistic and the audience thinks of the lighting as coming from the sun or clearly motivated sources, the composition, as an abstract form, creates an impression, albeit subconsciously.

In approaching compositional questions abstractly, we cannot ignore the realistic content of a scene, the values created by the production, or the attitude of the audience to the content of the play. For example, we may light actors on stage to create a certain abstractly conceived composition, but if one of those figures is nude, audience attention may generate a new focus that is entirely independent of the abstraction and which may totally disrupt the perception of any composition which disregards the values placed on visual content. Even though abstraction is the beginning point for compositional analysis, it is foolish to ignore the values placed on what is seen.

Later, in Chapters 10 and 11, we will discuss the relationship between content and lighting, between what is lit and how we light it. Particularly in Chapter 11, we will examine how compositional features of other aspects of design—scenery, costume, makeup, sound, and choreography—influence the lighting design. For the present, however, while recognizing that we see only light which strikes an object, we will concentrate on the compositional features of the lighting itself. Taking the psychological factors already discussed, we will apply them to the creation of an overall lighting design. All compositional choices must be made within the context of the perceptual conditions governing the audience's vision at any given moment in the production.

We will examine three major areas of composition: the creation of the overall visual framework, the arrangement of components within the framework, and the time dimension.

THE VISUAL FRAMEWORK AND FIELD OF LIGHT

One of the first decisions a painter must make is the size and shape of the canvas, or for a sculptor, the size of the stone. All that follows is within this framework. Of course a painter, for example, may choose to further restrict the composition within the overall frame or may arrange elements so they seem to extend beyond the limits of the frame, but once established, the edge of the canvas exerts a compelling influence over the work of art. The miniaturist must work in a different way from the mural painter, and an oval frame exerts pressures differently than a square frame. In a third dimension, the techniques of a bas-relief sculptor are quite different from the sculptor who works in full round.

In the theatre, the size and shape of the architectural space and, more particularly, of the performing space strongly influence the visual framework. A thirty-foot wide proscenium makes demands unlike those of a fifty-foot proscenium. Thrust, arena, proscenium, and open staging define the visual space in various ways, and so-called black box theatres allow even more flexible arrangements of the visual framework.

Even within a fixed theatrical form, the scenic designer may alter the visual framework. Teasers and tormentors may reduce the size of a proscenium, or a design may spill out of the proscenium into the auditorium. A director may contain action within a small portion of the overall space or expand it into the auditorium. The treatment of space in the theatre is accordionlike. The structure of the architecture fixes outer limits but considerable variation is possible within those boundaries.

Because lighting defines the limits of vision, it is obviously a major device for determining the visual framework. It can work in conjunction with architectural and scenic boundaries or it can work alone around those boundaries. It is an extremely plastic medium and therefore affords tremendous flexibility as a means of defining space. Under light, the visual framework is like a flexible film or balloon, capable of expansion or contraction in any direction. Light can change the compositional boundaries in an instant and provide a more pliable framework than any other artistic medium. This flexibility results in a great number of considerations in determining the influence of light on the size, shape, and quality of the visual framework.

Size of the Visual Field

The size of the visual field may range from the entire theatrical space to the tiny area lit by a pin spot. Until the latter part of the nineteenth century, the auditorium remained lit throughout the performance, and the spectator's total view included audience and stage. In this situation, the architectural style of the scenery often continued the style of the auditorium, and actors and costumes frequently mirrored specific audience members. In a sense, the total performance space included the audience, members of which came as much to see one another as what happened onstage. Some types of modern theatre also aim for audience participation, and in these cases the auditorium might appropriately remain lit. When this occurs, the lighting is more properly considered an environmental factor than a framework for a visual field detached from the viewer.

More commonly, the lighting helps to differentiate the performance space from the auditorium and to define the outer limits of the theatrical world. Within the architectural limits of the theatre, the decision as to how much space is used depends on the objectives of the production at any given moment. Even when the scenic design sharply defines the playing space, the lighting designer may light the entire scenic area or only a portion of it.

As a general rule, the more tightly the light focuses on a single actor, the more strongly the audience concentrates on psychological dimensions or the character's struggles with self. As an increasingly larger area is lit, the audience likely becomes proportionately more aware of environmental influences, either social or cosmic, on the character. If we pursue the analogy with painting, tight lighting on a single character is the light of portraiture. A large lit area is the lighting of the muralist or landscape painter. It has been observed that drama dealing with humanity's conflicts with nature or the gods tends to be set outdoors. Domestic and inner conflicts are usually set inside. The same principle applies to lighting: the more panoramic the space, the broader the issues involved. Obviously if the style of the production permits, the size of the lit area may vary as the type of conflict varies within a play.

The audience's perception of "an area of light" or a "lit area" depends on a large number of variables. If the floor or walls are visible, pools of light may define this area. The higher the contrast between bright light and the surrounding darkness, the clearer our sense of the boundaries of the lit area. On stages with enough moisture or dust in the air to allow beams of light to be seen, the ambience or glow of light in the atmosphere may define an area of light even if large surfaces are not clearly lit. When neither beams of light nor large surfaces are visible, the configuration of distinctly lit objects defines the area of light.

The same idea applies to dance lighting. If only the area around a single performer is lit, our concentration is on the interrelationship of the parts of one body. As the lit area expands, we become more aware of the dancer's use of the stage space or of the relationship of forms among dancers. Within a single piece, this focus may shift from moment to moment.

So far we have discussed the size of the lit area as if it were a single homogenous entity. Light can create multiple frames like pictures in a gallery or arrange frames within frames, each of variable size. For example, Hamlet's isolation from the court in Act I, Scene 2 can be emphasized by placing him in a small self-contained pool of light, separate from the larger lit area surrounding the court. In *Our Town*, Emily's attempt to struggle with the magnitude of the universe is made more poignant if, in addition to the pool of light on her ladder, dim ambient light makes us aware of the cavernous stage space around her. An audience presented with multiple frames compares one with the other or sees their relationship.

The question of the size of the lit area also relates to the distance of the viewer. The important issue is how much of a field can be seen at one glance. If an audience member can take in the whole of a lit area at one time, the response is quite different from a large illuminated area that must be scanned to determine points of concentration. It is easier to attain a unified composition in the smaller area. The viewer is less aware of the larger space as a unified whole and may concentrate more on elements within the space than on the entire thing. The smaller space requires less decision making by the viewer and results in greater objectivity. A viewer is more involved in the larger space and will find it more difficult to remain passive. This variable depends largely on the distance of a seat from the playing area, and a spectator may experience the performance space very differently from the front row than from the last, but the lighting designer must still make allowances for the size of the auditorium. To obtain the same compositional unity within an area of light, a small theatre with the audience close requires a much tighter focus than in a larger auditorium. Similarly, a panoramic scope is possible with a smaller area of light in the smaller theatre.

Field Proportion

Lighting may vary the apparent ratio between the height, width, and depth of the stage space. The absence of light at the outer perimeter will cause the space to contract accordingly. Inversely, brightening at the outer edges causes the space to expand as long as the contrast with the surrounding border of darkness is not so sharp that it gives undue emphasis to the frame. Therefore lighting the top of vertical elements and darkening the side ends emphasizes height. Moving quickly to darkness just over the performers' heads and brightening the sides emphasizes width.

We can vary proportions even without scenery. If the theatre has sufficient dust or humidity in the air for beams of light to be seen, the direction of the beam will pull the eye along that axis. Even the direction of dim lighting on masking drapes influences the perception of space. Similarly, the flow of lighting, with or without scenery, tends to expand the space in the direction of flow.

Lighting alters the apparent depth of the performing space by either emphasizing or deemphasizing visual cues for depth perception. A downstage to upstage progression from warm to cool colors and from sharply focused to diffused lighting and a heavy reliance on side lighting which stresses different planes in depth will deepen the space. Reversing these progressions or using flat front light will make the space seem more shallow. The color and diffusion progressions are not workable when the audience surrounds the playing space, but any variations of color, intensity, or lighting angle arranged to vary according to the distance from the viewers will accent the lateral dimensions of the space.

Shape of the Visual Frame

We discussed proportion in terms of three dimensions, but the visual frame does not have to be thought of as an expandable box. Diagonals may dominate, one side of the stage may soar while the other side runs off into the distance, or the entire space may bulge like an odd-shaped balloon.

Different frame shapes produce different responses and expectations and imply different treatments of composition and movement within the frame. If the space is

indeed boxlike, we expect a degree of formality with straight lines and real balance. Of course, much theatre depends on tension, conflict, and surprise; so our expectations may be upset. The creation of the expectation, however, is a necessary prerequisite for reversing it.

The illuminated box allows a good deal of audience passivity, but if we divide the space into separate frames, the viewer must begin to make choices. Fragmentation of the playing space is the stuff of conflict, but excessive fragmentation may only produce confusion. A three ring circus may offer one or two rings too much for the spectator's concentration. The simpler the division, the stronger the potential for conflict. If a number of separated frames are related in form, the viewer may respond to the pattern as a whole composition, but apparently random differences in form with considerable overlap may produce disorder.

An oval or rounded frame produces an even more relaxed atmosphere than one with straight edges. A degree of formality is still implied if the shape is symmetrical, but rounded forms and circular or sinuous movements seem more in place. In most instances the spectator will judge lit areas with curved edges to be more normal on the stage than straight edges, and the rounded frame calls less attention to itself.

The more unusual the shape of the frame of light, the more unrelated it is to scenic forms, or the more unmotivated it is in relation to natural illumination sources, the more attention it attracts. The danger is similar to a painting overpowered by a frame that is too large or ornate. For example, a sharply defined star-shaped area of light or an imposed pattern of bars of light may distract from what is happening within the lit area. There may be justification for these effects, but we must assess the distraction risk.

Any lit space with a strongly linear shape takes on the association of that line. If a narrow, vertical space is framed with light, height will be emphasized in the composition. A lit area which meanders over steps and platforms, suggests asymmetrical composition and indirect lines of movement.

If scenery has sufficient vertical scale, the vertical dimension of the lighting frame is easily determined by the height at which the lighting stops. An atmosphere which allows lighting beams to be seen makes it difficult to prevent the space from rising up to the level of overhead masking or instruments. It may be difficult to push the vertical dimension up in clean air without tall scenery. Without scenery, the style of the production may allow lighting instruments to be hung in view, which rapidly heightens the space.

Edge Sharpness

The transition from light to darkness at the boundaries of the lit area may be sharp or gradual. Available stage lighting instruments offer a range of beam diffusion from the indistinct spread of floodlights, through the relatively soft-edged pool of the fresnel spotlight, to the sharp edges of the ellipsoidal spotlight. Further modification is possible by using diffusion filters, taking instruments out of focus, or by removing lenses.

Sharp edges emphasize the frame and the separation between the lit and unlit space. Soft edges blur the frame and blend the performing area in with the surrounding space. Hard edges require more compositional clarity within the frame and may suggest more overall sharpness in execution or even in the delineation of thematic material. Sharp edges make the lit area appear brighter for a given level of illumination as a result of border contrast.

If there are to be frames within frames, the boundaries must be relatively sharp for the effect to be noticed. The eye is not sensitive to gradual changes in the level of brightness.

It is frequently difficult to cut off the lit area sharply with lighting control alone. Light bounces off of stage surfaces onto the surrounding area. Careful selection of hanging positions can at least assure that light bouncing from stationary objects will not reflect into the otherwise lit area. If the overall level of brightness is increased, the spill light may be less noticeable. Even though a proportionately larger percentage of light is reflected into unwanted areas, the eye is less sensitive to brightness differences at high levels and will accordingly take less notice of secondary reflections. Glare and mood considerations or the brightness in relation to surrounding scenes may prohibit this increase.

Outdoor stages are surrounded by a glowing halo of light resulting from the diffusion, scattering, and reflection of moisture particles in the air. Before the advent of air conditioning, all stages had this glow from suspended dust particles. Air-conditioning removed the dust and moisture from the air, but now that energy conservation is with us, many units are not operated at their designed temperature level, and the glow is beginning to reappear in the theatre. This may compromise a bit our sharply defined areas of light, but the glow adds a compensating aura of theatricality.

Openness and Closure

A given area of light may create the impression of being a small part of a greater whole or it may seem to be a complete entity unto itself. In other words, the space may seem to open up beyond the frame or to close down within the frame. Much of the impression is beyond the control of the lighting. For instance, if we see on stage only parts of things which seem to continue out of sight, such as the trunk of a tree or large portions of the sky, we are reminded of the larger space. Our prior experience compels us to think of the whole when only a part is shown. If a building or room seems complete on stage, we assume no larger structure. Even with abstract settings, lines and forms which seem to continue beyond the audience's sight lines expand the feeling of space.

Lighting may accentuate these physical cues for space perception, and the designer must pay close attention to the spatial demands of the scenery. If tall walls extend beyond the teasers, a failure to provide some light on their upper surfaces may compress scenery designed to tower. Insufficient light at the side edges of a sky drop will reduce its effectiveness as a space expander. Light on the outer edges of platforms designed to disappear into darkness may convert a sweeping design into an ineffectual pile of stage platforms. Inversely, too much light beyond the limits of a self-contained space designed for claustrophobic effects may open an area intended to be enclosed.

Even without scenery, lighting can open or close the apparent space within its frame. For example, sharply defined edges tend to contain a space more than diffused edges, but if the lighting is brighter at the edges than in the center of a space, there is a compensating sense of openness. Because lighting tends to accumulate in the center of a lit stage, it requires some careful planning to assure that the outer edges are brighter than the center. A dimly lit area without distinct edges of darkness, surrounding a more intense pool of light, also generates a feeling of greater space. Multiple shafts of light that seem to radiate out from the stage or a flow of light from off stage opens the space. Any linear shape taken by the lighting, which seems to continue out of sightlines, will expand the space in that direction.

Closure is created by having the light beams converge to a point on stage, by having the edges sharply defined but slightly dimmer than the center of the lit space, by keeping as much spill light as possible out of the surrounding darkness, and by creating a lighting shape that seems self-contained on the stage.

Grounding

The apparent weight and stability of a visual composition partly depend upon the shape of the visual frame and the relations of the frame to the audience's perception of the visual ground or floor. We live in a world controlled by gravity. Our sense of what is up and what is down and the solidness of the ground are central factors in our perception of space and form. Architecture, sculpture, dance, and painting all depend on tension and equilibrium generated by our understanding of the force of gravity. A form that totters on a small point creates tension because we expect it to fall. A mass on a large base seems stable because we see no way that it can fall.

We do not think of light itself having any weight. It seems to function outside of gravity; so its ability to change our perception of the stability of a composition depends on its capacity to influence our perception of objects which are subject to gravity.

In most instances the overhead mounting position of lighting instruments results in heavy illumination of the stage floor. Particularly if the audience is seated above the stage, the floor is often the brightest part of the visual field and only portions of the forms above are equally bright. In this situation, the composition is always firmly grounded. Because beams of light from overhead spread, the top of the beam is always smaller than the bottom, which also creates a sense of stability.

It therefore requires special effort if we wish to make the visual frame "float," resisting the natural tendency of the lighting to emphasize the ground. A vivid example of this is the dance lighting made popular in the 1960s by Alwin Nikolais. With low-mounted 3-1/2 inch ellipsoidal spotlights, "shinbusters," coming from the sides or diagonally from the front and focused so that light strikes the dancers but not the floor, the dancers appear suspended in space. Because the only light seen strikes the dancer, the darkness around the lit body becomes the visual frame. Separate instruments are used to wash the stage floor or for the backing cyclorama so the composition can expand at will.

The general principle is that any object

will appear to float if the lights are mounted low and kept off the floor. Even the floor of a small platform provides some grounding if the audience sees it. If we want a godlike dream figure suspended over the action, light must be kept off of his supporting platform and a band of darkness should separate the figure from any stage lighting below. If the only light is on the figure and the lit area is sufficiently small and intense, an autokinetic response will develop and the figure will seem to move in the air. This can be visually fatiguing if it lasts too long. The sense of a form being suspended works only when the audience has some vague idea of where the ground *ought* to be. If the frame of light is suspended for too long without reference to the actual floor, the viewer will adapt to the bottom of the suspended visual frame as the new visual ground. We do this when we watch a movie screen and will do the same thing to a drop or projection screen suspended over the stage.

If the audience is seated below the stage level or if the floor is not heavily lit, the grounding of vertical forms can be altered with light. An area of light broader at the top than at the bottom, areas with a strong diagonal axis, or areas separated from the ground will assume a more dynamic quality than frames more clearly grounded.

The stage floor itself is a relatively neutral space until surrounding walls, floor painting, carpets, or light define the playing area. Once that definition occurs, the floor remains a strong grounding influence even when not lit.

Stage settings sometimes have foreground forms in shadow or silhouette while mid- or distant planes are in light. Normally the dark area around a lighted space is viewed as the visual frame, but in those cases where the foreground is clearly part of the total composition, even though unlit, the frame becomes the recognized limits of the playing area, such as a proscenium. This dark foreground may exert a strong downward pull on the composition. This also applies to shadowy forms or distinct silhouettes at the sides or tops of the frame, but their influence on the grounding effect depends on their shape (see Figure 5–1).

Part/Whole Relationships

The compositional frame is not simply the boundary of a single expanse of light. There may be areas of light and darkness within a larger composition, and the limits of a composition are not defined only by light. If the lit sections appear to be part of a larger form, the audience imagines the total shape. The lit segments must relate to one another in an orderly fashion, and enough of the complete form must be shown to clearly imply the larger shape.

When areas of light overlap or when one area is within another, the relationship of the parts to the whole is usually easy to see, but when the areas are separated by dark-

FIGURE 5-1 Joseph Urban's setting for the opening scene of *Parsifal* at the Metropolitan Oprea House in 1919. [From George Altman, Ralph Freud, Kenneth Macgowan, William Melnitz, *Theatre Pictorial* (Berkeley, Cal.: University of California Press, 1953). © University of California Press. Used by permission.]

ness, their connection may be less clear. Certainly the audience's impression of the stage as a single, unified place tends to impose a degree of unity on all that happens there, but there is still a difference between separated areas of light seen as parts of a whole composition and areas which seem to frame separate compositions. The content of the lit area is important in determining the amount of unity. If we seem to be looking at two lit portions of a single form, we bridge the gap. If the objects in each pool of light seem self-contained or unrelated, we see them as disparate. For example, the use of a shared angle for key lights, that is, instruments providing highlights, tends to unify otherwise separated pools of light, but the use of a different key angle for each pool emphasizes the separation, particularly if the highlights appear to come from opposite wings of the stage.

Apart from content, the characteristics of the lighting itself can either subdivide, fragment, or unify lit areas. Similarities in color, size, or shape invite consolidation. Differences in these factors encourage disjunction, particularly if the colors are complementary to one another. Extreme differences in brightness may simply relegate one area to secondary focus without creating independent frames. Proximity produces unity, but the amount of darkness needed between two pools of light to make a compositional separation depends on the size, shape, intensity, and color of the lit areas. Similar areas span a greater interval. Intense, sharply defined pools separate more readily than diffuse, less intense pools. The closer the spectator is, the more significant is the intervening darkness between areas of light.

In daylight, physical barriers control the limits of vision. In a darkened theatre, lighting shapes the visual field. All of our discussion of composition to this point has concerned edges or boundaries of illumination. We have considered the size, proportion, shape, edge sharpness, degree of openness or closure, and grounding of the area of light on stage and the manner in which multiple areas of light relate to one another. Having examined the outer limits of the lighted space, we must now turn to the arrangement of components within that framework.

Composition:
Arranging Light
within the Visual Frame

The lighting designer can produce an even wash of light over the entire performing space, like classroom or office illumination, where the primary objective is maximum visibility. Indeed, theatre practitioners such as Bertolt Brecht and Jerzy Grotowski echoed Aristotle's suspicion of the emotion-producing power of visual design and called for stage lighting that is "neutral," a "work light" environment for actors. But too often this is the *unintentional* effect of lighting by unimaginative or inexperienced "designers." This sort of stage lighting has no compositional component other than the frame, and even that is likely to be determined by the scenery or architecture of the theatre.

The serious lighting designer should take a cue from the first line of Gerard Manley Hopkin's poem, "Pied Beauty": "Glory be to God for Dappled things—." Theatrical interest and beauty come from variety and texture, and from the moment any recognizable variegation arises in the lighting, the compositional arrangement of light within the frame becomes an important concern.

Line and Axial Direction

Most textbook discussions of visual composition begin with line, the simplest of visual forms other than the point. Because most stage lighting instruments produce a pool of light, however, we usually think of theatrical lighting in terms of areas or expanses of light. This assumption ignores an important element. Of course lasers generate a thin line of light, but the use of shutters, gobos, and projections also enables us to create lines of light from conventional instruments. In addition, when we can see light beams, they have an axial direction with linear characteristics. Lighting can also pick out linear features on stage or emphasize the linear aspects of a solid by highlighting edges or receding surfaces, which appear as thin lines to the audience.

Lines have weight (their thickness or thinness), direction, contour (whether they are straight or curved), varying degrees of connectedness (whether they are broken or solid), and, in certain combinations or configurations, lines create the impression of a multidimensional shape. Any examination of the work of an engraver or sketch artist shows the extent to which line alone can express form and composition. Even the crudest pencil sketch of a stage lighting design quickly reveals some basic linear features (see Figure 6-1).

Ideally, the lighting, particularly for a proscenium production, can emphasize either line or mass in the three-dimensional setting. Lights positioned to illuminate both front and receding surfaces, usually from angles near 45° from the floor and central vertical plane, stress mass. High-angled light from the top, sides, and back accentuates line. Generally, the more emphasis given to line, the less weight the composition appears to have. This effect, however, may be offset if it produces large areas of shadow which tend to weigh the visual picture. Maximum airiness results when front surfaces

are filled with light but edges and receding surfaces are highlighted.

Shadow can also emphasize line. The visibility of facial lines, for example, depends on a sufficient lighting angle to leave furrows in shadow. Shadowed receding surfaces may outline a front surface lit from an acute angle (see Figure 6-4). This is analogous to highlighting, but a dark background obscures the effect, which works only in front of a separate plane of brightness.

Increasing figure-ground contrast with lighting accents the linear features of any skeletal structure (see Figure 6-3). The structure may be silhouetted against a bright background or lit against a dark background, or structure and background may be lit with contrasting colors. The same light on both the figure and the ground will lessen audience consciousness of the linear structure.

The lighting designer must carefully analyze the scenic design to determine which lines, if any, are to be emphasized. For example, the straight top edge of a conventional interior setting with no ceiling usually should be made to disappear into darkness, but the cut away edges of a fragmented wall are frequently a major feature of the design and should be stressed. The effectiveness of

FIGURE 6-1 A lighting design's sketch for *Fiddler on the Roof*.

FIGURE 6-2 Jo Mielziner's design for *Cat on a Hot Tin Roof*. [From Jo Mielziner, *Designing for the Theatre* (New York: Bramhall House, 1965), p. 182. © 1955. Reprinted with the permission of Atheneum Publishers.]

scenic designs often depends on the proper treatment of linear elements (see Figure 6-2).

A complex setting includes a variety of forms, some with straight faces, some with curved, with edges and surfaces going in a variety of directions. The lighting designer may choose which of these lines to stress and can shift emphasis from moment to moment as the production progresses. For example, Jo Mielziner's famous setting for *Death of a Salesman* (Figure 6-3) includes a very angular roof line, a strong horizontal line separating the lower and upper levels of the house, and the confused vertical lines of the surrounding apartments on the backdrop. By stressing the horizontal line, the design assumes considerable stability and solidness, but a shift in emphasis to the diagonal roof lines creates a more dynamic feeling. The backing apartments are two-dimensional, so this part of the design must either be in darkness or taken in its entirety; but the

strong vertical lines which extend out of sight create the feeling of a confused but monumentally oppressive environment. This particular design contains no significant curved or rounded elements, but that feature could be introduced by the curved edge of pools of light. Color and mass arrangements are also important parts of the design, but changing lights to stress one and then another linear feature could alone vary the composition and mood of the design.

Lines of light projected onto a surface with no inherent linear features can add linear properties to a scenic element that otherwise contributes only mass to the composition. Gordon Craig's design shown in Figure 6-4 gains much of its dynamic quality from the interaction between strong vertical forms and diagonal lines of light. Except for the bending figure in the foreground, the lighting provides the only diagonal lines, and without them the design would be

FIGURE 6-3   Jo Mielziner's design for the opening scene of *Death of a Salesman*. [From Jo Mielziner, *Designing for the Theatre* (New York: Bramhall House, 1965), p. 146. © 1949. Reprinted with the permission of Atheneum Publishers.]

much more staid and less energetic. It is interesting to note that even though we are aware of the volume of the towering forms, the dark shadows on their receding surfaces create vertical lines which leave a stronger impression than the lit mass of the front surfaces. Any examination of the work of good scenic designers will show that they frequently highlight portions of the scenery or include shafts of light in the total design to create forceful linear features.

Shafts of light in the air can also add clear linear elements to the visual picture, sometimes inadvertently. At a recent modern dance production in an old, dusty civic auditorium, the stage was lit entirely from behind the proscenium. The light on the dancers was interesting enough, but the beams were clearly revealed by the dusty air, and the eye was drawn up to a chaotic jumble which was very discordant with the well ordered choreography below. In this case, a careful adjustment of the mounting positions could have organized the shafts of light so that the entire composition encouraged the eye to concentrate on the dancers where attention belonged.

Josef Svoboda is the best known modern designer to struggle with the problem of using light shafts as a feature of stage design in air-conditioned theatres. He experimented with different string structures and suspended balls to provide a medium in which the light beam could be seen in three dimensions. He developed a special aerosol technique so that tiny droplets were suspended in the air, which exposed the light beams. By using low-voltage, high-intensity lights which cause very concentrated beams, he created curtains and three-dimensional forms with strong linear characteristics (see Figure 6-5). Illuminated space thus joins reflective surfaces as a major design component. This approach adapts well to outdoor theatre where there is enough dust and moisture in the air for beams to be seen. However, out-of-doors, long throw distances and a limited choice of mounting po-

FIGURE 6-4 Edward Gordon Craig's design entitled *1907*. [From *Scene* (London: Oxford University Press, 1923). Reprinted courtesy of Oxford University Press.]

sitions make it difficult to get narrow beams of highly consolidated light from desired angles.

Whether we are talking about beams of light, streaks of light projected onto surfaces, or highlights which accentuate linear features, the compositional concern is to create a meaningful pattern of lines. Lines draw the eye and represent shape. Is the eye carried where it should go? Is the shape ordered in such a way that a unified composition is created which is in harmony with production objectives? Jo Mielziner in his design for *A Cat on a Hot Tin Roof,* cleverly indicated how lighting emphasized important linear features in the setting (see Figure

FIGURE 6-5   Josef Svoboda's scenery and lighting for *Tristan and Isolde*. [From Jarka Burian, *The Sceneography of Josef Svoboda* (Middletown, Conn.: Wesleyan University Press, 1971), p. 76. Copyright © 1971 by Jarka Burian. Reprinted by permission of Wesleyan University Press and KaiDib Films International, Glendale, California.]

6-2). The inverted pyramid at the top fills the overhead space, focuses the eye back onto the large platform below, echoes the shape of the thrusting platform, and imposes a threatening form over the action. The vertical stripes represent the columns of a Southern plantation appropriate for the play, but they also provide a vertical counterthrust for the overhead pyramid, seeming to support it, and balancing what would otherwise be a predominantly horizontal composition. These structures are asymmetrical, three on one side, two on the other, which compensates for the fact that the point of both the pyramid and the large thrusting platform are off-center. The shadow cast by rear illumination on the stage right column helps to fill the floor on that side and balances the composition which is otherwise weighted to the stage-left side of center. The columns are unevenly lit so that in some instances they blend with the background. This breaks the strong upward pull which would otherwise be further exerted by the fact that the vertical lines converge toward the top. The straightness of all the structural lines emphasizes the roundness of the human figures and further contrasts with softly rounded pools of light on the background and stage floor. The scenery is emphatic but lit much more dimly than the figures in the foreground. This

simple but carefully controlled and very effective design relies heavily on line. The lighting is cleverly modulated to produce the total effect, which would be quite different if the setting were simply washed in light or if the lighting were significantly changed in any way.

Any setting could and should be analyzed in the same way to ascertain how linear features are to be used. Others may make less conspicuous use of line, but there are always linear components. A quick sketch will usually reduce a design to its major lines and some decision can then be made concerning the interaction of light with these. The control of line is in many respects the core of design, and the lighting designer should make as careful a study of it as the sketch artist does.

Focus

The focus of a composition is the object or area that holds an observer's greatest attention. It is not necessarily the first thing that catches the eye when a scene is first revealed. A complex composition may have a visual entryway, a series of forms which attract initial attention but lead the eye to the primary focus. A complicated visual picture may also have more than one focus, but these are usually arranged in some sort of hierarchy with one dominating. The need for a focus is partly a recognition of its ability to unify a composition and partly a product of the artist's desire to control the attention of the observer. Unfocused scenes, scenes with multiple focuses of equal attraction, or scenes with split focus have a place in the theatre during moments which emphasize confusion, tension, or conflict, but the use of these approaches still requires an understanding of the principles for controlling focus.

Focus may result from the predisposed attention of the audience, the attention-getting value of a given stimulus in relation to others, or by the arrangement of components in a composition. To a large extent, compositional focus must include considerations of the first two. If the audience knows that a character is about to commit murder, that character is likely to be the focus of attention even though all abstract compositional precepts place him on the periphery. If the audience needs to see something in darkness, it will strain to do so, and will view an area of brightness as no more than a distraction.

Various attempts have been made to describe a hierarchy of stimuli in terms of precedence of attention. As long as only one attribute is in question, this can be done fairly easily. Brighter light, more saturated color, the greater degree of movement, the larger area, the more dynamic form will attract the greatest amount of attention. But is color more attention-getting than brightness? How much brighter must an achromatic stimulus be than a colored stimulus in order to take focus? What happens when we further complicate the question by making the colorless area larger but moving the color? It is fairly simple to test the relative attention-gathering powers of any two stimuli, but it is extremely difficult to categorize all of the possible variables to derive a workable system for mechanically predetermining which will take focus when each possesses a different attention-getting attribute.

When comparing the relative attention-getting power of dissimilar stimuli, a few general principles do apply. Any stimulus that changes more likely invites attention than one which remains constant. The more features a stimulus has that attract attention, the more likely it is to take focus. The more different or discordant a stimulus is in relation to its environment, the more it will draw attention. However, when it comes to practical application, the only safe way to be sure that features take the relative degree of focus intended is through experimentation, experience, and our ability to visualize. Preliminary sketches, designs, and lighting rehearsals test options in the most concrete form possible short of the actual production. Even the greatest artists do preliminary sketches to resolve compositional problems before undertaking the final work.

An artist also attains focus by ordering or arranging features within the visual field, the compositional aspect of focus. Again with complex variables, some guidelines are available. A composition with clear linear features having a sense of direction creates a focus where the lines appear to lead or stop. If lines converge on a point, that point is an even stronger focus. If the lines form a shape, the eye moves to the center of that shape if anything there holds attention. If the line is without shape or direction, the focus will be at the center of the line. In simplest terms, if a line of light crosses the entire width of the stage, the focus will be center stage. If the instruments are angled so that the line of light extends from the wings to a point one-third of the way in from the opposite side, the line is given a sense of direction, and the focus will be at that point where the light stops. Converging beams of light obviously create a focus where they meet, but a secondary focus is possible at each light source because the beam edges converge there. For example, Robert Edmond Jones' design for *Macbeth* shown in Figure 6-6 creates a primary focus on the three witches standing center stage because all beams converge on them. How-

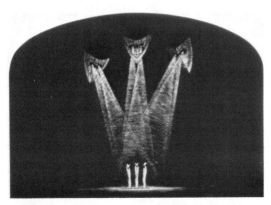

FIGURE 6-6 Robert Edmond Jones' design for *Macbeth*. [From Robert Edmond Jones, *Drawings for the Theatre* (New York: Theatre Arts, Inc., 1925). Copyright 1925 by Theatre Arts, Inc.; copyright © 1970 by Theatre Arts Books. Used with the permission of the publisher, Theatre Arts Books, 153 Waverly Place, New York, N.Y. 10014.]

ever, focuses are created at each of the overhead masks because the beam edges of two lights converge on each mask. In addition there is another secondary focus in the air above the witches' heads, the center of the shape created by the six beams of light.

A symmetrical composition creates a focus at its center. Even if the composition is asymmetrical but balanced, the center of balance becomes a focus. Other elements may be strongly enough conceived to draw

primary focus, but at least a secondary focus remains in the center of the composition. In Norman Bel Geddes' design for the *Patriot* shown in Figure 6-7, the eye initially focuses on one of the bright areas in the field of vision, but eventually the silhouetted figure in the foreground, partly framed by the rectangular door, becomes the primary focus. Taken by itself, this figure is hardly distinguishable from the background, but the bright areas to either side balance one another and pull the focus to the compositional center, which in this case is not center stage.

Note that Bel Geddes created this composition primarily with light. The actual scenic structure is indistinct in the rendering and only those portions which are highlighted are important to the visual composition.

An overriding geometric shape into which major components fit frequently unifies a composition. Different shapes create different focuses depending on their orientation. For example, a triangle with its base on the ground has a focus at its vertex. If the triangle is equilateral and the base not on the ground, the corner to which the triangle seems tipped will take the focus. If the triangle is not equilateral, the focus is usually at its most acute angle unless this is offset by a strong sense of the center of weight being tipped toward another angle. The

FIGURE 6-7 Norman Bel Geddes' sketch for *The Patriot* (New York, 1928). [Norman Bel Geddes Collection, Hoblitzelle Theatre Arts Library, Humanities Research Center, The University of Texas at Austin. Used by permission of Edith Lutyens Bel Geddes, executrix.]

FIGURE 6-8 Edward Gordon Craig's design entitled *1907*. [From *Scene* (London: Oxford University Press, 1923). Reprinted courtesy of Oxford University Press.]

strong focus on the human form in the Gordon Craig design shown in Figure 6-8 largely results from her placement at the acute angle of a right triangle. Here again, light forms the composition. The scenic shapes are all rectangular, but the diagonal shafts of light suggest a triangular form.

The triangle is a closed shape and has a secondary focus at its center, the point equidistant from all sides. All static, closed shapes will have some focus at their center, but dynamic compositional shapes which have a strong sense of direction push the focus in that dominant direction. In Craig's design for the sleep-walking scene in *Macbeth* (see Figure 6-9), the stairs and their supporting base form a triangular shape with curved edges. The focus here is clearly on the apex of the triangle, the platform at the base of the stairs. The fact that Lady Macbeth is not in the focus adds a strong

pull to move her down to that platform. In this instance, the rendering is washed with light, and the pull could be even more accentuated by darkening all but the dominant shape just described.

It is common practice in the theatre to create tension by having a character move outside of the compositional focus. Of course the actor or dancer is part of the total composition and changes it by moving, but if a strong focus is maintained in an area of the stage in spite of this movement, the audience subconsciously wishes to resolve the compositional tension by having the performer move into the focus.

To the extent that the lighting defines, changes, and creates form, it is an important element in determining the compositional focus. One need only take a series of screens and rectangular columns such as those shown in Figure 6-8 and imagine the

FIGURE 6-9 Edward Gordon Craig's design for *Macbeth*, the sleep-walking scene. [From Edward Gordon Craig, *Towards a New Theatre* (London: JM Dent & Sons, Ltd., 1913). Reprinted by permission of the estate of H. E. Robert Craig. © the estate of H. E. Robert Craig.]

changes in composition that could result from altering the pattern of lighting, and it will become apparent how important lighting is in this matter.

Balance

A composition may be symmetrical or asymmetrical; and the latter may be balanced or unbalanced. Balance means that the entire composition is in a state of equilibrium, that the components to right and left of the center of a visual frame somehow equal one another. In a sense, any visual composition has some point of balance, but if that point is outside the center of the visual frame or creates tension with the frame, we view the overall composition as unbalanced. Do not think of the term "unbalanced" as a value judgment, because frequently in the theatre we want the tension created by an unbalanced composition. The notion of asymmetrical balance may seem self-contradictory, but it only means that unlike elements balance one another and that one-half of the composition does not mirror the other.

The question of balance is at least as complicated as that of focus. In both cases, the perception of the viewer and the value placed by the viewer on visual elements are important components difficult to categorize. Here too we must compare different attributes of the visual experience without an easily defined objective basis for comparison. Color may balance mass, but how much or how bright a color balances how large and what-shaped mass? Experiments can measure simple comparisons, but the possible variables are so complex that they limit any systemization. The eye of the artist or artistic observer usually resolves the problem. General principles apply, but ultimately a composition is balanced if it looks balanced.

If we isolate any one visual attribute of the stage picture, balancing is relatively simple. For instance, a sense of equal brightness in both halves of a composition enhances

the balance. A small area of greater brightness balances a larger area of less intensity. Because the impression of brightness increases as the area decreases, the measurable intensity of the smaller area does not have to increase directly in proportion to its diminishing size. Differences of brightness are also more significant when the overall level of illumination is lower because the audience perceives smaller brightness differences at lower intensities.

The compositional center of balance shifts depending on the position of areas of light. Think of a composition as a seesaw with area of light balanced at either end. A large area of light near the center requires a small area of greater intensity to be near the edge of the composition to generate an impression of balance. A number of smaller areas on one side may balance a larger area on the other. In Lee Simonson's setting for *Elizabeth the Queen,* shown in Figure 6-10, the compositional center is on the floor between the two figures. The light on the queen alone does not balance the relatively intense area of light surrounding the man, accentuated by candles, his white shirt, and the lit trap door. The window, overhead flags, and dim light on the stage left doorway are necessary to maintain the balance. If the queen were removed, the entire composition would shift stage-right. For that matter, the center will move if you place your hand over any of the lit areas in the picture. Note that here again, the details of the setting are not visible. The composition consists wholly of those objects highlighted and presumably an entirely different arrangement of light would produce a totally different composition and view of the scenery.

If we take brightness of light area as our beginning point and add visual attributes, we will see how quickly the problem of balance complicates. If the lit area has a distinct shape, particularly if that shape has a strong sense of direction, a new variable influences the balance. A clearly shaped or dynamic area of light creates more compositional

FIGURE 6-10 Lee Simonson's setting for *Elizabeth the Queen.* [From Lee Simonson, *Part of a Lifetime* (New York: Duell, Sloan, and Pearce, 1943). Copyright © 1943 by Lee Simonson. Copyright renewed 1971 by Lee Simonson. Reprinted by permission of the publisher, E. P. Dutton, Inc.]

weight than a nebulous or extremely stable area of light. Any distinctness of shape produces visual pull, but particularly a shape with directionality moves the effect of the lit area in the direction in which the shape seems to move. For example, if the axis moves offstage, the compensating area of light on the other side will have to move off to maintain the center of balance at the same point. In Robert Edmond Jones' design for *The Green Pastures,* shown in Figure 6-11, the indistinct wash of light on the large scenic unit stage-right balances the much smaller, but highly directional slash of light on the stage-left floor. The dynamically curved body of the stage-left figure further balances the brightly lit but more stable

block of light on the apparition, even though it is difficult to imagine how the light rendered by Jones on the apparition could be translated literally into stage lighting.

Color influences both visual weight and perceived spatial balance. Colors of approximately the same hue to either side of the center pull the composition together and balance one another. A colored area of light with greater saturation, higher brightness, or a dynamic shape will balance a larger, less saturated or less bright, static area of colored light. Colors that are the complementary afterimages of one another seem to move apart and divide the composition. However, in a generally achromatic field,

FIGURE 6-11 Robert Edmond Jones' design for *The Green Pastures*. [From Ralph Pendleton, *The Theatre of Robert Edmond Jones* (Middletown, Conn.: Wesleyan University Press, 1958), p. 77.]

any colored light can be a component in achieving a balanced composition.

Dissimilar visual attributes can also balance one another. A small area of color offsets a large area of white light. Shadow can even be counterpoised against light. In Jones' design for *Othello* (see Figure 6-12), the deep shadow stage-right of the bed partly balances the area of light around the candle. The silhouetted figure in the fore-

FIGURE 6-12 Robert Edmond Jones' design for *Othello*. [From the collection of The Museum of Modern Art, New York.]

ground further helps to balance the larger but less distinctly shaped shadowed area. In this design, areas of darkness are the main compositional features, but of course, areas of light define the shadows. The overriding starlight above and the symmetrical shape of the back wall also accentuate the balance in the *Othello* design. Even though we cannot see the entire wall, we see enough of its shape to give us the sense of a complete form.

An arrangement of elements may create the impression of an overall compositional shape, itself balanced, even though the components emphasize mismatched visual features. Jo Mielziner's design for *The Red General* (see Figure 6-13) contains a variety of scenic forms with a strong diagonal cutout forcing the entire composition to the stage-left side, but the lighting picks out human figures and portions of the scenery in such a way that the dominant form is not the trian-

gle but a dumbbell shape which seems perfectly balanced.

Our discussion thus far has concentrated on the balance of elements to the left and right of the compositional center, but for a three-dimensional space, the compositional balance must work in all directions. Rather than a seesaw, a more proper image might be a balancing block. Composition in depth is particularly important to thrust or arena staging where something which is to the left of the visual frame for one audience member is in the center for another. If we think of the stage as a sculptural space, we can balance the visual form on its center in such a way that it always appears balanced as we move around it.

Any quick survey of books illustrating scenic designs will show that the centrally balanced composition is by far the common form. The positioning of performers or the lighting may upset this balance to create ten-

FIGURE 6-13 Jo Mielziner's design for *The Red General.* [From Jo Mielziner, *Designing for the Theatre* (New York: Bramhall House, 1965), p. 74. © 1929. Reprinted with the permission of Atheneum Publishers.]

sion, but we must establish the balance itself to accentuate the deviation. As a general rule, any lighting design must be capable of establishing, disrupting, and restoring this visual balance as the tensions of the production change.

Positive and Negative Space

In a composition, positive space is made up of forms that appear to have volume, and negative space is the area between these forms or the background seen around them. Generally the positive space contains the important information and dominates the attention of the audience, but the negative space also has a distinct shape, albeit defined by the limits of the positive form, and can make a compositional statement. Some so-called optical illusions are based on ambivalent relationships between positive and negative spaces. In Figure 6-14, if we take the black area to be negative, we see a vase, but if the white area is negative, we see the silhouettes of two identical faces.

It is tempting to assume that light always defines a positive space and that darkness or shadow is the negative, but this is not the case. In Jo Mielziner's famous design for

FIGURE 6-14 The "urn phenomenon" illustrates figure/ground ambiguity.

Maxwell Anderson's *Winterset* (see Figure 6-15), the lightest areas are the background elements: the blank alley wall stage right and the V-shaped opening between the tenement building and the bridge abutment. This thrusting negative space is the strongest visual element in the field and gives the composition its greatest impact. Lighting that lessens the contrast between the foreground and background would diminish the awareness of this negative space and change the effect of the design. If areas of darkness are seen as silhouettes of solid form, the lighter area may become the negative space. This is commonly the case for settings placed in front of a lit sky drop or cyclorama.

A given area of light may function as a negative space with respect to one form and a positive space with respect to another. In Jones' design for *Othello* (see 6-12), the candlelit wall serves as negative space for the foreground silhouette but positive space against the starlit sky. The latter contrast is accentuated by the shadow of the wall against the sky drop, which gives a black outline to the top of the wall. This layering of positive and negative spaces could continue on additional planes and would increase the sense of stage depth.

The more regularly shaped the negative space, the more emphatic is its contribution to the design. We are not particularly aware of the negative areas in Bel Geddes' design for *The Patriot* (Figure 6-7) because they assume no distinct order.

A clearly shaped negative space can often provide a source of unity for a series of scenes within one production. Each of the scenes in Mielziner's design for *Cat on a Hot Tin Roof* emphasizes the area bounded by the stage platforms and the ceiling piece (see Figure 6-2). Even though the place changes, the shape of the surrounding space remains constant. One of the reasons for giving emphasis to a scenic or architectural frame around the stage is to define the outer limits of the negative space. If the composition is framed only with light, the

FIGURE 6-15 Jo Mielziner's design for *Winterset*. [From Jo Mielziner, *Designing for the Theatre* (New York: Bramhall House, 1965), p. 89. © 1935. Reprinted with the permission of Atheneum Publishers.]

negative space dissipates into the auditorium. Some light on the physical frame contains the negative space within the frame.

Light can impose a feeling of negative space where none exists scenically. For example, a production of *Romeo and Juliet* used a high platform for Juliet's balcony, but with conventional front lighting, the height of the platform did not seem a sufficient obstacle in view of Romeo's ardor. The substitution of higher-angled lights focused sharply on the balcony and on Romeo beneath clearly defined the negative gap of darkness between the two. Suddenly the distance and the sense of separation seemed much greater.

Josef Svoboda uses visible beams of light to create both positive and negative forms. In Figure 6-5, the column of light seems an almost solid and positive form, but for several of Svoboda's productions, strong backlight obscures any upstage scenery and becomes a highly luminous negative space surrounding the foreground figures.

The treatment of negative space helps to determine the openness of the composition. With a high ratio of negative to positive space, a setting seems open and more airy. The higher the contrast between positive and negative space and the greater the apparent transparency of the negative space, the more open the composition seems. Transparency is a matter of appearance of depth. A solid, blank wall is a more opaque negative space than a well-lit sky cyc. Relatively low-angled, well-blended, lightly hued lights on a sky cyc give a greater impression of transparency than any lighting which calls attention to the surface of the cyc. Where darkness is used as a negative space, the more absolute the appearance of blackness, the more transparent the space is. If we are even dimly aware of black curtains, for example, the space is still negative but somewhat opaque.

The color of light as well as brightness contrast can differentiate negative and positive space. To the extent that warmer colors always seem nearer the observer, if all other stimuli are equal, which rarely occurs, the warmer-colored space would seem to be positive. This principle is useful as a means of accentuating the contrast between positive and negative space by making the latter always a cooler color. Any contrast, particularly of hues that are complementary afterimages, will emphasize the separation between positive and negative space, but if the negative area is the warmer of the two, it will appear more opaque and the entire composition will be somewhat flatter than otherwise.

Similarly, the more saturated hue tends to be associated with the positive form. For example, a sunset effect on a skydrop using colors severely more saturated than the hues of foreground lights, may completely destroy the illusion of the skydrop as a transparent negative background.

If similar hues light both the positive forms and the negative space, other lights will have to be added to accentuate the modeling of the three-dimensional form in order to maintain any sense of negative space. More diffusion of the light in the background and more sharply focused, high-angle light on the foreground forms help to differentiate the positive from the negative space. We have also seen how back lighting can highlight solid forms in the foreground and give the negative space overall luminousness.

We cannot distinguish a form without some background contrast; so we always see some negative space in any composition, but if the negative space is small or poorly differentiated, the composition seems cluttered, flat and uninteresting. High contrast and a high ratio of negative space to positive form make stronger, more dramatic visual

statements. For example, Robert Edmond Jones' use of light to accentuate negative space in his designs in Figures 6-6, 6-11, and 6-12 creates a sharper contrast than Bel Geddes' design in Figure 6-7, and as a consequence Jones' designs are stronger and more dramatic.

Pattern

The arrangement of visual components into an orderly design creates a pattern. By contrast, an overall wash of light or an apparently random confusion of light would be without pattern. The concept of pattern implies a discernible shape or systematic organization of elements, usually with some aspect of repetition. A pattern projector creates a pattern of light and dark within the pool of a single light, but the arrangement of many lights on a stage and the interrelationship betwen these lights and stage forms produce an overall pattern.

Because so much of stage lighting is done with spotlights that produce distinct pools of light, the arrangement of these pools into a particular pattern is one of the most basic levels of lighting design except when the pools overlap to blend amorphously. In modern dance lighting, for example, pools of light on the floor are often a conspicuous portion of the design. By exploring the variables in arranging areas of light, we can isolate some of the elementary principles of pattern design.

A regular arrangement of separate but identical areas of light creates a sense of order, but if maintained for too long, this becomes monotonous. Some variety results when performers move in and out of these lit areas, which generates tension against the regularity of the pattern. Visual interest also increases if there is tension within the pattern itself. For example, in a circular arrangement of pools of light, if one pool is different—slightly larger or smaller, another color, or a little out of line—we still see the total pattern, but the anomaly sparks special interest. We wait in anticipation for the difference to be explained. Perhaps this one little discrepancy calls our attention even more to the complete pattern.

Ways for organizing parts of a pattern other than repetition include either diminishing or increasing progressions of size, brightness, hue, saturation, diffusion, or any other feature capable of being organized into a hierarchy of values. Contrasting elements may alternate regularly, or one element may recur in the midst of contrasting ingredients. A variety of components may be organized into a cohesive shape or into regular groups.

In keeping with the principle that the best works of art are those which maintain a sense of order while encompassing the greatest possible complexity, the visual interest of our pools of light on the floor increases when we begin to interrelate separate patterns. The patterns may simply overlap with each pattern maintaining its own identity, but the more stimulating situation occurs when one pool of light fits into several interlocking patterns or when the patterns interconnect simultaneously on different levels. For example, a downstage circle of light may be (1) part of a warm-to-cool color progression from down- to upstage, (2) part of a series of concentric pools of

light, and (3) one component in a V-shaped pattern of lit circles, therefore functioning as part of three separate patterns.

A pattern does not have to be symmetrical or geometric. The outlines of pieces of a jigsaw puzzle frequently form distinct patterns even though their separate shapes are not regular. Both Alwin Nikolais and Josef Svoboda, for example, use projectors to cast very complex, sinuous, multi-colored patterns of light onto layers of scrim, projection screens, or mirrors. (See Figures 6-16 and 6-17). Cutouts for trees, leaves, or clouds used as gobos in ellipsoidal spotlights project very irregular but distinct patterns. As we noted in our earlier discussion on the psychophysical aspects of pattern perception (pp. 62–65), the pattern of light can easily distract attention from the form of the lit surfaces. Occasionally this may be desirable (Plate IV), but otherwise use strongly patterned projections with care.

Light can either impose pattern, as in Jones' *Macbeth* design (Figure 6-6), or discover pattern in the scenery by emphasizing the regularity of certain scenic features, as with Mielziner's treatment of the vertical strips in his *Cat on a Hot Tin Roof* design (Figure 6-2). The number of patterns possible is almost infinite. The point is that the lighting designer must analyze pattern ele-

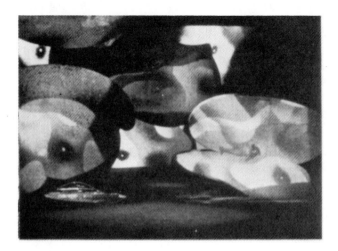

FIGURE 6-16 Josef Svoboda's setting for *Tannhauser*. [From Jarka Burian, *The Scenography of Josef Svoboda* (Middletown, Conn.: Wesleyan University Press, 1971), p. 76. Copyright © 1971 by Jarka Burian. Reprinted by permission of Wesleyan University Press and KaiDib Films International, Glendale, California.]

FIGURE 6-17 Alwin Nikolais' staging of "Cross Fade." [Photo by Tom Caravaglis.]

ments in the stage picture and then decide the extent to which lighting should emphasize specific pattens or add needed patterns at specific moments in the production. The designer must also maintain a wary eye to be sure that patterns of light or highlighted scenic patterns do not distract from other aspects of the production. Here again, a quick pencil sketch of the stage picture will usually isolate and reveal the major components of the visual pattern.

Harmony

Harmony is the interrelationship of the parts of a design to create unity of effect and an aesthetically pleasing whole. There is unmistakably a place for disharmony on the stage, but its ability to express tension, climax, or conflict depends partly on the establishment of a prior state of harmony, a process which differentiates disharmony from mere confusion.

Harmony of design results partially from unity of style, which we will discusss in detail in Chapter 8. But let us briefly examine two other aspects of harmony that influence the lighting design: color harmony and spatial harmony.

At least since the Renaissance, writers on art and aesthetics have attempted to discover principles governing combinations of colors which seem pleasing to the observer. Even though there are exponents for various systems, no one approach emerges as essentially more correct than another. It is apparent that taste (which varies with historical time and from individual to individual), the visual sophistication of the observer, and the context in which the colors are seen all influence judgments of color harmony. Therefore while recognizing that there is no absolute law of color harmony, it is useful to describe some of the major approaches and known variables.

There is agreement that similar—or related colors, at least—are harmonious. The trick is to determine the basis for relatedness or the tolerable degree of dissimilarity. Considering only hue, we can develop a continua of color from the spectrum or arrange a color wheel so that secondary colors lie between their component primaries. If we place the purple made by combining colors at the end of the spectrum between those two ends and wrap the spectrum in a circle, the resulting color wheel is basically the same whether we are talking about painter's primaries, light primaries, or the spectrum. Figure 6-18 shows such a wheel.

Some writers contend that harmonious hues lie within a given number of steps on this circle. For example, Maitland Graves in *Color Fundamentals,* states unequivocally that harmonious hues are six steps apart or less on a twenty-step color wheel.[1]

Colors also have two additional attributes: saturation or chroma, and brightness or value. If we expand our color wheel in three dimensions, one for each attribute, we produce a color cone, the most commonly known of which was developed in 1912 by

Albert Munsell, a Boston artist. Elaborate versions of the Munsell cone have 100 hue variations, 10 variations of brightness, and as many as 14 levels of saturation.

Harmony may presumably be accomplished by similarities of saturation or brightness as well as hue. Graves allows harmonious values to be only four steps apart but accepts the full chroma range.

Are there not harmonious relationships of colors outside of this narrow range? Graves uses the term "complementary" to describe hues opposite one another on the wheel, which combine to make black with pigment or white with light, and "contrasting" for other hues outside of the six-hue range. Both of these terms are differentiated from "harmonious," but numerous other writers have included complementary colors in the broader view of harmony. For example, Itten, a teacher at the Bauhaus in the 1920s, argued that the idea of harmony implied balance and symmetry of forces and that, for equilibrium, the eye demands medium grey and becomes disquieted in its absence. Therefore, any two or more colors are mutually harmonious if their mixture yields a neutral grey.[2]

There is a psychophysical basis for including both similar and complementary colors in this broader concept of harmony. When we juxtapose two colors, successive contrast and chromatic adaptation may cause the apparent hues to shift. If the colors are similar, there is no significant shift, or if the colors are complementary to one another their apparent brightness or saturation may alter, but their hue remains unchanged. Ralph M. Evans argues that this stability of apparent hues makes a given pair of colors go well together while colors seem inharmonious if there is a hue shift.[3]

Another theory of color harmony—based on the premise that the observer needs to make unambiguous hue distinctions—was advanced by P. Moon and D. E. Spencer, who argued that there are two areas of inharmonious ambiguity, the first where the observer is unsure whether the colors are in-

FIGURE 6-18 A color wheel showing Maitland Graves' range of harmony. Any six consecutive steps would be harmonius. [From Maitland Graves, *Color Fundamentals* (New York: McGraw Hill, 1952), p. 172.] © 1952 McGraw-Hill. Reproduced by permission.

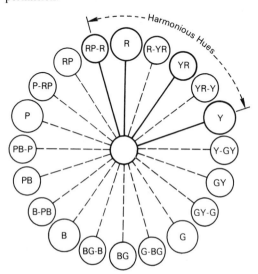

tended to be identical, the second where he is not sure whether the colors are definitely similar or contrasting. Using the Munsell color circle of 100 steps, the areas of ambiguity are between 2 and 7 and between 12 and 28 hue steps to either side of the chosen color (see Figure 6-19).[4]

The fact that spatial variables seem to influence our judgments further complicates the question of color harmony. The absolute size and relative size of areas of color, their degree of proximity, the shape of the elements, and the overall design of the visual field cause variations in affective determinations of color harmony. For example, a greenish-yellow area and a blue area of equal size, saturation, and brightness seem discordant, but increasing the relative size, saturation, or brightness of any one of the two colors restores considerable unity to the composition.

The value which the observer places on each of the component colors in a composition also influences the appraisal of har-

FIGURE 6-19 A color wheel showing P. Moon and D. E. Spencer's system for determining harmony. The shaded sections represent areas of color ambiguity, expressed on the left as steps on the Munsell hue wheel and on the right as degrees of the full hue circle. [From *Colour 73* (New York: John Wiley & Sons, 1973), p. 503.

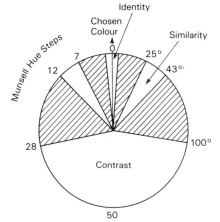

mony. The so-called "pure" spectral colors, red, blue, green, and yellow, for example, seem less discordant together than combinations of dissimilar "impure" hues.

While no one reliable system emerges for determining color harmony, there are a few reasonably safe guiding principles. Any group of colors will be in harmony to the degree that they share a common attribute, particularly hue. If the relationship between colors is "ambiguous," that is, lacking in clear similarity or contrast, the colors will more likely seem inharmonious. A clearly perceived and orderly plan for combining colors increases the probability that they will appear harmonious. A color combination familiar to the observer is more likely to seem harmonious than an unfamiliar combination. The changing dictates of color combinations in clothing fashions, however, shows how rapidly audiences can become familiar with new ideas of harmony.

The stage lighting designer frequently works with a base tint or wash which creates an overall color tone for the stage. If the wash is even, a fairly slight deviation can become obtrusive. One mismatched blue color on the lights for a sky cyc, for example, quickly calls attention to itself and seems out of place. White light, to the extent that it contains all colors, seems to "go with" virtually any lighting tint; so colors which complement the general color tone of the stage seem in harmony. Tints to either side of the complementary color call attention to themselves but will not disrupt the harmony if confined to small areas. Variations in tint that are clearly motivated or conform to changes in the scenic structure are less likely to create disharmony than the same tints arbitrarily used. If an overall color tone is not established, more variation of hue can be tolerated, but it is more difficult to establish a sense of color harmony.

A general stage tint tends to impose color harmony on a design that does not otherwise possess it for the simple reason that the tint emphasizes objects which reflect the component colors of the tint and suppresses all other hues. The danger, of course, is that the sameness of tint may produce harmony and boredom at the same time. A mixed palette of related tints will keep both harmony and visual interest.

To shift attention to the problem of spatial harmony, note that unity of composition and compositional harmony are not always the same thing. The idea of harmony implies concord, mutual reinforcement of elements, and parts fitting comfortably into a whole. Some visual compositions, particularly on the stage, entail conflict, collision of elements, and unity maintained through mutual tension. These may be unified compositions, but not necessarily harmonious ones. Some conflict and contrast can be maintained without destroying the harmony of a composition, but at some step, discord produces disharmony. For example, the design for *Troilus and Cressida* shown in Figure 6-20 uses a nearly symmetrical setting with clean simple lines. This is clearly a unified composition, but the lighting creates a strong sense of tension and disharmony. The diagonal shadow across the stage-right screen divides the composition vertically and forces the eye to the left of the visual frame, in tension with the desire to focus on

the central figure. The greater brightness of the stage-right side is a contrary force to the attention and body position of the human figure, which leads the eye in the opposite direction. Silhouetted structures divide the composition into separate horizontal planes with the top of the backing screens demarcating upper and lower halves of the stage, but even here the division is made ambiguous by the V-shaped split. The patterns of light and darkness on the screens create tension with one another, and their cloud-like shape intrudes into an otherwise geometrically conceived composition. There is nothing wrong with this design. Certainly the lighting adds interest to what is otherwise a fairly stark and plain stage structure. However, analyzed just in terms of the relationship of light to shadow, it is not a harmonious design.

Spatial harmony results from an ordering of elements into a cohesive unit without unresolved or undue tension. A balanced composition is frequently harmonious, but counterpoised dynamic features having no harmonic relationship also produce balance.

Frequent methods for attaining compositional harmony are repetition, blending, inclusion, progression, and closure.

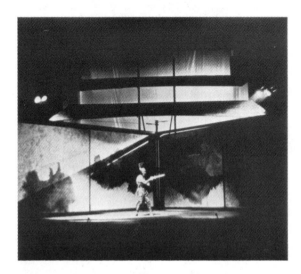

FIGURE 6-20 Andre Acquart's setting for *Troilus and Cressida* at the Theatre de la Cite, Villeurbanne, France, 1964. [From International Theatre Institute, *Stage Design Throughout the World Since 1960* (New York: Theatre Art Books, 1972), p. 49.]

Repetition. Just as the use of a color wash can establish a basis for color harmony, any line or form used with enough consistency tends to pull a composition together. Craig's use of vertical rectangles and diagonal streaks of light in the design shown in Figure 6-4 or Mielziner's use of silhouetted lines in the *Death of a Salesman* setting, Figure 6-3, impose overriding visual structures which relate portions of the design to one another. The more rhythmic the pattern of repetition, the greater the harmonic effect is. Rhythm implies an underlying regularity and the repetition of variety at fixed intervals. In this context, rhythm applies to the movement of the eye over a composition. In Craig's design in Figure 6-4, for example, the height, width, and brightness of the vertical blocks vary, but he maintains a fairly regular interval in the alterations between the lit front faces and the shadowed receding edges. As the eye moves into the composition, this rhythm of light and shadow establishes a sense of harmony. Even the ratio between streaks of shadow and streaks of brightness in the diagonal lighting maintain roughly the same ratio as the pattern of light and shadow on the vertical screens.

Blending. By emphasizing the connections between forms, blending helps to establish harmony. Color blending is a familiar concept, but light can also help to blend objects in space. In Bel Geddes' design in Figure 6-7, for example, the foreground figure has the same tonal value as the group in the doorway, which connects the two in spite of their separation in space. In painting, this technique is known as *bridging*. Notice also how the scenic unit stage-left blends into both the foreground and background. This approach works contrary to the objective of using light to reveal form or emphasize three-dimensionality. Obviously we do not want to blend the stage into a homogenous mass, but it is also unnecessary to carve out every form with light. The lighting designer makes decisions moment by moment concerning which forms to differentiate from their surroundings and which forms to blend. The first approach emphasizes contrast, the second, harmony.

Inclusion. Blending is one method for stressing inclusion, the embodiment of one form into another. The impression that all of the parts of a design contribute to the whole, like a well-conceived machine, helps to establish harmony. If an area of light encompasses smaller patches of light, the entire effect seems harmonious. Patterns of light created by sunlight shining through leaves on a tree or through a stained glass window make this effect. We see little splotches of light, but we sense the overall unity. To the extent that most stage lighting is composed of pools from spotlights, the same principle works by analogy. Just as we view the light passing through the leaves as part of the total illumination, we should sense the spotlit areas as part of a total composition. There are times when we wish to subdivide the stage space, and in these cases we correctly sacrifice harmony for contrast or the idea of the multiplicity of space, although a degree of harmony can be maintained by other methods.

Progression. An overall sense of progression also incorporates the parts into a harmonious whole. Returning again to Craig's design in Figure 6–4, the angle of the diagonal lighting duplicates the angle made by the tops of the screens as they recede upstage. This regular progression to the furthest reaches of the stage space binds together the lighting and the scene design. Frequently a progression of lighting intensity from a bright foreground to a dark background, or the reverse, will help to create visual harmony. Harmony is enhanced only by those progressions that complete themselves onstage or provide enough information so the audience surmises their offstage continuation. Otherwise the incompleteness of the form creates tension.

Closure. Completeness largely depends on closure, the containment of the design within an overall compositional shape. This shape also gives a way of relating parts to the whole. The more balanced and static the shape, the greater the degree of harmony, although one must guard against monotony. A great deal of effort has been devoted to identifying "naturally" harmonic shapes. There are defenders of circles, spheres, cubes, equilateral spirals, figure eights, egg shapes, and others as candidates for the title of the perfect harmonic form. Any shape which is itself pleasing and stable will add similar values to a composition. For example, Mielziner's design for *Winterset* (Figure 6-15) is very stark and dramatic, but the fact that the central lit area is in the form of a catenary curve, the natural line taken when a piece of string is suspended between two fixed points, adds a considerable degree of dignity and harmony to the design. Mielziner's design for *Death of a Salesman* (Figure 6-3) contains a very faint central oval, beige against the purple field, defined by the curve of the steps behind Willy, the boys' beds overhead, and the parents' bed stage-right, with the kitchen wall at its center. This provides a harmonious core for the otherwise dynamic silhouette of the house. Craig's designs (Figures 6-4 and 6-8) use balanced, inverted pyramids, defined largely with light, as central motifs in otherwise vertical designs. In all of these cases, a contained, stable form provides a harmonic dimension for the design.

Light naturally radiates from reflective surfaces in variations of a spherical form. Unless the lit areas are fragmented or strong linear features are added to the lighting, spherical radiation naturally imposes a degree of harmony into a design. Maintaining the rounded form of a pool of light even when multiple areas are lit, carries out this harmony. In this situation, the designer must carefully control the outer edge of the lit areas to be sure that sharp shuttering at peculiar angles does not disrupt the desired effect. A slight variation in intensity and color such as is used for the oval shape in *Death of a Salesman* requires subtle control of the lighting.

Variation and Simplicity

The impulse in any art form to make the art experience as complex and richly textured as possible counters the need to clarify and simplify the artistic expression. If art extracts order from the apparent chaos of experience, it must simultaneously reflect order and the diversity of its subject matter. The history of any art form tends to swing between these two poles and, at its worst, art disintegrates into either clutter or starkness.

The period or style of a specific play or production may require a specific emphasis in the composition of the lighting on either complexity or simplicity, but otherwise the goal of the designer should be to strike a balance between the two. To state this goal in another way, the composition should be as varied as possible without sacrificing the sense of artistic control and order. Even the dramatic treatment of chaos requires some degree of control, perhaps more than other situations, or there is a danger that the artistic experience itself will become chaotic. Extreme realists may argue that theatre should present the chaos of reality itself, but others recognize that the unique element which distinguishes theatre from life is just this sense of order and control.

Perhaps the best rule of thumb is to eliminate anything that is unnecessary. The technical requirements of lighting should not impose complexity. Complexity should grow out of the richness of the subject matter and the artistic statement. If a design seems starved, the solution is not to use a more complicated technique, but to see if the design can say more and accomplish more.

The advantage of variety is its potential for holding attention. Its danger is that excessive complexity can confuse, clutter, or distract. The advantage of simplicity is in the clarity and strength of its statement. The danger is that it can become monotonous.

An ideal solution is a composition which leads from simplicity to complexity or through complexity to simplicity. In the first case, the initial impression is of the overall form, but as we examine it more closely we become aware of more and more detail that enriches the experience. In the second case, the spectator first sees the complexity, but then discovers the overriding form which gives all of the parts unity. Even though these two approaches can be controlled by manipulating such variables as the visual entryway or having the overall form depend on objects and shapes that take either primary or secondary focus, the difference is often in the ways two spectators will approach a single composition. In either case, the end result is the same: a composition has both variety and simplicity.

The designs of Robert Edmond Jones almost provide a casebook for the application of this principle of complexity within simplicity. Lighting was an integral part of Jones' scenic conception from the first renderings, and the initial response to any of his designs is that he made a very bold, strong, and simple statement, principally with the interplay of light and shadow. Closer examination reveals very subtle and intricate control of effects. For example, his design for *The Fountain* (Figure 6-21), a play by Eugene O'Neill, which Jones also directed, seems at first to be lit by a single spot of light which focuses on the tortured central figure, throwing the foreground figure into silhouette, and casting an ominous tombstone-shaped shadow of the torture block on the stone wall in the background. The brightly lit area slightly off center counterbalances the large background shadow which is off-center the other direction. The near symmetry of the composition plus the blockiness of the tortureboard and its shadow give the design a great degree of formality and emphasize the contrasting sinuousness of the human forms. The visual image is simple, striking, almost stark. How-

FIGURE 6-21 Robert Edmond Jones' design for *The Fountain*. [From Robert Edmond Jones, *Drawings for the Theatre* (New York: Theatre Arts, Inc., 1925). Copyright 1925 by Theatre Arts, Inc.; copyright © 1970 by Theatre Arts Books. Used with permission of the publisher, Theatre Arts Books, 153 Waverly Place, New York, N.Y. 10014.]

ever, when we look closer, we realize that no one light or even a natural arrangement of lighting could produce this effect unless we assume, as in a Rembrandt painting, that the light is generated mysteriously from within the figures or the setting. A front light of sufficient size and intensity to project the shadow on the back wall would have to come low from down-right or from a down-right overhead light reflected off the floor. Yet the right side of the tortured figure is in shadow and the foreground character seems to catch no light at all. Notice the shadow over the head and shoulders of the tortured figure. It gives the figure a sense of bulk and strength and emphasizes the crucifixion like body position. How is this shadow produced when the highlights suggest a light coming from overhead, placing all shadows below the body? Of course, this is only a rendering. Has Jones simply created an internally inconsistent lighting design which we could not possibly reproduce on stage? Try sketching a lighting plot to produce the effects of light and shadow suggested by Jones. It can be done.

The pool of light on the floor, the highlights on the hanging figure, and much of the light on the torture block come from a spotlight hung overhead and slightly to the stage-left of the central composition. On an up-to-downstage axis, it is hung between the two characters so that it lights only the upstage side of the foreground figure. Notice the heavy shadows at his feet. The fainter shadows over the shoulders of the tortured figure may come partly from floor bounce, but could be emphasized by a low-angled light in a footlight position down-left-center, focused sharply to the torture block and off the foreground character. The shadow on the back wall cannot come from a realistically placed source because this same light would destroy the silhouette effect of the foreground person and wash out the strong shadows which give the hanging body such a cavernous, tortured look. A

completely independent system of lights must be used for the backdrop. In Jones' day this would have been done with shuttered spotlights. Today, we might use a full stage projector. The impression is that the shadow comes from the light on the torture block, but in fact this is impossible. An examination of the other Jones designs illustrated in this book will reveal similar use of very strong, simple lighting effects, conceived with a great deal of imagination.

In his advice to a young stage designer, Jones quotes Michaelangelo: "Beauty is the purgation of superfluities."[5] Jones also asks that stage lighting be "penetrating," that it reveal "the ultimate in the immediate."[6] For a designer of Jones' talent, and ideally for all lighting design, simplicity and complexity are the same thing, or to state it in other words—there is a point where simplicity becomes very complex.

Gradation and Tonal Effect

Variation in lighting intensity and, to some extent, color, provide major cues for figure discrimination and depth perception; but homogeneity of brightness or color is one method to enhance harmony by blending. The lighting design can run the full range between these two extremes. To use the terminology of the photographer, a scene may be lit either with high or low contrast in intensity or color.

Adaptation level fixes the limits of brightness contrast. The black point or the intensity level below which all stimuli are seen as black varies according to intensity and sets the bottom end of the brightness range. Further increase in brightness once the adaptation level is established will only increase the level of the black point. The apparent spread between the brightest and darkest objects in a field is greatest when the overall intensity is low and when the brightest area occupies a relatively small percentage of the total field. In this situation or whenever there is a big difference between the brightest and darkest portions of the stage, glare is a potential danger.

The ratio between the brightest and darkest portions of a field is called the *brightness ratio* or *luminance ratio*. For the eye to detect a noticeable difference in brightness, the ratio must be at least two to one. Illumination engineers prescribe various brightness ratios for different working spaces, the ideal range usually being between three to one and ten to one. In fact, the ideal ratio varies considerably according to the lighting conditions and the desired effect. For instance, if the direction of the light is poor, the ratio should be low. If the bottom end of the ratio is complete darkness, this limits the maximum brightness that can be comfortably viewed. However, if there is a good relationship between key and fill lighting, and the bottom part of the ratio is bright enough to reveal some detail, the audience can tolerate a ratio higher than ten to one.

Brightness contrasts may be either sharp or gradual. We obtain the sharpest differences when a person or object is lit with a single light with little or no light reflected from surfaces other than the primary object. Maximum gradation results from using multiple illumination sources or having a number of reflective surfaces to provide full light. Extremely sharp, well-focused light tends to reduce objects to their simplest forms and obscure details revealed by finer gradations of brightness.

The brightness ratio and degree of brightness gradation tends to have an emotional effect on a viewer. Dramatic tension increases with a high ratio and sharp contrasts so long as we keep brightness levels below the fatigue-producing point. Tonal variations make a scene visually interesting and help to sustain attention. A decrease in the brightness ratio tends to increase blending and produce a more soothing effect. However, at some point, usually around a three-to-one ratio, the differences are not sufficient to maintain visual interest and a feeling of lethargy or gloom may set in.

The distribution of brightness gradations in the field also helps to shape audience response. Large areas of contrasting brightness tend to have a more dramatic impact than smaller areas or than larger areas with less contrast.

The effect of variations in brightness gradation on a scene can easily be illustrated by using darkroom techniques to vary the contrast of a photograph of a stage setting. The scene shown in Figure 6-22 takes on quite different moods according to the type of contrast. One can imagine how similar changes in the type of contrast could be obtained for one setting using lighting instruments on stage.

Gradations in the color of light are also important factors in the composition and work in a manner analogous to brightness gradation. Just as there is a level of brightness adaptation, color adaptation decreases the sensitivity of the eye to a dominant color in the lighting. Small hue differences result in a low-contrast composition, whereas the use of highly saturated complementary or contrasting colors increases the compositional contrast. Differences in hue may be either abrupt or gradual. The first more likely creates a discordant or vibrant effect, but it is also the more dramatic. The second produces more harmony and is more soothing, but may be less interesting. The distribution of areas of color also influences the way gradations are perceived. Finer variations of hue are more noticeable when a large area of a given color dominates the scene. Without a tonal or focal color, we accept a much wider range of lighting hues as "normal." We have also seen how gradations in the color of a field, particularly with the blue shift of distant objects in aerial perspective, can be a cue for depth.

When we talk about the lighting for a given scene being "hard" or "soft," we are

FIGURE 6-22(a) Variations in brightness contrast produce a marked difference in the mood created by a setting [Figures 6-22(a) and 6-22(b)]. [Act 1, scene 4 of *A Streetcar Named Desire* by Tennessee Williams, produced by the William and Mary Theatre, lighting by Christopher J. Boll.]

FIGURE 6-22(b)

discussing gradation and tonal effect. Just as the words "hard" and "soft" may also have dramatic and emotional connotations, so do different lighting effects associated with those words. An important part of lighting design is the determination of the amount of contrast appropriate for a given moment in a production or the way in which contrast should change as the performance progresses.

The fact that other designers and the director seem initially to control the compositional arrangement of features within the visual framework may mislead the lighting designer into the mistaken idea that stage lighting has no compositional function. Even though all of the compositional elements discussed in this chapter could still function on a generally lit stage with no specific lighting composition, the insertion of any variation in brightness, color, or distribution of light introduces a new dimension of composition. The lighting may enhance, obscure, or change the composition or add an entirely novel composi-

tional aspect. The lighting designer may not control the initial compositional choices, but the lighting design ultimately determines the final appearance of the composition.

Composition: Time Factors

Theatre is essentially a time art, unlike painting but like music. The unfolding of events in time is basic to all theatrical forms: drama, dance, and opera. Any resequencing of events changes the artistic experience. The basic form of the dramatic experience develops over time: tension growing out of conflict, rising and falling in mounting waves to a climax, until the conflict resolves and the tension lessens. Plays may take other forms, but the great majority are variations on this proven pattern. Dance choreography may progress in a less linear fashion and follow other modes of organization, but it often uses classic dramatic structure. This structure seems to have developed in response to the fundamental fact that spectator attention in most cases flags after a while, and to maintain even a constant level of interest any experience must become progressively more rich. Tension attracts interest.

Even a static composition can induce some feeling of movement and rhythm by a careful control of features which draw the eye along certain lines at a definite rate. The visual entryway or pathway may be a subtle dimension of time, but the results do depend on a sequence of visual encounters controlled by the designers.

Scenic designs for multiset plays usually attempt to find a visual parallel to the dramatic structure; so scenic compositions may move from balanced and harmonious forms to arrangements which express increasingly more tension and conflict. In more abstract designs, portions of the setting may move or disintegrate in order to directly state the dramatic development. However, the play requiring a single setting with no justification for significant changes is common. In these cases particularly, the burden for making dramatic changes in the setting rests with the lighting.

110

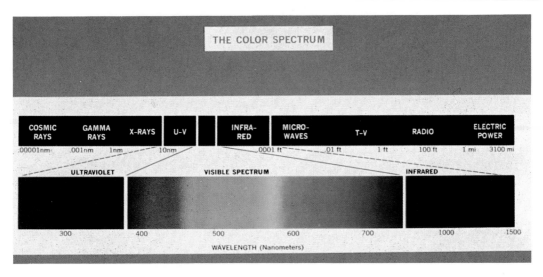

THE COLOR SPECTRUM

| COSMIC RAYS | GAMMA RAYS | X-RAYS | U-V | | INFRA-RED | MICRO-WAVES | T-V | RADIO | ELECTRIC POWER |

.00001nm   .001nm   1nm   10nm   .0001 ft   .01 ft   1 ft   100 ft   1 mi   3100 mi

ULTRAVIOLET   VISIBLE SPECTRUM   INFRARED

300   400   500   600   700   1000   1500

WAVELENGTH (Nanometers)

PLATE I Electromagnetic spectrum including the visible light spectrum.
[Courtesy of General Electric Co., Nela Park, Cleveland, Ohio.]

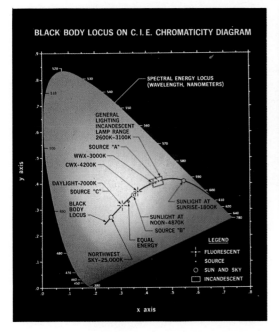

BLACK BODY LOCUS ON C.I.E. CHROMATICITY DIAGRAM

SPECTRAL ENERGY LOCUS
(WAVELENGTH, NANOMETERS)

GENERAL
LIGHTING
INCANDESCENT
LAMP RANGE
2600K-3100K

SOURCE "A"
WWX-3000K
CWX-4200K

DAYLIGHT-7000K
SOURCE "C"

BLACK
BODY
LOCUS

SUNLIGHT AT
SUNRISE-1800K

SUNLIGHT AT
NOON-4870K
SOURCE "B"

EQUAL
ENERGY

NORTHWEST
SKY-25,000K

LEGEND
-¦- FLUORESCENT
·   SOURCE
○   SUN AND SKY
☐   INCANDESCENT

y axis

x axis

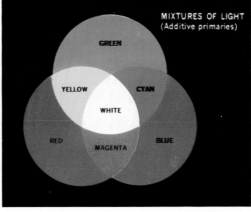

MIXTURES OF LIGHT
(Additive primaries)

GREEN

YELLOW   CYAN

WHITE

RED   MAGENTA   BLUE

PLATE IIa C.I.E. Chromaticity Diagram. The outside curved line
represents the range of spectral colors, decreasing in saturation toward
the center of the diagram. The chromaticity of any color in relation to
the three primary colors may be graphically represented by a point on
the diagram. [Courtesy of General Electric Co., Nela Park, Cleveland, Ohio.]

PLATE IIb Overlapping circles of the three traditional color primaries of
light show how they mix to produce secondary colors and white.
[Courtesy of General Electric Co., Nela Park, Cleveland, Ohio.]

PLATE III Side lighting (bottom) enhances the perception of stage depth. Predominantly front lighting on the model (top) tends to flatten the stage space.

PLATE IV *The Tempest* at the Dallas Theatre Center. Lighting by Frank King. A variegated color pattern blends costumes with the stage space. [Photo courtesy of the Dallas Theatre Center.]

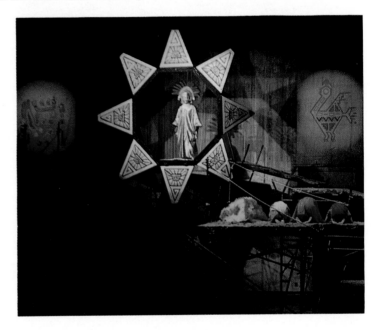

PLATE V *The Royal Hunt* of the Sun by Peter Shaffer at Washington University in St. Louis. [Lighting by Jack Brown.]

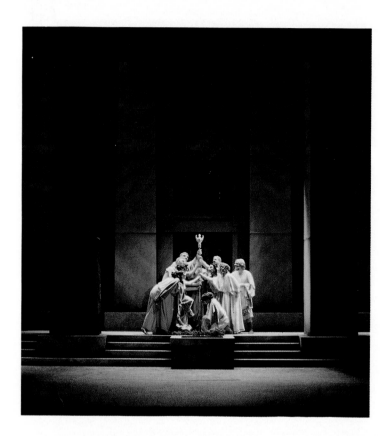

PLATE VII *A Streetcar Named Desire* at The College of William and Mary. [Scenery by Jerry Bledsoe. Lighting by Christopher J. Boll.]

To the extent that lighting can both make its own visual statement and change the apparent form of the stage space, it is the most flexible of the scenic media in the theatre and the most accessible means for changing the visual composition over time. It is therefore not enough to think of the lighting composition as an unchanging picture or even as a series of static arrangemens. The lighting designer must compose in a temporal context, thinking of the movement of light and the sequence of effects.

Movement and Rhythm in a Stationary Composition

The manner in which lighting creates or emphasizes certain forms or lines determines how the eye moves over a scene and, to some extent, how the observer responds to a composition. Movement and rhythm in this context refer to values assigned to a fixed composition as a result of the movement of the spectator's eyes.

Eye movement is in fact the beginning of a kinetic response of the entire body of the viewer. When we actively watch something in motion, the muscles in our body actually undergo a miniature sympathetic response, duplicating the action of the thing observed. This muscular movement may be barely perceptible but can be measured electrically by highly sensitive instruments. A static composition with strong dynamics produces a similar response. Thus a tall building or monument causes us to straighten up and stretch a little. Whether these physical responses are triggered by the emotional reactions to dynamic visual experiences, or vice-versa, there is certainly a strong link. These reactions may vary considerably from person to person and any description of them must be highly subjective, but we can predict some fairly general patterns of response with considerable reliability.

For example, vertical lines or forms give a composition a sense of majesty or dignity. Craig's designs in Figures 6-5 and 6-9 amply illustrate this. There may be few theatres with sufficient stage height to use these designs, but the vertical pull is unmistakable and greatly accentuated by the lighting. In contrast, horizontal forms tend to be restful and oblique lines add a dimension of dynamism and speed. Using light to stress the roof line in Mielziner's design for *Death of a Salesman* (Figure 6-4), for instance, adds considerable vitality to an otherwise staid composition.

Waving or curved forms create a feeling of graceful motion and languor. The silhouetted banister in Jones' design for *Swords* (Figure 7-1) curves slightly and creates a

FIGURE 7-1 Robert Edmond Jones design for *Swords*. [From Robert Edmond Jones, *Drawing for the Theatre* (New York: Theatre Arts, Inc., 1925). Copyright 1925 by Theatre Arts, Inc.; copyright © 1970 by Theatre Arts Books. Used with the permission of the publisher, Theatre Arts Books, 153 Waverly Place, New York, N.Y. 10014.]

long, dipping wave as the eye moves across the stage. Draped forms in front of the landings, the curved arc of the lit door openings, the central arch, and the softly rounded pools of light further emphasize the curved forms in the composition. If the banisters and doorways had straight tops, the feeling of the design would be quite different. In Jones' design for *The House of Women* (Figure 7-2) vertical and horizontal linear features predominate, but highlighting emphasizes the rounded forms of the chandelier, the lamps on the mantle and piano, and the white dress of the woman. A sense of opulence results.

The curves in *Swords* and *The House of Women* are fairly regular in form, but spiral or twisting forms create an impression of tension and conflict (Figure 7-3). Any composition with abrupt changes in line direction or a staccato repetition of motif seem more animated than a setting with blocky forms and smooth line progression. Pointed figures, zigzags, fragmented forms, and broken lines convey images of tension, excitement, or disorder (Figure 7-4). The lighting design can use beam edges to create these patterns or can emphasize specific features of the set, underscoring particular compositional characteristics.

The Physical Movement of Lighting

Lights can literally move across the stage, as in the case of follow spots, or lighting can appear to move by means of cross-fades or chasers. As long as followspots continue to require an operator for each instrument, their use is somewhat limited. In most cases, the spotlight follows the movement of the performer with the intention of highlighting that performer without calling great attention to the light itself, but there are times when the followspot itself attracts more notice. The "searching light" probes the darkness looking for the performer, building expectation as it goes. A moving spot can become a performer in its own right, substituting for an apparition or missing actor. The famous circus clown, Emmet Kelly, developed a comic routine where he used a broom to sweep away intractable spotlights. Rapidly circling spotlights used to introduce the major acts in a circus can have a similarly stimulating effect onstage.

Because of image persistence, rapidly moving lights create the impression of bands or circles of light, and controlling the direction of movement can vary the composition of these bands. This creates a very dynamic image, but if sustained too long it be-

FIGURE 7-2 Robert Edmond Jones' design for *The House of Women.* [From Ralph Pendleton, *The Theatre of Robert Edmond Jones* (Middletown, Conn.: Wesleyan University Press, 1958), p. 63.]

FIGURE 7-3 Ludwig Sievert's design for *Don Juan*. [From Walter Fuerst
and Samuel J. Hume, *XXth Century Stage Decoration, Vol. 2: The Illustrations*
(London: Alfred A. Knopf, 1928), plate 205.]

comes bothersome; the spectator's eyes are compelled to try to resolve a fixed image in a field where the light disappears before the eye has time to focus on anything. The rate of movement of these lights obviously influences the effect created. Rapid movement in random directions can be exhilarating but disorienting. More leisurely movement in graceful patterns stimulates without confusing, but a regularly repeated pattern sustained for too long can be downright annoying.

The cross-fading of lights is a much more common aspect of movement and more important in determining the rhythm of the production and the temporal dimension of composition. With the advent of memory-controlled lighting systems, very complicated and precise patterns of cross-fading are possible and have become part of the lighting designer's stock and trade. Cues can be engineered in which different lights dim or brighten at different rates, various

portions of the dimming curve are executed at varied speeds, or a lighting change pauses in the middle and begins again after a fixed interval. Of course, many of these effects are possible on a manually controlled board; the skilled operator has an advantage over a memory system if changes must be timed to the often variable movements of performers. Memory systems only provide an opportunity for greater complexity and precise duplication of the timing of cues.

When the lighting changes rapidly, the audience may be aware of and respond to the tempo of the change, but will view the composition in before-and-after terms. If the cross-fade is slow enough so that the audience can resolve the visual picture in the middle of the shift, they will be aware of the composition as a moving form with visual characteristics that change from moment to moment, with a distinct sense of flow and direction. The patterns of change possible are virtually infinite, but we can examine

FIGURE 7-4 David Gibson's lighting of Virgil Beaver's setting for *Of Time and the River* at the Dallas Theatre Center. [Photo by Windy Drum.]

some of those most frequently used and demonstrate the importance of carefully controlling this aspect of the design.

The scene can close down to a smaller area or open up to a larger. In both cases, even if we keep the foot-candle reading constant, the initial impression on the audience will be greater brightness. The change can be a simple subtraction or addition of lit areas, or we can arrange the distribution to give emphasis to a particular part of the stage. For example, we can expand the lit area by first bringing up the light on a new point of focus and then filling in the gap. The scene can break into smaller areas, or fragments can coalesce into a larger area.

This may take place as a single shift or occur in stages, in which case the position of new areas of light or darkness and the direction of the progression will influence the composition. Plays such as *The Rimers of Eldritch* with multiple vignettes that flow in and out of the central action frequently require this approach.

Light can alternate between two or more major areas. The rate of change, like the speed of a rising or falling curtain, does much to set the mood for the coming scene or to punctuate the concluding scene. One area may completely darken before the other comes up; the second may come to full intensity before the first dims; one may brighten while the other darkens; the darkening scene may remain slightly illuminated; or there may be various combinations of these. The manner of the shift determines the relationship between the two scenes and the extent of the visual frame. For instance, a slight glow on the newly darkened scene "keeps it in the picture." An instant of total darkness between the two tends to divide them into separate compositions. The areas may occupy entirely separate parts of the stage or they may overlap. If they overlap, the sense of changing to a different area is maintained as long as their compositional centers remain outside of one another.

Portions of a composition may brighten or darken. If any area abruptly changes brightness, even by darkening, it instantly draws attention. Therefore a portion of the stage may not be taken out of immediate focus simply by darkening it. The element of change is a more important attention-getting device than the greater brightness of the surrounding area. However, brightening an area does bring it immediately into focus because the change reinforces the attention-getting value of the brighter stimulus.

The brightening or darkening of a portion of the stage may establish a clear linear flow to the lighting which can become an important compositional device and means of creating focus. Realistic devices such as opening and shutting curtains and doors which block the light or the use of a moving light source frequently motivate these changes. For example, a curtain or a window opened to stronger exterior light generates a shaft of light which leads the eye to a pivotal focus in the room. The speed with which the curtain opens to some extent motivates the speed with which the shaft of light seems to advance into the room and may make the difference between a sudden revelation and more slowly mounting tension.

Bringing a new light source into the set-

ting is a somewhat unrealistic but accepted convention for creating a new flow of light with greatly increased illumination. A character enters with a lantern and crosses the stage. As the lantern moves, new areas of the stage become successively brighter. When the lantern passes out of an area, that space again darkens, but not to its previous low level. A new lighting composition results with a brightness level too high to be coming from the new source alone, but it "feels right." In a more abstract production, these linear movements of light can be executed according to the mood of the moment or for compositional change without concern for realistic motivation.

The lighting for the opening or closing of a scene may emphasize the movement of the light and the change in the composition. Rather than all of the lights coming on or going off at one time, the lights may change in stages. The lighting designer can thereby control both the first and last things seen by the audience and can also give added weight to these points of focus by having the light appear to close in on or open out from them. Thus, during an end-of-scene dimout, a compositionally minor but dramatically important object onstage may take attention away from the previous point of focus within the fully lit scene. This is an effective way of foreshadowing or punctuating a scene, but it requires a fairly slow blackout or brightening for the audience to have time to register on the new focus.

Changes can be made in color or in key-and-fill relationships on the entire stage, or on a single object, without any significant changes in the overall level of brightness. One convention for indicating the passage of time on an empty stage is by changing the apparent direction of the light source, and extreme changes in the composition can even signify that a unit setting has switched locales. Altering the composition of light on the setting or on a single actor conveys major shifts in mood. The emphasis here is on change. We can presumably make a mood shift in the lighting slowly enough so that the audience remains consciously unaware of it; but if we want to emphasize the act of changing moods, the motion of the shift should be apparent.

How slowly can the lights change without losing the sense of motion? Or to state the same problem in another manner, how slowly must we change the lighting for the audience not to be aware of the shift? How sneaky must a sneak be? Of course the audience may become aware that the lights have changed, but this is different from the perception that they *are* changing. There is no absolute answer to this question. It depends on too many variables. If the audience knows that the lighting is going to change and they are concentrating on that change, the shift would probably have to be very subtle indeed to go undetected. However, the audience's attention is rarely fixed so exclusively on the lighting. If a great deal is happening on stage and the attention of the audience is drawn strongly to other matters, fairly bold alterations in the lighting may go undetected. Indeed, one way to mask lighting changes is to make them coincide in tempo, direction, and space with the movement of a performer on stage. If the lighting change anticipates the movement slightly it calls somewhat more attention to itself, but emphasizes the performer's move. If it lags behind the actor or dancer's movement, the effect may be annoying; and if the lights move while all else is still, they may steal focus.

Rhythm

The rate of change in lighting, the length of intervals between changes, and the temporal relationship of different compositions establish an element of rhythm in the lighting. If the changes are too far apart, the audience will notice contrast or the tempo of a single shift, but will not necessarily perceive the lighting design as a whole with rhythmic changes. How long the interval must be be-

fore the shifts break into disparate experiences depends on how noticeable the changes are and how regularly they occur. Shifts which attract attention and occur at regular intervals may contribute to the rhythm of the production even when the shifts are far apart. Subtle changes at variable intervals will have less effect on the overall rhythm.

The rhythm influences both the perception of structure and the mood of the audience. In simplest terms, the three-act division of a play is indicated by three periods of light. Scenes within any act may be further marked by blackouts, but more subtle French scenes or beats may also be designated by lighting changes. It is not suggested that changes ought necessarily to occur whenever the action of a play takes a new direction, but the designer should be aware of these structural features to decide if a shift is appropriate. A *French scene* begins whenever a character enters or exits, and usually the business of the play takes a slightly different direction when this occurs. A *beat* is a portion of the play during which a character pursues a single definable action in order to obtain a specific objective. The director may not wish to call attention to these structural elements or may use means other then the lighting to set them off, but lighting changes are a major tool for emphasizing the architectonic aspects of the play.

Choreography has similar structural divisions, defined in terms of movement rather than plot or character motivation. Units or beats may last from a few seconds to several minutes. For example, a single dancer turns in the center of the stage. After the completion of the turn, two additional dancers enter from opposite corners and carom off the central figure onto the downstage corners. The central dancer then leaps into the arms of the down-right dancer while the third closes into a tight ball on the floor. We have described three distinct beats: turn, carom, and leap/contract. These three may be part of a larger unit which fits into a yet larger structure, and we may choose to emphasize these divisions with lighting changes.

Whenever dance, drama and, of course, opera are accompanied by music, the musical structure may provide a key for the rhythm of lighting changes. Presumably a light show for a rock concert might choose a musical unit as small as a note on which lighting changes could be based, but this tempo will be too frantic for most productions. Phrases, key shifts, or changes in musical tempo, as well as major divisions in lyrics, may cue lighting shifts which reinforce the musical cadence.

To pursue the musical analogy, the rhythmic aspects of a lighting design must be scored, and the more conspicuous the lighting or the more abstract the production, the more important this lighting score becomes. Just as multimedia artists have had to develop new methods of notation to control the arrangement of events over time, the lighting designer may find it necessary to go beyond a conventional cue sheet. Because production demands are so diverse and there are so many variables at the lighting designer's disposal, it is impossible to prescribe any one method for noting the lighting score, but a large sheet of paper with a time line is a good starting place, and a stop watch is an essential piece of equipment.

Traditionally, cues are assigned a place in a script and the length of time required for their execution is noted. If the interval between cues is also timed and a scale of apparent brightness is established on a range of one to ten, an interesting schematic presentation develops for this one aspect of the lighting design. If the use of the lights can be grouped in any logical way—for example, cyc lights, right side lights, central acting area lights—a separate line can be used to indicate the apparent intensity of each group, and their temporal relationship becomes clearer (see Figures 12-1 and 12-2). Actual control board readings may not be a

reliable indicator of brightness from the audience's point of view because the settings cannot easily reflect such matters as brightness adaptation; so the designer will have to subjectively evaluate the apparent brightness. The use of colored markers to indicate color toning, of arrows to indicate direction of flow, and of circles and other contours to show the extent and shape of the lit area make a schematic time diagram of the lighting more expressive. Crude though these methods may be, they often reveal rhythmic and structural features of the design, particularly when the changes are frequent as in the case of much lighting used for modern dance.

If we now add to this scheme some graphic representation for the structure of the play or choreography, we can see the relationship between its structure and the lighting design. We will examine the development of the lighting score in further detail after we have discussed ways of analyzing the structure on which the score is based.

The temporal aspects of lighting design can be so pronounced that dance can be choreographed to lighting changes just as it is to music. The Mimi Garrard Dance Company programmed both sound and lighting cues into a memory system which controlled the actual sound and light used during performance. Any memory system for lighting control that includes a time function could create a fixed sequence of lighting which would be as dependable a foundation for choreography as sound. The important difference is that the dancers would have to be able to see the changes if lighting were their only time cue.

The rhythm of light changes shapes the mood of the audience as much as the quality of the lighting at any given moment. As an extreme case, flashing lights can induce alpha patterns in brain-wave functions, but most other effects are much more subtle and consequently more difficult to measure reliably. Noticeable, but gradual, changes in the lighting, executed over a period of about ten seconds and occurring at intervals of only a few minutes, induce a calming and relaxed effect. Fast changes, particularly at short intervals, are more disruptive and produce a certain amount of excitement, even tension. Obviously, a whole continuum of responses lies between these two poles. The rate of change may also accelerate or decelerate, producing an attendant change in mood. Tempos may alternate or contrast. Slow lighting changes may introduce or conclude scenes or areas of the stage associated with one character or theme while faster changes bracket other scenes associated with another character or theme. The intrusion of faster shifts may suddenly disrupt the equanimity established by a slow rhythm. The lighting may create an overall rhythm for the whole stage space but a contrasting tempo for a particular portion of the stage or for one character or group on the stage.

Unfortunately playwrights, particularly of realistic plays, often fail to make provisions within their scripts for motivated lighting changes. In these cases the lighting designer must work with the director to add business that will motivate lighting shifts which help to establish a dimension of variety and rhythm to the design. For interior scenes, curtains over windows may be opened and closed, lamps may be turned on and off, doors to bright offstage areas may be left open or closed, or we may even assume the passage of clouds or change in the weather outside in order to motivate lighting shifts. In less realistic plays, the style of the production may allow more theatrical changes without so much concern for realistic motivation.

Even in very prohibitive situations, the beginning and ending of scenes offer some opportunity to establish a rhythm to the lighting design. There is a great difference in emotional effect between scenes that suddenly black out and ones that gradually fade. Particularly today, as the front curtain is used less for act or scene divisions, the tempo of lighting becomes increasingly im-portant. Even when the curtain is available, many directors choose to raise or lower it in darkness so the more pliable and expressive medium of lighting can be used to set the tempo for the start or conclusion of a scene.

Different kinds of plays or scenes traditionally aim to evoke different audience moods, each of which requires a specific rhythm in lighting changes. For example, a mounting tempo in the lighting which climaxes with the obligatory chase scene underscores the crescendo of a farce. "Swells" of strong light give a classical tragedy a sense of dignity. The lighting changes for romantic scenes or romantic songs within musicals "balloon" warmly out of the surrounding material. Violence calls for abrupt, clashing rhythms, but the feeling of fear that melodrama tries to induce often comes from "oozing" lights which seem to creep into our consciousness, almost unnoticed. Strong, clear lighting changes reinforce our feeling of order for a tightly constructed play, whereas broken, discordant rhythms of change reinforce the apparent chaos of stream-of-consciousness or expressionistic drama. Even though specific types of plays share rhythmic approaches, each play ultimately has its own rhythm which the lighting designer must capture and express.

Temporal Harmony

Just as elements of a lighting design can create a harmonic whole at any given moment, so the relation of elements to one another as they change over time can be harmonious or not. The deciding factor is consistency. Once a pattern of change is established, any major deviation will seem incongruous. Incongruity may be the desired effect, but the designer must be able to produce it at will rather than inadvertently as a result of losing control over the rhythm of change. Even inconsistency can create unity if it is a recurring inconsistency, or—to restate it—a consistent inconsistency.

For example, in a modern production of

Shakespeare's *Antony and Cleopatra* the contrast between the Roman and the Egyptian worlds could be expressed by different qualities of light: stark, high-contrast white light for the *Realpolitik* domain of Octavius; diffuse, colored light for Cleopatra's opulent realm of the senses. Antony's vascillation between the two could be indicated by the quality of light around him at specific points in the play, and, when appropriate, the two types of lighting could be shown together. The changes in and out of the Egyptian scenes should be slow and fulsome, but the beginning and end of the Roman scenes could be sharp and abrupt. The intrusion of Rome into Egypt and the eventual destruction of the world of Cleopatra could be suggested by the gradual predominance of the stark lighting. The play itself is organized into increasingly shorter scenes; so the structural crescendo would be accentuated by the rhythm of the lighting shifts and contrasts. This design concept is built upon conflict, but if the contrasts are handled consistently the overall effect will be unified and harmonious.

Unity within change is also gained by keeping one aspect of the lighting constant while varying others. A consistent color tone or key/fill configuration can tie together diverse intensity levels or shifting shapes to the area of light. Of course the lighting is not the only aspect of the visual picture, and we can maintain a sense of unity with a wider range of changes on a static setting than on a setting where the scenery changes as the lighting changes.

In fact, the sense of harmony rarely comes from the handling of lighting changes alone. The movement of performers, scene changes, music, and the cadences of the voice interact with the lighting to create a whole effect. The parts must be carefully orchestrated to produce an overall sense of harmony or disharmony where desired. In this respect, the lighting designer plays his or her instruments under the synthesizing baton of the stage director or dance choreographer. Like a good musician, the lighting designer must control those instruments while keeping a close ear and, in this case, eye on the other performers.

To summarize this discussion of composition in stage lighting, the designer must be able to use light to compose moving stage pictures that express the values of the play or production; realize the full visual potential of the scenery, costumes, makeup, and blocking; stimulate the desired responses by the audience; and create a meaningful aesthetic experience. The specific components of composition have been isolated for the sake of analysis; they provide a checklist of controllable variables. The end result however, must synthesize them into a whole visual statement. Many good designers will be able to produce an effective design based on the simple premise that "it looks right." This does not mean they ignore the components examined here, only that they have incorporated them into an aesthetic sense which responds to the product without necessarily being aware any longer of the process. The great pianist may not think about the fingering, but it is still there.

Style in Lighting Design: Production Styles

Style is a distinctive way of doing anything: hitting a tennis ball, composing a painting, or designing lighting. In one sense, every theatrical production has its unique style, but we generally use the word to describe *a recurring way of doing things characteristic of a given director, designer, or actor, typical of a specific theatrical period, or peculiar to a certain theatrical form.* Thus we speak of Richard Burton's style of acting or Ming Cho Lee's style of design, the style of the Baroque period, or the style of expressionism.

Obviously, style can be expressed on a number of different levels simultaneously within a single production, and this is a frequent problem in the theatre. Even though there may be justification for combining conflicting styles to attain a certain effect, too often incompatible styles are inadvertently mixed because all facets of a production have not been adequately coordinated. The result is confusion without purpose.

The style of the lighting design must grow out of the style of the production. The designer lights not just objects, but a play, a dance performance, or an opera. It is not sufficient for the lighting to provide visibility, modeling, coloring, and focus; it must also make a stylistic statement consistent with the entire production.

Many times erratic, unmotivated lighting shifts destroy the believability of an otherwise realistic play, or a dull, static but realistic design dampens the effect of a highly theatrical production that cries out for a more imaginative, artificial lighting. Various "methods" for arranging lights based on prevailing practice or assumptions about the demands made by a specific stage configuration are applied indiscriminately to production after production, regardless of the changing performance styles. In all of these cases the lighting designer has failed to understand or exploit the stylistic potential of the lighting design in order to reinforce the style of the production as a whole.

Stage lighting does have styles, just as surely as any other aspect of the production, and lighting styles can be influenced by a number of different factors: theatre architecture, historical period, genre, conventional systems of lighting, and the style of other aspects of the production. It is common to prescribe different lighting styles depending on whether the stage is proscenium, thrust, or arena, indoors or out, whether the production is dance, drama, or opera, or whether the play is comedy or tragedy, whether Broadway or McCandless approaches are to be used, or occasionally, whether the setting is modern or in a past period. We will discuss all of these approaches to style, but first let us examine the more important question of the theatrical style of the play or production itself, defined in terms of commonly accepted modes of artistic expression.

When a theatrical style is given a label, that is usually an acknowledgement that enough productions share common characteristics so that they may be grouped under a single heading. Once a term describing style gains usage, we tend to use it to describe productions which do not possess all of the defining characteristics of the style but have at least enough to be subsumed under the category. In other words, we tend to shove single productions into these pigeon holes. For example, the term "expressionism" is used to describe plays and productions having certain conventionally accepted features. A given production of Georg Büchner's *Woyzeck* may contain some features fitting this category and not others, but it will still be considered expressionistic if it generally fits. This process is useful for identifying major stylistic features of a production, and, to the extent that an audience recognizes a specific style *per se*, it may help to direct expectations. The approach is limited, however, if we use the terminology for evaluation, or to condemn a specific production because it does not fit neatly into conventional categories. To say that a play is expressionistic is not to say that it is good or bad, nor that it must conform completely to some imagined list of characteristics.

Another difficulty in discussing style is the variety of terminology and the confusion as to exactly what is being described by any term. Is musical comedy a style? Can there be both realistic and impressionistic musical comedies? Some terms seem principally to describe content (e.g., historical drama); others, structure (e.g., the well-made play); and yet others, theme (e.g., absurdist drama). We are interested here in the manner (style) in which content, form, and theme are presented.

Nothing is sacred about the stylistic terms used here. Most are derived from art forms other than theatre and are useful partly because they are somewhat in vogue. Divisions between categories are not sharp, and individual productions rarely fit neatly into one category.

In discussing production styles, we will begin with the more realistic and work toward the more artificial, or from representational to presentational, from those which attempt to literally duplicate the world outside of the theatre to those which overtly recognize the theatre as a performance space and a tool for communication. We will begin with several forms of realism and gradually make the transition to more presentational styles: symbolism, expressionism, formalism, and theatricalism. Some styles such as cubism, constructivism, surrealism, impressionism, and romanticism require lighting effects much like other styles and will be grouped with those similar styles.

To better understand this subject, it will be useful to discuss differences in the motivation for light sources and changes depending on the style of a production, as well as to examine the different conventions that have come to be associated with individual lighting styles. For example, one style demands that the brightening of a stage area be justified by a realistic change in the light source, while another insists that the brightening be motivated by something happening in a character's mind. As to convention, an unmotivated spotlight would upset us in a naturalistic play, but the array of stage lights coming through the fourth wall—so that the audience may see—bothers us not at all. With some styles, we take great care to conceal all lighting instruments from the audience, but with others we go out of our way to make sure the instruments are in full view. Different styles have different conventions.

REALISTIC STYLES

Realism attempts to imitate on stage the surface appearance of the world outside the theatre. Therefore, for all realistic styles, we must justify lighting effects by reference to the sources of light in that external, perceptual world: sunlight, street lights, fires, etc. The task of the lighting designer is to discover realistic motivation for all effects and to produce a lighting impression as near to the thing being imitated as possible.

In practice one is immediately confronted with the necessity to compromise some reality for the sake of visibility and modeling. The only *realistic* light source available may come from an upstage window, but the audience needs to see clearly the downstage side of the actors. What do we do with a night scene illuminated by moonlight only, or by no light at all? We therefore sacrifice some degree of reality for theatrical necessity. Vaguely defined sources of light from behind the audience, blue lighting for night scenes, the supplementing of light from onstage sources, and the general increase in the brightness of light from any realistic source are conventions meant to be accepted by an audience and then shifted into the subconscious area of perception.

The rule is simple: once the conventional lighting pattern has been accepted by the audience, any variations in that pattern consciously perceived by the audience must be justified by reference to external reality. It is not enough to "sneak up" a special spot on an actor so that the audience is unaware of the increasing brightness. At no point must the audience perceive that a change has occurred unless that change has been motivated. In a strictly realistic play, an "actor special" must be accounted for by a shaft of sunlight, a floorlamp, a mirror, or some realistic motivation. It may be argued that the "actor special" is a convention which, if repeated enough in a production, moves into the area of subconscious response by the audience. This is true, but the convention has then been taken beyond the boundaries of strict realism.

Naturalism

The most extreme form of realism is naturalism, with its slavish attention to detail presented with photographic accuracy (Figure 2-10). This style of production is rarely seen on the stage any more. The naturalists viewed the theatre as something of a laboratory for demonstrating with scientific objectivity the effects of heredity and environment on character. Because the setting was partly a determinant of human behavior, it had to be depicted with utmost exactness. The lighting designer must consequently pay close attention to any features of the lighting environment that could conceivably influence the character's actions. The depressing gloom of a northern winter, which figures into so many of Ibsen's plays, is an instance of such an effect and is not easily reproduced on stage.

Even though a lighting design for a naturalistic play should adhere to a strict sense of reality, the designer should still strive to add as much of an artistic statement as possible without offending the appearance of reality. As with photography, the replication of reality in theatre can be either dull or visually interesting. The necessity of strictly observing realism may complicate the designer's task, but compositional concerns are still relevant. The plays usually offer sufficient latitude in the selection of apparent light sources, directions, intensities, and tints to provide considerable room for important decisions regarding the composition of the lighting.

Selective Realism

In contrast to what George Bernard Shaw described as the "bric-a-bracism" of naturalism, the form of realism most frequently encountered in today's theatre is "selective." Rather than attempting to reproduce the most trivial detail of the external world, this theatrical form chooses features that make a total impression of reality without slavishly filling in unimportant trivia. Groundcloths replace truckloads of dirt, and scrim may be substituted for the glass panes in windows.

The lighting for selective realism must be just as firmly rooted in believable reality as for naturalism. Indeed, even more emphasis may be placed on the lighting as a means of creating a feeling of reality in the absence of exact verisimilitude. In addition, the lighting designer must exercise particular caution not to call undue attention to areas where realism has been compromised. If a setting uses real wood and plaster walls, as David Belasco did early in this century, the lighting angle is less critical than for canvas substitutes where hinges and dutchmen at joints are easily revealed when lit at acute angles. Selective realism is always at the brink of believability; so any miscue which calls overt attention to the artifice can destroy the illusion of reality.

Fragmented realism is a variety of selective realism which uses a part to represent the whole. To the extent that walls are removed from interiors to allow the audience to see, all stage settings are fragmented, but the style goes even further and uses only one corner of a room or one wall or a portion of a wall to depict the entire setting. Whatever is shown is realistic.

Here again lighting must be realistically motivated, with the exception that the space outside of the fragments exists in sort of a theatrical no-man's-land. At times some portions of this neutral space may be treated as extensions of the fragments, in which case the lighting must extend the impression of realism. At other times, the neutral area may be used for scenes in entirely different styles or may be simply acknowledged as theatrical space, part of the stage machinery. It is not unusual for fragments unused at any moment to be left in full view of the audience without being lit or for the lighting within a fragment to be treated quite realistically while the lighting instruments themselves are in full view. Fragmentation is realism within an unrealistic surrounding, and the treatment of the lighting design may parallel this dualism.

Pictorial Realism

A better term for pictorial realism might be "the picturesque." This is a style strongly associated with romanticism, opera, some musicals, and realistic treatments of classical drama. The objective is to stimulate the senses of the audience with as much beauty and visual interest as possible within the confines of realism. The beautiful or dramatic visual effect is almost its own justification with this style (see Figure 7-2).

Here the lighting designer has an opportunity to select and duplicate those specially striking impressions of lighting that one encounters over a lifetime and mentally files away for future use: sunsets, light diffusing through trees or stained glass, shimmering firelights, headlights in the fog, the color of light at dawn on a clear spring morning. You may add your own favorites. In this style of realism, the audience may be moved by the sheer visual impact of a scene. Applause is not out of place. It is not so much a matter of lighting calling attention to itself as beauty calling attention to itself.

The temptation is to treat all forms of realism as pictorial. While the lighting designer may wish to strive for the most interesting, perhaps the most beautiful composition possible, the purposes of the production may demand otherwise. Every setting with a window doesn't profit by a shaft of sunlight streaming through it. There are times when the setting needs to be humdrum, or when the emphasis should be on the performers alone and the surroundings should fade into a background of visual indifference. The trick is to know when the striking effect is appropriate. The designer's challenge is to light the production, not just to show off the lighting.

Suggestive Realism

Suggestive realism evokes a sense of place by presenting only its essential features. It emphasizes, and sometimes exaggerates, those aspects of a setting which are unique to that place and somehow define it. For example, the dungeon in O'Neill's *The Fountain* is described in the playwright's stage directions in realistic detail, but Robert Edmond Jones' design (Figure 6-12) creates a memorable sense of the place with no more than a carefully lit backdrop of a stone wall and a torture block on a platform. As Jones said, a production should present, "not a picture, but an image."[1] This is not simply a matter, as in selective realism, of using a part to indicate a whole or of eliminating unnecessary embellishment; it is an attempt to capture the essence of a locale. The design uses realistic details in the same way that a poet uses metaphor: to suggest a larger reality. Jones, one of the finest practitioners of this style, said that a setting is "a presence, a mood, a warm wind fanning the drama to flames. It echoes, it enhances, it animates. It is an expectancy, a foreboding, a tension. It says nothing, but it gives everything."[2]

The scenic economy of this production style emphasizes lighting and the evocative power of light. Because attention may be more on the impression created by an object than on the object itself, the designer must be extremely sensitive to the qualities of light reflected from any surface. This light alone may bear the entire burden of representing the unseen but implied objects. For example, the design may suggest a beachside by the shimmering light that would reflect from the water surface, a forest by the mottled light passing through unseen trees, or a cabaret by moving patterns of jewellike color.

An interesting exercise for developing an awareness of the light *ambience* for any locale is to imagine the lighting that would convey the sense of any place without the aid of specific scenic cues. Beginning with a bare stage or a unit setting of abstract blocks and platforms, is it possible with lighting alone to create the impression of a busy city street at night, a carnival, the control room of a space center, a heath in a storm, or a cathedral? Obviously the lighting cannot define all places as easily as these, but it is remarkable how many locations have a distinct pattern of light. The lighting designer, in practice, does not work alone; suggestive scenery as well as the context of the play or production assist in establishing the sense of a specific place.

Even though simplification and overstatement may be necessary for the lighting design used for suggestive realism, the lights are still tied to realistically motivated sources. In fact, because other parts of the production teeter on the brink of unreality, the lighting may need to be more literally realistic than when the scenery carries most of the burden of establishing the illusion of reality. Some vagueness in the lighting may be tolerated when the specific place is firmly established by the setting, but when the lighting is largely responsible for creating the sense of reality, it must be true to life.

Cartoon Realism

Many productions, particularly musical comedy, take realistic elements and simplify and exaggerate line, color, form, or detail so that a very distinct style is created, firmly rooted in realism, but which self-consciously distorts that reality. This is sometimes described by the all-embracing term "stylization," and in many respects this category is more a collection of different styles than a single style unto itself. It borrows from realms beyond that of scenic design, including styles used by illustrators and cartoonists, demonstrating how varied its treatments of reality can be.

The trick for the lighting designer is to discover the basis for the stylistic distortion and to exaggerate the lighting along similar lines, or at least to insure that the lighting does not interfere with the overall visual statement. For example, a scenic designer may choose to use large, clearly defined areas of evenly saturated primary colors for a village street. The design premise is to eliminate variegation, simplify contour, and sharpen major color distinctions. A lighting design which stressed texture and subtle gradations of brightness would probably be out of place here. The imposition of highly saturated colors in the lighting might confuse the scenic designer's treatment of color, but the lighting should stress sharp divisions between areas of different intensity, with a good deal of evenness within a given area of brightness. Sources should still be realistically motivated, but simplified. Multiple shadows would be particularly objectionable within this treatment.

Another production might create a sense of opulence by emphasizing curved lines, brilliant pastels, and soft gradations between colors and forms. In this case the lighting should be diffuse with light tints of color in rounded pools. In each of these examples the light source may be presumed to be the same, but the effects would be different. In the first case, for instance, the light shining out of a window would cast a distinctly rectangular pattern of even brightness. In the second case, the light coming from the window would cast a soft, rounded pool of tinted light. In each event, the audience would probably view the light-

ing as realistic within the context of the production. Once the style has been established, the audience adapts to it and accepts everything that is consistent within the style as believable. Only inconsistency will disrupt the illusion.

The possible variations of this style are almost limitless, and it is therefore impossible to prescribe any one approach for the lighting. It should be remembered that even though distorted, the stage picture is still firmly grounded in realism, and there is no justification for lighting effects which do not grow out of realistic sources. This is realism seen through the glasses of artistic convention, and the lighting designer must be sure to operate within the same conventions as the rest of the production.

In all of the styles thus far discussed, the lighting designer strives to create the illusion of reality. The designer must therefore both master the technical means needed to recreate realistic lighting and possess a storehouse of observations on which to draw. Unlike so many other observers, the designer cannot look through the light to the object but must store a mental catalog of the lighting *ambience* for any situation. Even though audiences may lack the visual self-consciousness of the designer, they still sense when supposedly realistic lighting fails. They may not know the reasons, but it still "looks wrong."

For the various forms of realism, the lighting designer's range of expression is largely limited to that lighting which is realistically feasible under the circumstances provided by the production. At times this may be a frustrating restriction; but with so many choices still to be made within a given realistic situation, the designer need not be content with the ordinary. Truth offers many extraordinary experiences. In addition, there are the added challenges of deceiving the audience into accepting stage illusion as reality and of discovering the most visually exciting and expressive moments of reality to recreate on the stage.

NONREALISTIC STYLES

Realism's fragmented, suggestive, and cartoon forms already make major concessions to artistic or theatrical convention, but the nonrepresentational styles which follow, in many cases, completely abandon the restriction that lighting effects be realistically motivated. Even though realistic light sources may still be established as need demands, the conventions of each style provide their own justification for the lighting. Indeed, for these styles, too strict adherence to realistic motivation may be a bothersome incongruity and betoken a missed opportunity to fully exploit the range of lighting effects possible within each style. This does not mean that "anything goes" with the lighting. Nonrealistic these styles may be; nevertheless they operate within a fixed set of conventions that raise audience expectations about the lighting and impose boundaries on how the lights are handled. The designer must still be able to identify the style and operate within its conventions, although the conventions themselves now constitute the major motivation for the lighting.

Formalism

The abstract or formal setting has no significant representational identity independent of the play. A series of screens, blocks, and platforms may be at one moment a cliff, at another, the walls of a chamber; or they may function in a totally theatrical context without reference to the external world. The stage of the Elizabethan public theatres, of bare-stage productions, of cubist and constructivist settings, and of much of the scenic design from the so-called New Stagecraft fit within this style. The designs shown in Figures 6-4, 6-5, 6-8, and 6-20 are good examples.

Light serves three important functions within the abstract (formalist) setting. It establishes the sense of place, varies the three-dimensional composition, and—in itself—adds a formal structural element to the composition.

Formalism does not necessarily abandon all representational functions. The style is often chosen as a solution to the problem of a play with many short scenes which would be extremely difficult and expensive to stage with realistic scenery. Particularly in these cases, the lighting may help to restore some of the reality lost by the process of abstraction. In these instances, the treatment of the lighting is the same as suggestive realism, but with the added flexibility of additional effects which are not realistically motivated. Once the lighting establishes the idea of a specific locale, special effects may be added for purely theatrical purposes. Josef Svoboda's design for *A Sunday in August* consisted of several platforms and step units backed by two scrims that met each other horizontally at an angle of 45°. Onto these scrims various projections were cast which could quickly transform the scene from a wooded area to a lake side (see Figure 8-1.) The only changing element was the lighting, but a strong impression was created of two different locations. In Svoboda's design the lighting projected fairly realistic images, but similar results are possible with less specific lighting. Jones used curtains to change portions of his unit setting for *Hamlet* (see Figure 4-5), but much of the sense of two different places this single setting allows stemmed from changes in lighting.

Even when an abstract setting is not physically altered during a production, changes in lighting can provide considerable visual variety. For plays, the shifts frequently mark changes of time or place, but the justification may be no more than a mood change. Given a setting with sufficient structural complexity, the variety of compositions possible by careful control of lighting angles, light and shadow distribution, and color is almost limitless. Realistic light sources may motivate these changes, but as often as not the dramatic need to change the stage pic-

FIGURE 8-1(a) & (b) Josef Svoboda's settings for *A Sunday in August*.
[From Jarka Burian, *The Sceneography of Josef Svoboda* (Middletown, Conn.:
Wesleyan University Press, 1971), p. Copyright © 1971 by Jarka Burian.
Reprinted by permission of Wesleyan University Press.]

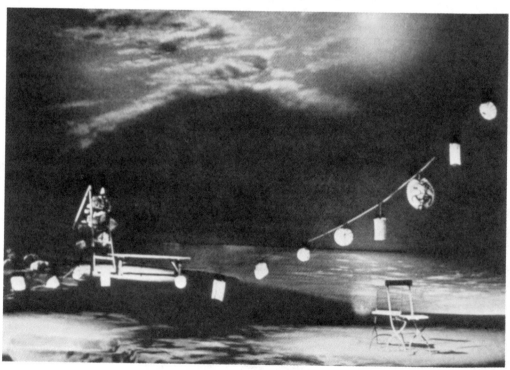

ture provides a sufficient excuse for the transformation. The abstract form of the setting makes the somewhat mechanical treatment of the lighting seem appropriate.

The light itself may provide an additional abstract scenic element. We have seen how Svoboda used a column of light in *Tristan and Isolde* (Figure 6-5) as a major piece of the scenery in a platform setting. The setting by Kaoru Kanamori for Giraudoux's *The Trojan War Will Not Take Place*, shown in Figure 8-2, demonstrates how squares of light continue the cubist pattern begun by square platforms. Only close examination reveals which of the lit areas are cubes and which only squares of light. Patterns of light and shadow, abstractly conceived, add an easily changed new dimension to an already abstract setting.

In practice, we identify formalism in lighting design by shifting patterns of shadow-casting light, often highly saturated in color, striking surfaces at acute angles, thereby emphasizing the form and quality of the lighting as well as providing optimum means for discovering the varied visual forms of the setting.

Symbolism

A symbol is a concrete expression for something invisible or metaphysical. A theatrical symbol uses a real object or sensory experience rather than words to convey this higher meaning. The significance of a sym-

bol may grow out of preconditioned associations on the part of the audience, as with a cross or crucifix onstage, or the playwright or director may develop the meaning solely from the context of the production. For example, in *A Streetcar Named Desire* Blanche Dubois tries to soften the light in the bedroom she has taken over by placing a multicolored Japanese shade over the bare lightbulb. In the same manner, she veneers the sordidness of her surroundings with romantic self-deceptions. When Mitch exposes Blanche's own sordid past and lies, he rips the colored shade from the lamp, subjecting Blanche, quite literally, to the bare light of truth. Much of the effectiveness of this device comes from the audience's spontaneous response to contrasting moods created by stark white light and soft, multicolored lighting, but the full symbolic implications of the device grown out of the play itself. No one would automatically associate a Japanese colored shade with the idea of romantic self-deception.

The use of theatrical symbols is not restricted to any specific style. They may occur in the most naturalistic play or they may be used overtly in a very artificial style, such as the style termed *symbolism*. Here objects or actions frequently have no realistic or literal meaning, but function almost exclusively on a symbolic level. The isolation and exaggeration of specific sensory experiences is justified entirely by their symbolic function. In its purest form, this style was practiced

FIGURE 8-2 Kaoru Kanamori's setting for *The Trojan War Will Not Take Place*, Tokyo, Japan, 1969. [From International Theatre Institute, *Stage Design Throughout the World Since 1960* (New York: Theatre Art Books, 1972), p. 99.]

principally by neo-Romantics in the early years of this century, but vestiges linger on in more eclectic productions which rely heavily on overstated symbolic devices in an otherwise semirealistic context—as for example John Osborne's *Luther,* which calls for emblematic devices hung over the stage that are never referred to in the dialogue.

The symbolic use of light in the theatre predates the use of artificial lighting. Performances of ancient Greek plays may have begun at dawn and occasionally used the actual rising of the sun as a symbolic motif. The beginning of Aeschylus' *Agamemnon* provides a possible example of this. Certainly Shakespeare in *Romeo and Juliet* relies heavily on light imagery to convey both the idea of love lighting the darkness of civil strife and the notion that the love affair is like a brief flash of lightning or gunpowder which provides brilliant light but consumes as it ignites. Shakespeare's imagery is embodied primarily in the language, and—with the possible exception of candles or torches—there was little opportunity in the Elizabethan theatre to use real lighting effects. However, modern productions of Shakespeare's plays can use theatrical lighting to provide striking visual parallels for verbal imagery.

Light symbolism is deeply rooted in our culture. Numerous primitive societies or early cultures practiced forms of sun worship with strong associations between light and life-giving forces, and correlative links-between darkness and death. Yahweh appeared in a burning bush. The New Testament is infused with light images. Christian saints are traditionally depicted with glowing halos. Moreover, we speak of "the light of truth," and "love's light," among dozens of well-established light metaphors which have entered the common usage of our language.

There are numerous examples of the playwright's use of light imagery. The lovers in Maxwell Anderson's *Winterset* huddle in the safety of a streetlight while their murderers lurk in the darkness. As members of the Tyrone family unmask their suffering in O'Neill's *Long Day's Journey Into Night,* they gather around the room's one light while fog and darkness close in around them. The Antrobus family in Wilder's *Skin of Our Teeth* stave off the destruction of mankind by literally building up the home fires.

We can briefly demonstrate symbolic lighting by examining its use in one short verse drama, *A Phoenix Too Frequent* by Christopher Fry.[3] The heroine, Dynamene, and her maid, Doto, are starving themselves to death in the tomb of Dynamene's recently deceased husband. Tegeus, who is taking a dinner break from his duties as guard of the bodies of hanged criminals, enters. He gradually dissuades Dynamene, who is falling in love with him, not to commit suicide. Tegeus' life is jeopardized, however, because one of the corpses disappears during his absence. Dynamene saves the day by substituting her husband's body for the missing corpse, which also symbolizes the comic victory of life over death.

The play begins in darkness except for the very low light of an oil lamp. Doto, whose only attraction to death is as "a new interest in life," is also very much afraid of the dark and refills the lamp so it burns more brightly. This is the first in a series of encroachments by the light of life into the darkness of death. Tegeus enters, attracted, as we later discover, by the light from Doto's lamp which was shining under the door. In the love scene which ensues, Tegeus—renamed Chromis by Dynamene—is at first associated with light images, and Dynamene, with images of darkness; but he gradually transforms her by imposing his own point of view: "If I seem to be frowning, that is only because/I'm looking directly into your light," he says. She says that she is "entirely shadow without/a smear of sun," but he insists, "when I cross/Like this the hurt of the little space between us/I come a journey from the wrenching ice/To walk in the sun." Chromis' victory is inevitable. As Dynamene early observes, "Oh how the inveterate body,/Even when cut from the heart, insists on leaf,/Puts out, with a separate meaningless will,/Fronds to intercept the thankless sun."

In the middle of the love scene Dynamene has mistaken moonlight spilling into the tomb for a "a thin dust of daylight/ Blowing on to the steps." By the end of the play, bright moonlight is streaming into the tomb. Fry observes the reality of time and resists the temptation to end the play with dawn, but the effect is the same. The stage has progressed from dark to bright, from death to life.

Even though it is not specifically called for in the script, giving Tegeus his own oil lamp will emphasize further the symbolic use of light. He at first extinguishes the lamp so as not to disturb Dynamene, but later relights it as he begins to make headway in persuading her not to commit suicide. The minor reversals in his love pursuit can also be stressed by moving the lamps so that Dynamene is at various times in light and darkness. Even though this play is in verse and the situation somewhat bizarre, Fry handles the action with considerable realism and the lighting effects must be realistically motivated.

Symbolism as a style is not necessarily restricted to realistic motivation. Scenes may darken simply because the situation worsens, and the villain appear in unnatural light just for the reason that he is villainous. The design may link specific colors of light with individual characters in the same way that melodrama uses musical themes. This points to the influence of an absent character on the action just by introducing that character's light color. Lighting effects can even represent thematic motifs, emphasized at appropriate moments by repeating the lighting pattern.

The most common use of lighting in this style is to emphasize objects or parts of the stage which have special symbolic significance. The concentration camp watchtower in Arthur Miller's *After the Fall* lingers in Quentin's mind as a reminder of human fal-

libility, some sort of original sin, and it is lit when its thematic relevance demands, not for any reasons concerning realism. The statue of the angel in Tennessee William's *Summer and Smoke,* the Inca sun in Peter Shaffer's *Royal Hunt of the Sun,* or the gates of Troy in Giraudoux's *The Trojan War Will Not Take Place* are further examples of scenic devices whose symbolic bearing on the action must be pointed with lighting.

A symbol is a tool for communication. The designer must not try to force symbolic meaning where there is no basis for communicating the meaning to the audience. Devices which have highly personal significance only to the designer or director, or which represent extremely esoteric uses of symbolic lighting, have little or no place in the theatre. Certainly there is a degree of gamesmanship in the use of dramatic symbols: the audience enjoys making its own discoveries of things that are implied rather than directly stated. But if the audience is only confused, the symbol has failed. A good theatrical symbol is not just a sign—a substitution for something that could just as easily be stated directly; it is the embodiment of an idea that can only be evoked indirectly, enriched by its mystery and the wealth of associations supplied by the audience and the production. This is a big assignment for a lighting effect and probably one rarely achieved, but it is a goal well worth the effort. In its attainment, theatre and the lighting art approach the religious function itself, leading an audience to glimpse the metaphysical, the unknowable except by mysterious means. Jones speaks of a light of "god-like intellection," which "reveals the ultimate in the immediate."[4] This is the poetic medium of stage lighting.

Expressionism, Impressionism, and Surrealism

Although they invoke fairly distinct images in discussions of painting, the terms *expressionism, impressionism,* and *surrealism* tend to fuse in the theatre. All three styles entail a similar view: reality filtered through subjective perception.

Impressionism depicts the world through evanescent qualities of light and color, and to the extent that it focuses on the *impression* of reality, rather than literal reality, the style shares many characteristics with suggestive realism.

Expressionism as a specific movement in the theatre developed out of Germany after World War I and presented a world-view typical of that period: a dehumanized and mechanistic society oppresses the individual who struggles for identity. The plays abstract and exaggerate both the social and physical environment to nightmarish proportions in an attempt to dramatize either the protagonist's or the playwright's view of these threats. Apologists may argue that expressionism does not distort reality but rather presents essential reality, the truth which underlies surface impression, but in practice the form seems very solipsistic.

Surrealism, strictly speaking, is a twentieth-century artistic movement, developing out of France but influenced by Freud, which purports to express subconscious mental activities by presenting frequently distorted images without order or sequence, as in a dream. It has been less popular in the theatre than expressionism and is associated less with specific political or social themes.

Even though specific images used by these styles differ, all aim at creating an external, theatrical form for subjective reality; and in practice the lighting approach used by all three is similar. For ease of discussion, we will group them under the single term "expressionism."

The lighting for expressionism is the lighting of a dream, or more often, of a nightmare (see Figures 6-16 and 8-2). The effects may begin realistically, but they quickly move beyond realism as external reality loses its control. Street lights seem to turn into balls of fire; flashing neon lights madly build to a crescendo; stars twirl in dizzy circles; sunlight seems to burn; and spotlights have cutting shafts. The approach to meaning is similar to symbolism, but the tone tends to be hysterical.

The lighting designer may draw the audience into this nightmare by emphasizing attributes of light which frustrate and fatigue the viewer: lights are moved abruptly, forcing the audience to strain to see an object or character in darkness at one moment and blinding them with intense light the next moment; saturated colors in the light distort the appearance of things; and contrasting colors create persistent afterimages. With ultraviolet light on fluorescent paint or with pinpoint spotlights, the designer disembodies or dissects characters. The audience's sense of order is destroyed by reversing visual cues, making opaque walls glow, putting light where there should be shadow, making sunlight purple and the moon blood red.

Even though this style may seem somewhat bizarre and limited to more experimental forms of theatre, surrealistic effects commonly appear in stage productions of a variety of styles, particularly to mark the disintegration of the protagonist or complete disorder in the situation—a kind of theatrical Walpurgis Night. For example, in *The Glass Menagerie* Tennessee Williams describes a "turgid smoky red glow" for a climactic fight between Tom and Amanda. For a ballet interlude meant to symbolize the collapse of stability in *A Tree Grows in Brooklyn,* Jo Mielziner used expressionistic techniques:

The constantly repeated image of the bridge which had dominated the previous settings was now treated impressionistically. The solid masonry towers of the bridge became exotic and unstable; the suspension cables were torn loose and curled. I painted the bridge on translucent muslin which was lighted mostly from the rear. As the ballet reached its climax, a brilliant light from behind the drop illuminated the twisted towers and the tangle of released cables. At the same time, abstract forms were projected from out front onto the dancers themselves.[5]

This effect of Mielziner's was used in a production that otherwise was in the style of cartoon realism.

The primary reason for the expressionistic lighting effect is to invoke an emotional response from the audience as directly as possible without the intervention of a realistic context. Presumably there are any number of lighting effects which produce emotion because of the situation, such as Laura blowing out the candle at the end of *The Glass Menagerie* or Rebecca, isolated in a spotlight at the top of a ladder, contemplating the awesome size of the universe at the end of Act I in *Our Town*. With expressionism, however, we cannot depend on a normal, ordered, realistic context for the lighting; so we must discover the qualities of light which produce an emotional reaction without reference to any realistic framework.

To use expressionistic lighting effectively, the designer should be able to predict emotional responses to specific lighting conditions. This entails mastery of what Antonin Artaud called "the concrete language of the stage," the use of sensuous stimuli rather than words.[6] Artaud, in formulating the principles for his Theatre of Cruelty, which relied heavily on expressionistic techniques, described what he called "theatrical hieroglyphics," a nonlinguistic language in which the body and face, nonverbal sounds, the *mise-en-scène*, and lighting convey meaning directly. He described a particularly visionary function for stage lights:

The particular action of light upon the mind, the effects of all kinds of luminous vibrations must be investigated, along with new ways of spreading light in waves, in sheets, in fusillades of fiery arrows. The color gamut of the equipment now in use is to be revised from beginning to end. In order to produce the qualities of particular musical tones, light must recover an element of thinness, density, and opaqueness, with a view to producing the sensations of heat, cold, anger, fear, etc.[7]

Artaud, in effect, envisioned the development of a technique for lighting emotional states rather than objects.

Our investigation earlier into the psychophysical aspects of lighting (Chapters 2, 3, and 4) moves in the direction Artaud wished to go; but as we discovered, the effects of lighting on emotional response has up to this point received little systematic attention, still depending largely on subjective sensibility, not scientifically verifiable fact. Humans, nonetheless, are obviously phototropic and strongly influenced by specific qualities of lighting. The task remains to gain a better understanding of the finer shades of difference in the emotional responses to specific lighting conditions.

Theatricalism

Formalism, symbolism, and expressionism are all to some extent self-consciously theatrical, that is, they allow the theatrical conditions of production to elaborate or distort perceptual reality. The same is true to a smaller extent for the less naturalistic forms of realism. However, a number of productions, particularly in recent decades, have carried this process to its logical conclusion and acknowledged the theatre as the ever-present "place" for the performance. Rather than using theatrical resources to create the illusion that the stage is something other than a performance space, these productions call attention to the theatre, saying, in effect, "we have something to show you, the audience, and we are going to use the tools of the theatre to communicate. It isn't necessary for you to forget that you are in a theatre. Indeed, you may marvel at how well we use it." For these productions, it is no more necessary to conceal theatrical devices than it would be to disguise a boxing ring or a football field.

Though their specific techniques vary, the self-conscious theatricalism these productions share qualify it as a single style. Brecht's Epic Theatre, Jerzy Grotowski's Polish Laboratory Theatre, and Peter Brook's "Empty Space" productions are among numerous examples of this approach.

According to Brecht's theory of Epic staging, the audience's awareness of the theatrical medium distances them from the production so that they may objectively evaluate what they see without becoming emotionally involved. The desired response is rational and therefore quite opposite from the implied emotionalism of the surrealists. The production both presents and comments on the play, using the theatrical environment as one means of making a statement. To emphasize the theatricality of the production, Brecht advocated leaving lighting instruments in full view of the audience. To avoid the emotion-producing power of lighting, he proposed performing under work lights—bright, general illumination.[8] It is consistent with Brecht's general theory, however—and frequent practice—to carry the lighting design a step further and include it among the theatre arts used to comment on the action. For example, using macabre lighting for romantic scenes or spotlighting an otherwise insignificant character in a scene rather than the principal figure makes the ironic statement frequently suitable for Brecht's Epic style. The justification for lighting effects in the Epic theatre comes not only from the materials of the play but from the attitudes being expressed toward these materials.

Jerzy Grotowski reacted against what he characterized as the "Rich Theatre," which synthesized literature, sculpture, painting, architecture, lighting, and acting under the direction of a *metteur-en-scène*. He advocated the formation of a "Poor Theatre," abandoning all theatrical devices actors could not create themselves. So, for example, rather than using makeup, the actor manipulates his own face to attain the desired characterization.

Stage lighting is presumably one of the theatrical "tricks" abandoned by Grotowski, who, like Brecht, advocates using work lights or general illumination for public performances. Even in this austere theatrical style, however, lighting still crept back into the picture:

> We forsook lighting effects, and this revealed a wide range of possibilities for the actor's use of stationary light-sources by deliberate work with shadows, bright spots, etc. It is particularly significant that once a spectator is placed in an illuminated zone, or in other words becomes visible, he too begins to play a part in the performance.[9]

Grotowski discovered what oriental actors have practiced for centuries: the expressions and moods of a face, even a mask, can change dramatically when turned in different directions to a light source. And the encouragement of audience participation was, in fact, the common rule in theatre before auditoriums were darkened for the first time in the nineteenth century. Grotowski's productions still use stage lighting for theatrical effect, but—in theory, at least—they avoid designing light around existing stage business; instead actors begin with stationary light sources and discover for themselves ways of moving in and out of, or positioning their bodies within, the light beams in order to produce a desired effect.

The use of stage lighting instruments during rehearsals for some styles of drama and much dance is often an excellent way for actors and director to discover ways of using light to alter the expression or mood of the face and the appearance of the body. In this way, both lighting and the lighting designer can participate in the development of the production from its earliest stages.

Even though Brecht and Grotowski, for different reasons, seem suspicious of the power of stage lighting and prescribe, in theory, work-light illumination for productions, the lighting for theatricalism need not be so limited. Because this style abandons the need to create any illusion of reality, virtually any lighting effect is appropriate as long as it serves the objectives of the production. The motivation for the lighting, therefore, is theatrical effect. If a spotlight, a sudden change in color toning, a projection, a strobe, or a shift in key/fill relationship helps to make an appropriate dramatic statement, it can be done without need for concealment or reference to any realistic source. With theatricalism, the theatre calls attention to itself and the lighting may do so as well. The theatricality of lighting is emphasized by exaggerating the major properties of light, that is, by having intense light, highly saturated in color, coming from sources which are easily recognized as artificial.

The styles discussed here—realism in its various guises, formalism, symbolism, expressionism, and theatricalism—are but the major ones recognized. The modern theatre is extremely eclectic, and a practicing lighting designer should expect to encounter virtually any production style, including many that borrow from more than one major form or fit neatly into no general category. The theatre also changes rapidly as playwrights, directors, and designers experiment with new production methods. What new style will evolve next year? No one knows. So the lighting designer maintains a flexible attitude toward theories of style: they are useful abstractions, certainly, but not immutable laws of procedure.

The important factor is for the lighting designer to realize that stylistic assumptions differ from production to production and that the lighting design must be tailored in style to the rest of the production. The designer must ask what assumptions the conventions of the production make about the lighting. How does the production ask the audience to view the lighting? What is the audience led to expect from the light? Always in the process of developing a lighting concept for a production, the designer should articulate the stylistic conventions underlying the production and the accompanying lighting design.

Style in Lighting Design: Formulas, Genre, and Architecture

In practice, the various lighting styles discussed in the previous chapter develop within broader schemes, or systems, for lighting, which in turn result from the use of conventional arrangements of lighting instruments, from traditional attitudes about the lighting required by specific genres, or from responses to conditions created by various types of theatre architecture. These "systems" can be mechanical or uninventive, but, at their best, they represent proven solutions evolved by lighting designers over time in response to practical problems. Each approach stamps a clearly identifiable hallmark on a lighting design and represents a true style of lighting.

LIGHTING FORMULAS

There was a time when Stanley McCandless' *A Method of Lighting the Stage* was the virtual bible for lighting design in educational thea-

tre. Generations of designers learned the McCandless Method, which even today is a commonly used instrument configuration in schools and colleges. Broadway, however, lacks the large number of mounting positions in the front of the house required by the McCandless Method; so another approach, sometimes called "jewel lighting," evolved for commercial theatre. For decades a more-or-less uniform lighting plot existed for dance; this has undergone major change in recent years, but the new approach is beginning to be used with much the same consistency.

Whether these are appropriate lighting methods or not is largely a matter of opinion. Indeed, lighting designers can almost be grouped into loose "schools" of approach depending on their preference for a particular lighting configuration. In some instances directors are so firmly grounded in a particular lighting convention that they demand adherence to it, and audiences who are repeatedly exposed to one way of handling the lighting may come to expect that method and view it as "correct" simply because it is familiar.

Some of these conventional lighting styles are described here because they should be in the lighting designer's personal repertory. A particular director may demand a specific style or it may provide the "right look" for a particular production. These styles developed as answers to concrete production demands and physical limitations with respect to available instrumentation and hanging positions. Even though each style may have limitations, as noted, each also has much to recommend it, and the designer should be able to exploit the strengths when the occasion demands the use of a specific lighting convention.

The Washed Stage

The rows of "X-rays" or light battens found in old theatres and unfortunately still frequently demanded by the designers of school auditoriums are vestiges of lighting practices that evolved from the candle, oil, and gas-light eras. Before the invention of the high-powered incandescent light source in the second decade of the twentieth century, most stage lighting consisted of washes of light from vertical stands in the wings and horizontal rows of light overhead or at the front of the stage. The introduction of the limelight and carbon-arc electric light in the mid-nineteenth century provided an opportunity for special effects using concentrated light sources, but the remaining general illumination was diffuse. Techniques were developed for filtering light through various media, bouncing it off of silk or other materials, and providing changing gradations of intensity by uneven distribution of light sources or by a variation of methods for dimming anything from candles to gaslight. Considerable tonal variation was possible, but with the exception of the occasional use of lime or arc lights, there

were no sharp beams of light.[1] If a production required strong highlights and shadows, they were painted on the scenery.

When the stage setting relies on two-dimensional painted scenery, this wash of light is adequate, but three-dimensional forms need a less diffused light. Interestingly, Adolphe Appia, while realizing the need for a sculptural light for three-dimensional scenery, often rendered his own designs in terms of the hazy, diffused light available in the theatre of his own time. The effects he created resulted from gradual variations in brightness and from differentiation of scenic planes with brightness differences (see Figure 9-1). Gordon Craig's designs, coming just a few years later, depended on beams of concentrated light (see Figures 6-4 and 6-8).

The major problem with using washes of light, even with flat scenery, was to light the performers adequately. It was difficult visually to pull them away from the scenery, and the flood of overhead light cast heavy shadows under the brow and nose. Footlights eliminated these shadows, but objections arose throughout the eighteenth and nineteenth centuries to the "unnaturalness" of this low-angled illumination.

It is difficult today to imagine a lighting design using no spotlights or only a couple of follow spots. This washed-stage style is of interest from a historical perspective only or for occasional productions of period plays. However, we may have gone too far in the other direction. If the lighting inventory of a late-nineteenth-century theatre consisted almost exclusively of strip or floodlighting devices, the typical inventory today is almost devoid of these instruments. The variety of floodlights manufactured before World War II has vanished from the catalogs of stage lighting suppliers, available only by adapting instruments designed for television or photography. The art of subtly blending and changing washes of light has all but disappeared in favor of the bolder strokes possible with spotlights.

FIGURE 9-1 Adolphe Appia's design for *Tristan and Isolde*. [From Walter R. Fuerst and Samuel J. Hume, *XXth Century Stage Decoration, Vol. 2: The Illustrations* (London: Alfred A. Knopf, 1928).]

McCandless Lighting

When the American director David Belasco, in 1911, produced *The Return of Peter Grimm*, most of the stage was lit with spotlights, each of which required a separate operator. From this time on, the spotlight gradually gained ascendance in the theatre, but it was not a sudden process. First high-wattage incandescent lamps had to develop that allowed spotlights to be hung in a fixed position without operators. Highly efficient spotlights made long throws from the auditorium feasible for the first time, but only slowly were light mounting positions behind the proscenium abandoned for front-of-house lighting. The second and third decades of this century were troubled economic times for the theatre; so few new commercial theatres were built with ample front-of-house lighting positions.

During this time educational theatre was beginning to stir in the United States. This awakening brought with it new theatres, built to house school programs, theatres which boasted the latest in stage-lighting equipment, including ample space over the auditorium for powerful new spotlights. It is not surprising, then, that a major system for using these lights developed at an academic institution, Yale University, where Professor Stanley McCandless designed lighting for the new theatre built in 1926.

To briefly reiterate the principles of the McCandless Method (discussed earlier, p. 66), it uses warm and cool crosslights striking the stage at an angle of 45° from both the vertical and horizontal axes. The warm light comes from the general direction of the light source, and the cool light fills in what would otherwise be the shadowed area. If the warm and cool tints are complementary, we have three tints: warm highlights, white light where the two crosslights combine, and cool shadowed areas. The playing space is divided into smaller areas, usually of a size easily covered by one spotlight beam. McCandless tended to impose an arbitrary grid of areas, but in practice the arrangement of the stage and the patterns of movement on it determine the size, shape, and configuration of areas (see Figure 11-5). Each area has at least one pair of crosslights. If the apparent light source changes during the course of the production, the warm-cool relationship may also switch. This is done by double-hanging each area, or by using a neutral tint on one side that is cooler than the warm tint and warmer than the cool. Thus with a neutral-cool combination, the neutral light will seem warm, but with a neutral-warm combination, the neutral light will seem cool (see Figure 9-2).

While McCandless' system was rapidly becoming law in educational theatre, he was anathematized by many commercial designers. Howard Bay's attack is typical:

The holes between the Areas must be plugged up with added units, it all ending in an arbitrary patchwork. The static, symmetrical inflexibility of the superimposed Area grid cannot accommodate varying demands of assorted scripts. Why should an actor be blue when he faces left stage, pink when he faces right stage, and pied when he turns front?[2]

It isn't really that bad. Even though McCandless advocated floodlights to blend the areas, pools of light may also overlap to obtain as even a blend as is possible with any approach using spotlights for general illumination. As we have seen, the areas could be arranged to suit the production; and with a proscenium production, the actor does not arbitrarily change colors under well-matched crosslights. A wide auditorium or a

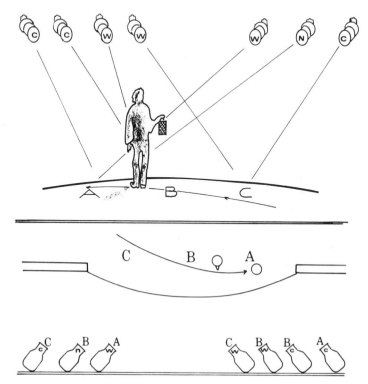

FIGURE 9-2 Diagram of a McCandless Configuration using a warm/neutral/cool combination for the central area in order to provide a shift in the direction of the highlight with a minimum number of instruments when the light moves to the stage left area. With the light source stage left, the neutral light becomes the crosslight when paired with the warm highlight. When the light source is stage right, the neutral light becomes the warm crosslight paired with the cool central area light.

thrust stage does present a problem for audience members seated to the side of the house which faces the predominantly cool lit side of the performers. In effect they see a figure lit with a cool front light and a warm side light.

The principal advantage of the McCandless Method is that it allows modeling while still providing some light in the otherwise shadowed area. If it is assumed that this cool light must always be blue, some unnatural effects will result. Out-of-door shadows usually do have a blue tint, but otherwise their color varies according to the tint of the light source and of reflected light. However, the perception of warm and cool color is a product of relative tint. If any two colors of light are juxtaposed, the tint nearest the blue end of the spectrum seems cooler. We do tend to associate the cooler light with shadow, which sustains the illusion desired by McCandless.

A more serious problem with the McCandless Method is that it requires a large number of circuits over the auditorium. Upstage areas may be lit from the first electric batten over the stage, but to maintain the ideal 45° angle from the floor, most of the area lighting must be from the front of the house. Many theatres simply lack these mounting positions. A related problem is the distance of throw frequently required. Lights over the auditorium are usually further away from the stage than lights behind the proscenium, and this may be an inefficient use of power. The need to have two instruments for each area, or more if the apparent light source changes, also increases the inventory of instruments required to light a production.

The 45° angle is a compromise between maximum modeling and maximum visibility. Even though it may be best to compromise, it is also nice to have the option to increase modeling with side lights or visibility with front lights. Even though nothing in the McCandless Method precludes the use of these lights, they are really outside the

scope of McCandless' scheme and involve further proliferation of instruments.

Regardless of how a designer feels about this method, productions lit accordingly do have a characteristic look or style. The convention of cooly illuminated shadows may enhance visibility, and audiences may accept this as an unnoticed theatrical necessity, but it does leave a somewhat idiosyncratic visual stamp on the production, particularly if applied with monotonous consistency. The McCandless Method has a place in the theatre, but if it is used as a universal technique and imposed in all stage-lighting situations, it obviously limits options.

Zone Lighting

While most plays abandoned the wing and drop settings of the nineteenth century in favor of more realistic arrangements, opera, dance, and musical comedy retained the older configuration well into the middle of the twentieth century. The lighting was therefore organized into "zones," a strip approximately the depth of the space between any two side legs, running the full width of the stage. As they had in eighteenth-century plays, scenes frequently alternated between those requiring the full stage depth and those "in one," where a drop shut off all but the downstage zone.

Border lights were retained to wash the scenery, and high side lights, cross-gelled with warm and cool colors, lit the acting areas. Strong back lights separated the actor from the brightly lit scenery, and a minimum of fill light was added from the low balcony rail. Because of the small amount of front light, particularly when the action was downstage, spotlights were frequently used and, in many instances, footlights were kept. When the action was upstage, front lighting could come from the first electric (bridge) position (see Figure 9-3).

This lighting arrangement placed instruments very near the object being lit, though maximum illumination was from the sides.

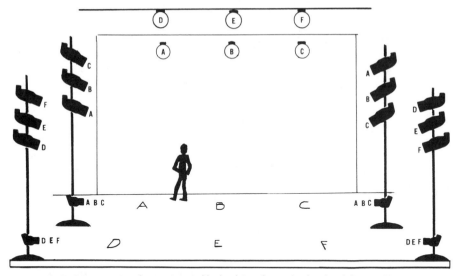

FIGURE 9-3   A schematic profile looking from the back of the stage towards the auditorium, showing an arrangement of instruments for zone lighting.

Such side lighting provided strong side entrances and exits for performers, particularly dancers and choruses who were often even more brightly lit at the edges of the stage than in the middle. The side lights gave good modeling, and often the production style placed more emphasis on singing, choreography, or broad acting; so subtle front lighting of the face was not necessary. The horizontal division of the stage space provided an opportunity for color differentiation which accentuated the depth of the stage. Scenic units were usually flown and arranged on the floor in the same "layered" effect; so the lighting actually complemented the structural form of the scenery.

The wing-and-drop setting, which is still used for many productions, implies a certain degree of artificiality and "hype" in the production style. Even though the strong emphasis placed on side lighting by this method may create an "unnatural" effect, it is appropriately theatrical for the staging style and remains a valid lighting technique.

Jewel Lighting

The premise that brighter is better and the continuing shortage of front-of-house mounting positions has influenced the method of lighting most commercial dramatic productions, particularly on Broadway. Howard Bay describes it succinctly: "In bold outline, modern lighting is a lucid pattern of paths of strong backlight, paths of strong sidelight, the necessary fill illumination from the fronts, plus specials as needed."[3] This approach evolved from zone lighting, but the areas are not necessarily horizontal strips on the stage floor and the side lighting has moved from the overhead pipes to offstage booms. Lighting stands placed in the house, often in old boxes designed for the audience (thus "box booms"), enable the side lighting to be carried out onto the apron. Very high wattage instruments are used: 1500 watt ellipsoidal spotlights for the cross side lighting and 3000 or 5000 watt fresnels to provide special punch for individual scenes.

Side lighting still dominates, even to the extent of using follow spots from platforms on the side. Box sets with closed side walls, particularly with a ceiling piece, throw havoc into this approach. There may be some attempt to compromise by grouping large numbers of instruments on booms just upstage of the proscenium, between the proscenium and the tormentors, but generally practioners of this lighting method will fight for open settings without side walls or ceilings, and this lighting style works best for these open settings.

Key and Fill Approaches

Lighting for film and television, particularly during the early decades of each, was dominated by the relative insensitivity of the camera to light. Early film was not very "fast"—that is, sensitive to light—and television cameras had the added disadvantage of being intolerant to high contrasts, which tended to burn an afterimage into the picture tube. Both film and television have now advanced to the point that they can operate effectively in candle light if necessary, but the method of lighting used still reflects the idea that sufficient general illumination enables the image to register on the camera (fill light) and modeling or compositional light is added from one direction (key light). In media work, large floodlights provide fill and spotlights furnish the key light.

Other methods which use warm and cool crosslights are really using the warm light as a key light and the cool light as a fill. To eliminate this color separation, which frequently looks unnatural, contrasting diffuse and directional light or low- and high-intensity light produces the same key/fill look.

When adapting key and fill approaches for stage use, floodlights may be used for fill light, but it is more common to use spotlights for both key and fill and to differentiate the lights with different wattage lamps or by dimming. The fill light also does not have to come from the front. It may be positioned in opposition to the key light so that it fills the maximum amount of area shadowed by the key light but still seen by the audience.

The positioning of the key light determines the location of the apparent light source. Front or back key lights are generally avoided because they destroy modeling. When key and fill are differentiated by color, the tints are likely to be more closely related than with the McCandless Method. Where there are plausible sources of directional light in nature, the key/fill approach has the most natural appearance. Alteration of the key/fill relationship can substantially change the form of a setting or the appearance of a face, can transform the mood of a scene, can signify a change of time or place, or can establish a rhythm for a production. Particularly if the key light is not locked by convention into a specific position, whether from the side or 45°, its variable positioning provides maximum compositional flexibility in comparison with other schemes for arranging instruments. Taken by itself, this approach may not provide enough variety for every theatrical production, but it is an excellent beginning point for any consideration of lighting design.

LIGHTING STYLE DETERMINED BY GENRE

Do different types of drama require different approaches to lighting design? Is a certain quality of lighting preferred for comedy, and another for tragedy? Indeed, strong back and side light with warm colors and a general high level of brightness creates a mood of festivity that we associate with comedy. Lower levels of brightness, with large areas of shadow and high-angled key lights may create the mood of mystery and conflict suitable for tragedy. Other lighting patterns probably come to mind for musical comedy, opera, dance, or even something as specific as Restoration comedy; and the capacity of the lighting to establish or fulfill audience expectation is important. The problem is that these generic terms are too broad to describe the variety of styles possible within one genre.

A comedy may be serious or trivial, or it may have sombre moments in an otherwise frivolous context. We may stage it realistically or theatrically on an arena stage or behind a proscenium. A bright airy mood is attainable with McCandless, wash, zone, or jewel lighting. There are simply too many stylistic variables to prescribe any one method of lighting for comedy. An understanding of a genre and any expectations an audience may have regarding it help to refine a lighting style for a production, but by themselves generic terms are not sufficiently descriptive to outline a consistent approach for lighting all plays of any one type.

This same principle applies to the idea that there are distinct ways to light dance, drama, or opera. In fact, the approach used for jewel lighting of plays on Broadway is very similar to the hanging scheme usually used for dance, with its heavy reliance on side light and faint front washes. Even though lighting approaches for different dance productions tend to be basically the same and dance offers certain opportunities, such as no scenery and open wings, that invite specific uses of stage lighting, there is no categorical imperative that dance should be lit in this manner. A modern dance production which uses scenery and places heavy emphasis on the dancers' faces would require a radical departure from usual dance lighting. Similarly, the lighting for opera evolves from its very theatrical mode of presentation. A more realistic manner of staging opera invites a more realistic handling of the lighting design.

STYLE DETERMINED BY THEATRE ARCHITECTURE

Much of our discussion has focused on lighting design for indoor, proscenium productions. Although most principles of pro-scenium lighting adapt to other theatrical forms, the unique problems created by other stage forms require special design solutions, which have evolved into distinct styles. For example, there is a customary way of designing for arena productions which gives their lighting its own special look. Other methods of lighting are possible, but rarely used. This traditional arena lighting method gives enough latitude to adapt the design to a particular production style. In other words, the lighting for an arena production of a realistic play should be quite different from an expressionistic play presented in an arena, but both will differ from proscenium productions of the same plays.

Every new audience/stage configuration or major change in provisions for instrument placement has the potential for generating a new lighting style, but we will concentrate our discussion on well-developed approaches for lighting arena, three-quarter, and outdoor theatres.

Lighting the Arena Stages

The most obvious difficulty of lighting arena productions is that the audience must be able to see from all sides of the stage. Where light just from the front can provide adequate visibility, if not modeling, on a proscenium stage, at least two lights are needed for an arena stage. Even here, if the lights are positioned opposite one another to provide maximum coverage, a person seated perpendicular to the axis of the beam directions may see a dark stripe down the middle of a three-dimensional form, similar to side lights with no front fill in a proscenium theatre. To really obtain even illumination on a solid form with audience on all sides requires at least three lights for each area.

A given spotlight in the arena theatre may be front light for one quarter of the audience, side light for half the audience, and back light for the remaining quarter. This fact may be used to advantage, but no one light can be thought of in terms of a single function. If four lights are focused on each area of the stage, they would theoretically provide front, side, and back lights for all portions of the audience. This is a configuration similar to Broadway jewel lighting except that the ideal brightness ratios cannot be maintained. The effectiveness of back and side lights for proscenium productions depends on their being at least twice as bright as front light. For realistic outdoor lighting, the ratio between key and fill should be more on the order of five to one or even ten to one. If we accentuate the brightness of any of the four lights on the arena stage, there is the danger of creating blinding front light for at least some portion of the audience.

A further difficulty of arena lighting is to keep the light out of the eyes of the audience. If spotlights are used, they produce very little glare as long as the eyes of the audience are not in the beam of the light. The lower an instrument is hung in relation to the stage floor the greater the danger of either direct or reflected light making glare problems. Instruments at a high angle are more easily focused off the audience and reflected light is more likely to bounce over the head of the audience. Of course the high angle introduces the old problem of shadow under the face. This is less of a problem if auditorium seats are steeply banked, but otherwise a light-colored floor treatment will add some reflected light to fill those objectionable shadows. However, a floor too lightly colored will bounce too much light into the eyes of the audience and create glare problems. If a trough exists between the raised stage and raised seats, footlights placed there will also eliminate shadows (see Figure 9-8).

One method to help solve the problem of light in the eyes of the audience is to focus the instruments along the axes of the aisles. The typical arena stage has four aisles at the four corners of the stage or, in some other way, spaced equidistant around the stage. Lights placed over these aisles tend somewhat to concentrate glare, spill, and reflected light down the opposite aisle. Of course there is no way to distribute three instruments evenly over four equally spaced aisles, and if we hang four lights for each area over each of the four aisles, we have abandoned the front-back-side configuration in favor of an arrangement where lights for any audience segment are arranged so that there are two front lights at approximately 45° to a central axis and two back lights at the same angle. This is analogous to the McCandless arrangement, and the modeling provided by combinations of warm and cool light can be maintained if the four lights alternate in a warm-cool-warm-cool pattern. If this is just mechanically imposed, it may create difficulty in maintaining the appearance of the warm light always coming from the direction of the apparent light source. Where this degree of realism is required, the colors will have to be ordered warm, neutral, cool, neutral. Thus the neutral lights will appear cool in combination with the warmer light and warm in combination with the cooler tint (see Figure 9-4).

This arrangement of four lights grouped near the aisles and focused on each area is the most common one used for theatre-in-the-round. Because of the large number of instruments required, a three-light arrangement is sometimes substituted with a warm-neutral-cool tinting order (see Figure 9-5), but this inevitably places light in a nearly full front position for some portion of the audience and sacrifices modeling for economy.

These three or four lights on each area can also serve as general fill lights which provide visibility and some modeling, with a single key light added to establish the impression of a directional source, create some modeling based on brightness differences rather than tint contrast, and add compositional interest (Figure 9-6). Of course this key light further increases the number of instruments needed, and changes in the color of the wash would even require additional instruments.

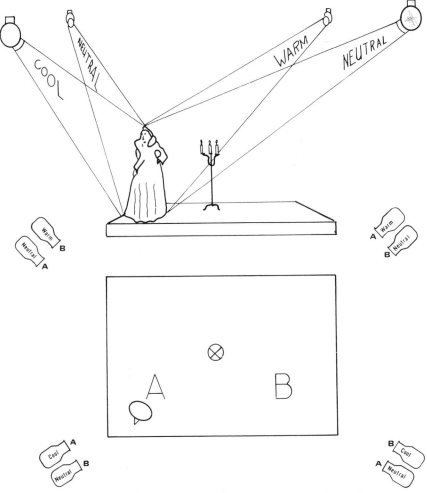

FIGURE 9-4 Hanging arrangement for two areas on an arena stage using a four instrument warm/neutral/cool/neutral arrangement. To an audience member seated in the 3 o'clock position, the neutral instrument at 4:30 appears cool while the same light appears warm to an audience member in the 6 o'clock position. The warmest light color always passes through the light source to the area being lit.

Because arena theatres are designed in large part to get the audience as near to the stage as possible, spectators can usually see more easily than in a proscenium theatre with the same number of people. Brightness levels can therefore be lower and effects made more subtle. Particularly if instrument angles are kept high to avoid glare, the lights are likely to be fairly near the stage; so arenas can use smaller wattage instruments than in most proscenium productions. Because of the shorter throw, instruments usually have wider-angled lenses and have shutters, barndoors, or top hats to keep light out

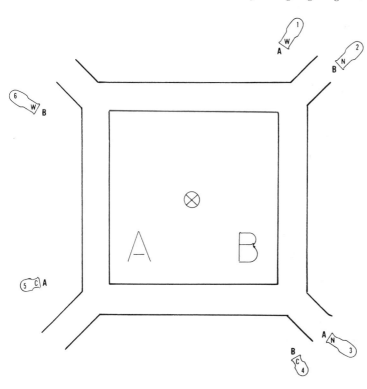

FIGURE 9-5   Diagram of lighting for an arena stage using three lights for each area, arranged in a warm/neutral/cool configuration. The warmest light passes through the light source on stage. This configuration makes it difficult to center lights on the aisles.

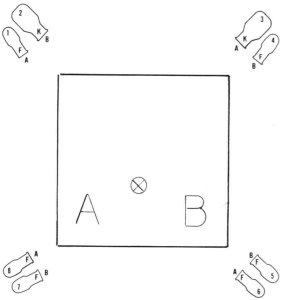

FIGURE 9-6   Hanging arrangement for two areas on an arena stage using a four instrument key/fill configuration. The key light is hung as nearly as possible on the axis of a line passing from the area through the apparent light source.

of the audience. Filter tints must also be more subtle. At one time it was necessary to burn filters in instruments for a time to obtain the lighter tints, but manufacturers now offer a wider selection of lighter colors.

Thrust-Stage Lighting

With the three-quarter or thrust-staging arrangement, the audience sits on three sides of the stage with the fourth side used for scenery. At first appearance, it would seem that we could alter the ideal lighting pattern used for the arena stage by eliminating the lights from the fourth side and lighting each area with only three instruments, but this is not really the optimum approach. Light coming from the fourth or scenic side is needed as back light for the audience seated opposite and as side light for the audience seated at the sides of the stage. A common solution for thrust staging is therefore to use the same arrangmeent of instruments we would for theatre-in-the-round, with the lights grouped near the four "corners" of the stage.

If only three spotlights are used for each area, it is probably best not to space them at intervals of 120°. There is no way to distribute this spacing over the 180° audience space without large portions of the audience viewing a stage lit by a combination of flat front light and two back side lights. The effect is the same as a combination of simple front and back light with no side light, and the result is poor modeling. The better arrangement is to place two lights as near to the front aisles as possible, 90° apart or 45° from the central axis. The third light comes directly from the scenic side just as a back light would be used in a proscenium theatre. The audience seated in the front section will see McCandless lighting. For the audience in the side sections, the front lights will be 130° rather than 90° apart with a back light coming in at an angle. This is not an objectionable spread of front lighting and is preferable to having a flat front light for a larger portion of the audience.

When three instruments are used, their filters may be arranged in a warm-neutral-cool sequence with the warm color from the side of the apparent light source. All seating sections will thereby face an apparent warm-cool combination with the neutral color switching according to which color is paired with it (see Figure 9-7). As with arena staging, the lighting for a thrust stage is often arranged in a key/fill configuration with three or four instruments used for fill lighting with an added key light.

Thrust stages present the same problems as arenas regarding light in the eyes of the audience and shadows under the face. Where there are exits for the actors or "vomitoria" leading down from the front corners of the stage, "shin busters" or low mounted spotlights can provide some low-angle fill for upstage areas. In some theatres a trough between the edge of the stage and the first row of seats allows lights to be positioned for bottom fill. Normal footlights cannot be used in these positions on the sides because they shine in the eyes of the audience on the opposite side. Small spotlights with a wide beam spread must be placed below the stage level and carefully focused so the bottom edge of the beam strikes the actors but goes over the heads of the audience (see Figure 9-8).

The scenery on the fourth side of the thrust stage is frequently three dimensional and often thrusts somewhat into the playing area. Because the audience is seated very near to it at the extreme sides, to avoid objectionable shadowing the scenery must be lit from two directions with a key/fill or warm/cool configuration.

Other Stage Arrangements

Particularly with the advent of so-called "black box" theatres—large studios in which seats and playing area can be arranged at will—the lighting designer is likely to encounter virtually any scheme of staging: audience on only two sides, audience in the middle, multiple playing areas with the au-

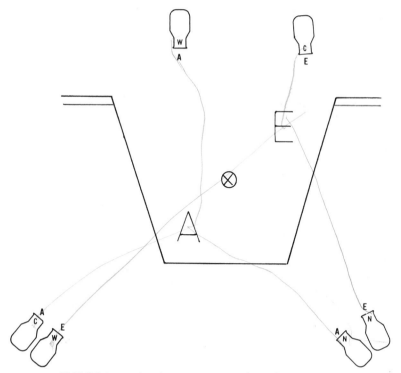

FIGURE 9-7 Hanging arrangement for a thrust stage using three instruments per area in a warm/cool/neutral configuration.

dience moving around, or a three-dimensional use of the space with audience and performers on various platforms.

In spite of the variety, a few basic approaches to the arrangement of lights will suffice. No audience member can view the action from but one side at one time. From

FIGURE 9-8 Footlighting for an arena or thrust stage production.

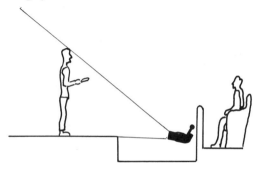

the perspective of any one audience member, lighting adequate for a proscenium production is adequate for any staging. Circumvential staging, for example, with the audience in the middle of the action, involves no more than a proscenium stage wrapped around 360°. There may be no place for side lighting; so a McCandless or key/fill arrangement will have to be used.

To the extent that arena lighting provides for an area seen from four sides, it will also provide good light for any area seen from any two or three sides. Arrangements with the audience only on opposite sides of the stage still require lighting as if they were full arena or back-to-back proscenium productions. In the latter case strong side lights can be used from the sides where there is no audience and a low-level fill from the audience sides, which produces an effect similar to jewel lighting. If the audience is seated on only two sides at right angles to one another or, in other words, only 90° rather than 180° around a thrust stage, a side/front arrangement may be preferable to the normal thrust lighting. Because there is no audience at the extreme sides of the stage, side lighting is possible without it becoming flat front light for some section of the audience (see Figure 9-9).

Arrangements with the audience above and below the stage do present some special problems, but not unlike those in other theatres with very high balconies or a steep auditorium rake, or in particularly old-style proscenium theatres, with most of the orchestra seats below the stage. As it is, probably not enough attention is given in lighting design to the vertical distribution of the audience in relation to the stage. For example, balcony front lights in the Broadway theatre are, in effect, footlights for that portion of the audience seated in the balconies. Similarly, the absence of light under the face is

no problem on a stage like the Vivian Beaumont Theater at Lincoln Center where the auditorium is steeply banked and few audience members can see the shadowed portions of the face.

Even though shadows under the face are a condition of natural lighting and therefore not extremely objectionable, we are not accustomed to viewing faces high above us; so an extremely elevated stage may require bottom fill. Footlights made more sense in nineteenth-century theatres with raised stages and large orchestra floors with little or no rake. In a theatre where the audience is divided so that a portion is below the stage and a portion above, it may be necessary to provide virtually a low-intensity mirror image of the overhead lighting with instruments from low angles. Obviously mounting positions are going to be less available on the floor or through the floor; so the design will have to make compromises. The point is simply that the lighting designer must eval-

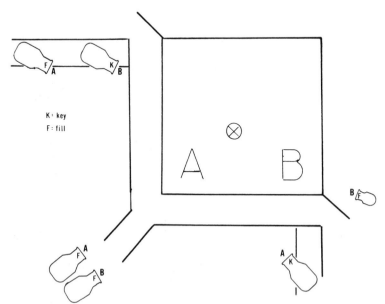

FIGURE 9-9 A key/fill configuration on two areas for a thrust stage with the audience only 90° around the stage.

uate the space spherically and not just in terms of a two-dimensional ground plot.

Lighting the Outdoor Theatre

Open-air theatres can have any architectural arrangement, although most have a proscenium-like configuration with the audience on one side and the stage on the other. Many so-called outdoor theatres are virtually indoor theatres without a roof or without some side walls, in which case the lighting approach is not significantly different from that used inside. However, an open-air theatre which tries to take advantage of a natural setting may lack conventional overhead hanging positions for lighting instruments, particularly over the stage. Some side lights may be concealed behind bushes or rocks, but the majority of the lighting typically comes from "towers" usually located at the sides of auditorium and/or at the downstage corners of the stage. There may be some additional lights at the very back of the seating space. This configuration lends itself to either McCandless or key/fill approaches. With sufficient scenery at the sides of the stage to mask side lighting, the design can use a modified jewel lighting scheme with the front fill coming 45° to the side of the central axis rather than directly from the front. The lack of hanging positions for strong back light, however, makes it difficult to completely reproduce the Broadway effect.

Outdoor theatres typically are large and, with the heavy emphasis on front-of-house lighting, instruments must be powerful and filter colors relatively saturated. Atmospheric conditions tend to scatter the light somewhat, resulting in more diffusion and somewhat more of a red shift or emphasis of warm colors than encountered indoors. The moisture in the air also enables the audience to see light beams fairly easily, which can be either a distraction or a compositional and stylistic plus if handled properly.

Natural scenery can provide marvelous lighting opportunities but, if extreme realism is an objective, any deviation becomes more noticeable when juxtaposed against real trees or a real moon. Most outdoor theatres aim for pictorial realism or realism enhanced by a good deal of theatrical grandioseness; so the lighting effects may be rooted in realism but extended well beyond a literal recreation of real lighting conditions.

It would be possible to continue our discussion of style into an analysis of work by specific lighting designers, many of whom have a characteristic way of designing, a design "signature" just as unique as the artistic style of Rembrandt, Andrew Wyeth, or Edward Hopper. Lighting designs tend to be evanescent, difficult to document or reconstruct. Even photographs or moving pictures cannot recapture the exact effect created on stage because the lighting demands of film are distinct from those of the spectator's eye in the auditorium.

Whether style grows from the conventions of the production, traditional arrangements of lights, the demands of stage architecture, or the methods of specific designers, the single most important factor is probably consistency. Audiences enter the theatre ready to use their imagination and will pretty well accept the theatrical world presented to them as long as its various components are internally consistent and treated consistently over time. Once the rules are stated, they must be followed. Inexplicable changes or purposeless incongruities only confuse the audience and call self-conscious attention to the mechanics of theatrical production.

The Designer's Approach: Analyzing the Script

Ultimately the designer must make a decision regarding what instrument to place where and when to use it at what intensity. The psychophysical mechanisms, the principles of composition and use of style examined so far, serve the lighting designer only to the extent that they translate into practical application. Just as mastery of equipment alone will not produce a good design, neither will mastery of design principles alone—without knowledge of how to apply them—produce an effective lighting plot.

This book does not deal with specific matters of lighting instrumentation. The reader should already be familiar with the equipment or seek that information from among the many texts available. Similarly, the mechanics of the design process, the drafting of plots and execution of instrument schedules are essential skills which must be mastered but will not be examined here in any detail.

Our focus in this section is on the complex task of developing the lighting image which governs the selection and arrangement of instruments. We will carefully examine the design process underlying the lighting plot on the assumption that instrumentation will vary from situation to situation and that the technically competent designer will find a way to adapt available resources. Before we can decide how to light something, we must know what to light, what we want the light to do and why. By way of analogy, it is not how we say it with lights, but rather what we have to say; not how we show it, but what we show.

This is not to say that the design is what the designer has in his or her head. The design is certainly not the lighting plot. It isn't even the light that shines on the stage. The design is what the audience sees, and it is complete only when the audience experiences it.

The stage lighting designer, however, more than any other theatrical designer, must rely on a mental image of the final product. Scenic and costume renderings or scenic models are much more reliable predictors of the appearance of final designs than any preliminary plan produced by the lighting designer. Even the handful of miniature lighting systems in existence give only an approximation of what the stage will look like with full-sized instruments. It is also impractical to "play with the lights" to any great extent in order to discover "how it looks" or "if it will work." In the professional theatre, time is money, and a lighting designer who wastes money with considerable rehanging, refocusing, or regelling will not easily find reemployment. Even in educational or community theatre, lighting rehearsals come at critical times when wasted effort can have a serious detrimental effect on other aspects of a production.

The conceptualization process is therefore extremely important to the lighting designer; that process will be examined in detail in the remaining chapters. In this chapter we will see how a designer analyzes a script, but first, let us take a brief overview of the evolution of a design concept. How does the designer get from the page to the stage?

All aspects of theatrical design—lighting, scenery, costumes, sound, and makeup—differ from the "pure" arts—primarily painting, writing, sculpture, and musical composition—to the extent that the theatrical designer controls only the "form," not the "content." In other words, a painter usually controls totally what he or she paints, but the lighting designer's work depends heavily on the work, often predetermined before the lighting designer begins, of the playwright, director, actors, choreographer, and other designers. For this reason, the lighting design process begins with a careful analysis of the given circumstances for the design: the script, the production concept, other design components, and the performances of actors, dancers, or singers.

In the best of circumstances the lighting designer is a major contributor to a production team, helping to shape the form of the final performance from its very inception. Ideally the design possibilities should develop as the playwright creates the script, and we can occasionally see the influence of specific designers on individual playwrights, such as that of Robert Edmond Jones on Eugene O'Neill or Jo Mielziner on Tennessee Williams. More realistically, the lighting designer may influence the script during the rewrite phase when the playwright responds to production contingencies. A large percentage of works produced are not new scripts, and in these instances the text is obviously more or less fixed, the influence of the designer limited to interpretation.

When the form of the script itself is fixed, the lighting designer should influence the next conceptual stage from its inception, the production concept. A wise director utilizes the creative talents of the specialists on the production team but, here again, actual practice too frequently falls short of the ideal. Directors are occasionally autocratic, and even among designers the lighting artist frequently comes in at the tail end, having to make the best of interpretative decisions already made by scenic and costume designers.

Lighting designers should use all available persuasive powers to attain their rightful positions as full members of the creative team, but they must also be prepared to obtain maximum effect from restrictive circumstances. At least let no lighting designer perpetrate what he or she suffers. Always carefully consider the influence of lighting on other aspects of the production and never be guilty of self-indulgent designs which exhibit lighting for its own sake alone.

Even though the degree of creative involvement by the lighting designer may vary radically, there is still a procedure followed hopefully with only minor variations. It begins with a careful analysis of the script, score, or choreography. After this all members of the production team meet to evolve an overall production concept, a guide to how the actual performances will realize the original artistic statement. This production concept may evolve and change as the actual execution of the work proceeds, but all members of the production team should participate in these changes or, at least, should know of them. Even during these first stages, designers may express ideas through sketches or preliminary drawings, but more detailed renderings follow. The lighting designer is at somewhat of a disadvantage at this point because the details of the lighting design must await further work by the scenic designer, but close communication between the two allows the scenic artist to incorporate the lighting concept into the renderings and gives the lighting designer an opportunity to make "in progress" sketches showing how the lighting will interact with other design components. Cooperation among the designers is crucial at this stage.

The designs may undergo further changes after subsequent discussions among the production team but, soon, finished elevations and renderings must go to the studios or shops in order to begin construction. Particularly when lighting instruments are rented and color media ordered, the lighting designer must design the lighting shortly after the scenic design is completed. However, the lighting designer now has a tremendous advantage; final details of design, focusing and cueing, often even the positioning of instruments and the selection of color, can come later; meanwhile the designer has precious time to experiment and rethink basic lighting decisions as other production elements begin to coalesce. Now is the chance to collect samples of fabric actually used for costumes and of paint colors used on the scenery in order to test their response under the colored lights proposed for the production. This is the opportunity to watch rehearsals in order to plot the movements of performers, observe tempo changes, and note the developing details of

the production. If it has not already been done, the brightness variations, cue intervals and durations, and color shifts can be developed, ideally with the director's cooperation, to produce a lighting "score" which shows how changes in the lighting over time will interact with scene shifts and actor movement to establish tempo and mood and to enhance the themes of the production. Hopefully only after this stage do the lighting plot, instrument and dimmer schedules and hookup sheets, color charts, and cue sheets reach their final form.

There are five distinct phases in the design process: script analysis, development of the production concept, analysis of other production elements, development of the lighting score and, finally, the carrying out of the lighting plot. Each of these may not be discrete in time. They often overlap and intermingle, but there is a natural progression from the rather speculative consideration of the script toward the increasingly concrete commitment to specific lighting.

We will examine each of these design steps in turn, applying the psychophysical, compositional, and stylistic considerations developed in earlier chapters as they are relevant. To illustrate the general principles developed here, we will demonstrate their application to a number of plays, but particularly to Tennessee Williams' *A Streetcar Named Desire* and Sophocles' *Oedipus Rex*, the first a relatively realistic play, the second a play open to a wider variety of stylistic interpretations. Illustrations of lighting used for these plays support our discussion but, unlike an actual production situation, no attempt is made here to conclude with a model lighting design. Any design for these plays must express the thousands of features unique to a particular performance, cast, director, design staff, theatre, audience, instrument inventory, dimmer capability, and time, Our analysis focuses on the design *process*. Each lighting designer applies that process in his or her own way to *create* a unique product suited for a specific production.

ANALYZING THE SCRIPT

During initial readings, the lighting designer approaches a script much as a director or any other member of the production staff should, except, of course, for the irresistible impulse to translate dramatic values into images of light. These first visions of light often indicate the evocative power inherent in a play's language; the designer should preserve these first impressions because the newness of an initial encounter with the script can never be precisely duplicated with rereadings, and because this first impression approximates in a superficial way the audience member's unbiased exposure to the finished creation. At the same time, the designer should warily avoid letting immediate reactions preclude the development of subsequent ideas. First impressions can be right, but they can also be superficial, and the ultimate value of the lighting is its ability to illuminate the complexities under the surface. The lighting designer must therefore be sensitive to first impressions but keep an open mind and guard against locking into rigid lighting ideas too early in the creative process.

Even though they rarely emerge from the reading process as totally independent entities, at least seven aspects of the text influence the lighting design: structure, characterization, theme, symbol, mood, style, and given circumstances. We will examine these and discuss how each influences the lighting design.

Structure

The dominant factor determining play structure is the need to hold the attention and interest of the audience over time. The richness and variety of the sensory or intellectual experience can do this for a while, but after a time even change loses some of its fascination. Structure itself seems to have an inherent appeal, and most aestheticians argue that form is a defining characteristic of an art experience in contrast to the randomness of life experience. Perhaps more importantly, a structured event is more easily understood, followed, and remembered and holds our interest longer than disordered episodes.

As the first order of business, the vast majority of successful plays establish a "need to know" in the audience; they identify a problem to be solved or a question to be answered. This *major dramatic question* (MDQ), or "dramatic spine," stimulates the audience's curiosity, drawing them forward into the vortex of the action, toward the answer provided at the play's conclusion. This question may focus primarily upon either action or the revelation of character, but in the most successful cases the answer comes through the behavior of the central character, the *protagonist,* whose course of action simultaneously solves the problem and reveals his or her moral makeup or "ethos." An episode near the beginning of the play, the *inciting incident,* raises the MDQ. The moment in the plot where the audience becomes aware of the MDQ is called *the point of attack.*

In formulating the MDQ, the subject of the interrogatory sentence should ideally be the protagonist and the principal verb should be the central action of the play: "Will Hamlet revenge the murder of his father by killing the murderer, his uncle, Claudius?" "When will Oedipus discover that he has killed his own father, Laius, and how will he react to that discovery?" "In *Death of a Salesman,* will Willy Loman commit suicide or recognize his own failure and reconcile with his son, Biff?" "Can Blanche Dubois find refuge by either alienating Stella from Stanley or by deceiving Mitch into marrying her?" Difficulty in formulating a MDQ may indicate lack of focus or some structural ambiguity in a play.

Obviously, if the audience can answer the MDQ quickly or easily, the play cannot sustain interest for very long. Dramatic complexity and structural intricacy arise from the *complications* placed in the way of the resolution of the MDQ. These complications grow out of the situation, the idiosyncrasies of the protagonist, the interference of outside forces such as the gods or society, or the machinations of characters other than the protagonist, principally the primary opposing character, the *antagonist*. In a classically constructed play, the action intensifies as the protagonist overcomes a series of complications. Each victory spurs the next entanglement, but every unravelment moves closer to the *climax* or crisis where the central character confronts the ultimate conflict that finally answers the MDQ. After this *resolution,* all that remains is the wrapping up of loose ends or the *denoument.*

Audience pyschology predicates three major features of this classical dramatic structure: *mounting tension, rising and falling action,* and *conflict.* As we have repeatedly seen, a constant stimulus produces a diminishing response. If we wish to maintain even a sustained level of interest, the source must increase in intensity. To build interest, the stimulus must increase in some multiple proportion. As a consequence of this, each of the *units* of a play involving a minor action, complication, and resolution should create a slightly higher level of tension and interest than the preceding unit. By the same reckoning, a scene with a disproportionately high level of tension early in the play may make it difficult to sustain interest in subsequent scenes, which thereby become anticlimatic.

Perceptual fatigue, however, requires a much more complex accommodation than an unrelenting rise in tension. Audiences also seek variety and require periods of relative relief from tension in order to prepare for the next intense response. Just as the sentience of the eye to a given color improves with periodic exposure to that color's complement or the discernment of brightness benefits from contrast, so does periodic alleviation of tension or the introduction of contrasting actions refresh the audience and restore its responsiveness to the next piece of action in the puzzle. The arrangement of these contrasts in tension can establish a pattern in the structure of a play just as surely as variations in the dynamics of a piece of music give shape to that composition.

If the need for increasing stimulation seems equated too easily with rising tension, that is because writers so often use conflict to hold audience attention, even to the extent that most modern dramatic theorists follow the lead of the early nineteenth-century German philosopher, G.W.F. Hegel, and contend that conflict is a defining feature of drama. Certainly a rich dramatic experience offers more stimulation than just tension and conflict, but these major components usually provide keys for understanding the structure of the action. The driving force of a play is a character doing things to obtain a goal, and structural complexity arises when obstacles to the attainment of that goal produce conflict, reaction, and the accommodation of increasingly difficult strategies to attain the desired end.

In analyzing the structure of a play, it is extremely useful to label the function of each episode or unit and to note specific lines or moments where major structural features occur. Where is the point of attack? Where is each new complication introduced and where is each resolved? Where does the protagonist learn significant new pieces of information or undergo major reversals? Where is the climax? This process begins the creation of a lighting score for the production.

By actually diagraming the major structural features of a play, the designer can grasp the overall shape as a whole, concentrating on the main configuration. Figure 10-1 shows such a diagram for *Oedipus Rex.*

After having completed the structural analysis, the designer must begin to decide the extent to which the structure of the play will determine the structure of the stage lighting. The final answer must await the examination of other parts of the script and production, but the options should be clear. At one extreme, the lighting may parallel

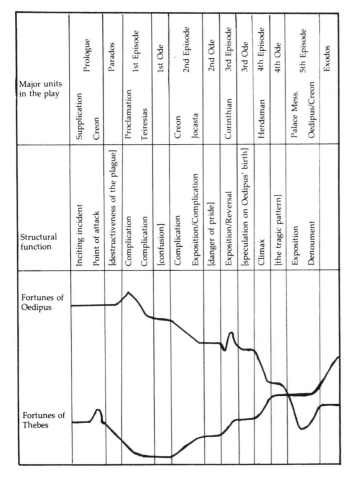

FIGURE 10-1 Diagram of the major structural features of *Oedipus Rex*

and reinforce the form of the play. For example, increasing brightness or darkness may underscore rising tension. A gradual heightening of the contrast in color or the use of progressively higher contrast between highlight and shadow may correspond to the intensification of conflict. Shifts to less flattering colors or lighting angles may mark the declining fortunes of the protagonist. Crises, reversals, and encounters can be underscored with lighting changes. Distinct types of light can differentiate separate plot lines. Special lighting on narrative sections can disconnect them from the main line of action. The repetition of lighting qualities can mark a return to a given time, place, or action.

At the other extreme, the lighting may obscure the play's structure. Constancy in the lighting may ignore major plot changes, or gradual shifts in the focus of the lighting to structurally unimportant points in the play may deemphasize the form of the plot. On first impression, this lack of reinforcement may appear to result from a failure to perceive the importance of structural elements (too often the case with poorly designed lighting), but the deemphasis may be carefully planned and quite appropriate. Just as an actor "throws away" a line for the sake of a more effective response to a later line, a director may wish to underplay a minor conflict or reversal in order to give greater emphasis to a later point. Playwrights do not always succeed in devising the best structures for their plays and may need assistance from the director, actor, or designer.

The more usual reason for not using light to stress a play's structure is that the form of the play is apparent without accentuation from the lighting, which can more appropriately be used for other things. Why belabor the plot structure if it is obvious?

The style of the production, particularly extreme realism, may also restrict the use of lighting to punctuate plot changes. In this case the lighting cannot change to emphasize a structural feature unless there is a realistic motivation for the change. Of course if the plot requires a lighting effect for clarification, an inventive designer should be able to discover a natural motivation even if it requires "planting" a light source earlier in the play just for the needed effect.

If a major shift in the plot seems otherwise obscure and if a lighting change would not be inappropriately obtrusive, use it, but otherwise no simple rule tells the designer when lighting should underline the play's structure. The designer and the director must judge how much underscoring the audience requires. However, the designer must clearly understand the structure of the play to make this decision.

Characterization

In discussing the plot structure, we have already touched on characterization by mentioning the protagonist and antagonist. Plot and character intertwine. The interaction of characters keeps the plot moving, and in a well-constructed play, the plot reveals character. Our analysis progresses logically from plot structure to characterization.

The lighting designer evaluates a play's characterization by asking six questions: What is the function of each character in the play? What are the important relationships among characters? Who should be in focus at each moment? Where is the character's attention focused? What happens to the character? What impression should the character make on an audience? The answers to these questions strongly influence the lighting; so we will examine each in turn.

What Is the Function of Each Character in the Play? The protagonist, as we saw, usually makes the choices which lead to the resolution of the major dramatic question, often resisted by an antagonist. Plot function defines other recurring character types. Many plays use a character who does not take action but functions as a *catalyst* for the action. An object rather than a character often fills this role, as for example the park bench in Edward Albee's *The Zoo Story* or the Italian straw hat in Feydeau's play by that name. As a character, the catalyst is often a similarly passive "bone of contention." The stereotyped "damsel in distress" of melodrama fame serves this use. In a modern play, Stella in *A Streetcar Named Desire* functions as the object of a battle for control by Blanche and Stanley. Stella repeatedly makes choices in Stanley's favor, just as the "damsel" invariably prefers the hero, but Stella is more acted upon than acting.

Another relatively passive character is the *chorus figure*. Ever since the abandonment of the chorus in ancient drama, playwrights have repeatedly compensated for the loss by using individual characters to comment on the action and frequently to voice the playwright's opinion. Moliere was particularly fond of this device and characters such as Cleante in *Tartuffe* or Philinte in *The Misanthrope* serve this objective. Comedy often counterpoises laughable deviations against this "normal" character.

Confidants are also commonly passive, providing opportunities for a principal character to reveal his or her thoughts to the audience. Theatrical styles which allow soliloquies have less use for confidants.

Foils accentuate the features of main characters by providing contrasts. George Bernard Shaw, for example, frequently uses a dialectic structure for his plays in which the point of view of any given character, the thesis, is opposed by a character representing an opposite view, the antithesis. The play progresses toward a synthesis of these conflicting ideas. For other playwrights, the foil may simply highlight a contrasting feature of another character. Creon's rationality in *Oedipus Rex* emphasizes Oedipus' occasional irrationality.

Creon is also one of several *messengers* in *Oedipus Rex,* characters who function to bring new information, usually concerning offstage events, to bear on the action of the play. The playwright sometimes develops these characters as a diversion for the audience, but their role is primarily functional.

Often in comedy, a character other than the protagonist keeps the plot moving. This *architectus* usually acts on behalf of a less effectual protagonist. The tricky slaves of Roman comedy or Harlequin in the commedia dell'arte provide good examples of this type.

Comedies frequently employ an *eiron,* a character who undercuts the excesses of the *alazon,* a self-inflated character whose extravagant behavior produces the audience's derisive laughter. The immoderation of the *alazon* parallels the extreme behavior of the tragic protagonist, only in this case the consequences are less catastrophic.[1]

Considerations other than plot requirements may determine the function of a character whose importance depends more upon symbolic or thematic demands. We will examine these functions in a later discussion of theme and symbol.

This functional analysis of characterization serves the lighting designer primarily as a basis for answering subsequent questions regarding focus and control of audience attitude. When we understand the purpose of a character in a play, we are better able to use lighting, where appropriate, to help the character fulfill that function.

What Are the Important Relationships Among Characters? One common adage of the theatre is that acting is the art of reacting. The sense of ensemble, of the wholeness of a production, comes in large part from the way characters interact, from the relationships established among characters. This interconnection is usually a product of plot function. The protagonist and antagonist are in opposition. The young lovers strive to connect, but the dissenting father blocks them. This interdependence also changes through time, and the lighting design provides a major resource for showing these shifting links.

Jean-Paul Sartre's play *No Exit* furnishes an excellent example of a triangular relationship. Three characters are in Hell. Each character depends upon another for some sort of satisfaction, but none cares to give satisfaction to the one who wants it. Estelle wants the man, Garcon, but he depends upon the approval of the cynical Inez who, in turn, desires Estelle. In short: "Hell is other people." Even though a strong argument can be made to perform this entire play in unmercifully revealing general illumination, more variety in the lighting may be desirable to show the gradually emerging relationships. The play progresses through a series of duets with each character trying to establish a relationship with another while the third hovers disruptively on the edges. The lighting offers several ways to express this relationship. The active character in the duet can be somewhat isolated while a link is established between the sought-after and the blocking character; the characters in the duet can be linked while a stronger focus is placed on the blocking character; or the characters in the duet can share a pool of illumination while the character sought after and the blocking character share a common light hue.

Careful foreshadowing, or perhaps more appropriately "forelighting," can create dramatic tension by anticipating developing links between characters. In Georg Kaiser's play *From Morn Till Midnight*, The Salvation Army Lass appears almost surreptitiously in early scenes, but it is effective for the audience to anticipate that she represents the ultimate solution for the protagonist's problems, a hope cruelly shattered at the play's conclusion. The lighting can connect the protagonist and the girl by similar lighting qualities during these early scenes even though the stage is crowded with other characters. Links in lighting qualities can also clarify the analogous relationships between characters in multiple-plot plays. For example, the use of parallel lighting early in *King Lear* between scenes in the main plot and the subplot establishes parallels between Lear and Gloucester, Cordelia and Edgar, or between Edmund and the evil sisters. Common lighting attributes may associate each of Olivia's four suitors in *Twelfth Night*, which enhances the fun of the play because the characters are so dissimilar in other ways.

A schematic diagram of character relationships often helps to clarify the play's structure, but by no means should the designer automatically assume that lighting should underscore these relationships. It is unnecessary to emphasize obvious relationships, and the director has many other ways to express connections between characters. However, the lighting designer should always know the relationships and be ready to clarify them when it is useful to do so.

Who Should Be in Focus at Each Moment in the Play?

The determination of focus is chiefly the responsibility of the director, who has many resources for this purpose, largely the blocking or arrangement of characters in the scenic space. However, except in an evenly lit space, any significant variation in lighting intensity, coloration, or angle will create focus within the space. Light obviously has a very strong pull on the audience's attention, whether consciously or subconsciously. The lighting can also be a valuable resource in the director's store of devices for creating focus. The task for the lighting designer, therefore, is never to inadvertently misplace the focus and to assist, when required, in the proper direction of the audience's attention. The director may spell out specific needs during production meetings but, in general, relies on the lighting designer's intelligent understanding of the needs of the play.

The matter is further complicated by the frequency with which a scene requires not a single strong focus, but a hierarchy of focuses or split focus. The designer must determine the relative importance of a number of factors in the visual field.

No simple rule determines which character should hold primary attention, but a few guiding principles aid in deciding where to place focus. When the protagonist is onstage, he or she usually takes the center of concentration, even if not directly involved in the conversation. For example, in Harold Pinter's play *The Birthday Party*, the main character, Stanley, spends much of the first part of the second act sitting silently in the middle of babbling characters at a surrounding party. He rarely speaks, but attention should be on his mounting disgust with the insipid babble around him, which leads to his explosive response at the end of the act. As Tesman and Thea make plans to reconstruct Lovborg's manuscript near the end of *Hedda Gabler*, Hedda drifts aimlessly around the room, but she should take focus as her feeling of superfluity drives her closer to suicide. Light from doorways, windows, or lamps should highlight her and keep the audience's attention on her responses to the conversation, rather than on the talking characters.

Characters entering a scene in progress

frequently change the course of the action and should receive at least momentary focus. The usual importance of entrances in a play explains why special lighting so often frames doorways to give them additional emphasis. The degree of highlighting depends on the relative importance of the character's entrance. Exists are less consistently important, but where the departure of a character influences the course of the action, that exit should take focus.

To the extent that messengers are relaying information important to an understanding of the play, they require focus, but sometimes the response of another character to this information is more important than the message itself. Oedipus should maintain focus during messenger scenes with Creon, the Corinthian Messenger, and the Old Shepherd, but the events related by the palace Messenger are more important that the response of the chorus.

Even a secondary character undergoing a major change usually takes precedence over a static protagonist. As Oedipus and the Corinthian Messenger reconstruct the Circumstances of Oedipus' rescue when he was an infant, Jocasta comes to the final realization that Oedipus is indeed her son. Even though she stays silent throughout most of this scene, she undergoes the greatest change of any character onstage and should have a strong focus.

Crowd scenes often provide the director and lighting designer the greatest challenge in maintaining proper focus. When Romeo invades the Capulet's party at the end of the first act in *Romeo and Juliet,* most of the characters in the play are onstage, but the focus must be kept on the young lovers, even a split focus as they mill among the partygoers before coming together. The use of followspots in musical drama simplifies this problem, but more realistic styles require inventive uses of motivated light sources. Torches, candles, and tapers furnish these sources for the *Romeo and Juliet* party scene.

Focus shifts according to the function of a character in a scene. As conflicts develop, new information emerges, or characters change, the center of attention moves. The lighting design cannot necessarily respond to all of these transitions without causing distraction, but the designer should always know which character or characters are properly in focus and be prepared to assist with lighting when required, particularly at key moments in the play or where other production factors create unwanted ambivalence.

Where Is the Character's Attention Focused? The lighting does not always have to center on the character. Particularly if the director or playwright has controlled audience attention by other means, the addition of a strong lighting focus may be redundant. In these circumstances the lights may create a secondary focus without distracting and add interesting complexity to the visual picture. The source of the principal character's own attention often merits special emphasis, maintaining cohesiveness by linking the character with his or her point of concentration. In other words, by calling attention to that which interests the character, we call further attention to the character.

As mentioned earlier, actors often analyze their roles in terms of "beats," segments of a play in which a character has a specific objective, a goal which motivates the character's actions and dominates the character's concentration. The objective can be internal, offstage, or abstract, but often the character's attention focuses on a concrete, onstage object. For example, in *The Man of La Mancha* Cervantes may be engaged in reenacting his story of Don Quixote, but his primary concern is his ability to confront the inquisitors who may reappear at any moment down the stairway to summon him. Even when the stairway is folded above the stage, it should remain somewhat in focus. Banquo's empty chair in the banquet scene of *Macbeth* is another famous example of an onstage point of concentration.

Even when offstage events take a character's concentration, the lighting can communicate that focus by emphasizing the exterior space. In *Riders to the Sea,* the women on stage anxiously await news of their missing men with the premonition that the men have drowned. The exterior door and window should stay in focus. When Oedipus rushes inside the palace after learning that he indeed murdered Laius, the chorus has an ode on the King's vulnerability, but the focus should remain on the closed doors behind which Oedipus, the theme of the ode, has fled.

Playwrights working in a realistic style often depict an onstage action which functions primarily to show reaction to offstage events. Sean O'Casey's characters engage in petty and often comic conflicts while their brothers, sons, and daughters die in revolutions on the streets outside the windows. The characters in Chekhov's *The Cherry Orchard* have a party, but the principal characters concentrate on the news of the offstage auction where the future of the family is being decided as Gayev struggles to save the manor house. An earlier playwright might have shown the actual auction, but Chekhov prefers to work with counterpoint and irony of tone. However, this juxtaposition works only if the exterior action stays in focus.

Doors, windows, and other openings in the setting provide important opportunities for the lighting designer to compose the stage picture with shafts of light and variegated intensities and color. However, one must beware of generating false focus and keep in mind the difference between focus placed on the opening itself and focus placed onstage by light coming through the opening. A shaft of light not occupied by a character but striking the floor, furniture, or scenery may, in effect, pull the eye outside of the setting. A translucent curtain on a window may make the window itself brighter than characters standing in its light and draw focus outside. These can be useful effects if the exterior appropriately demands attention.

The amount of focus placed on a character may depend on the importance of that person in the mind of a more central character. For example, in *Death of a Salesman,* Ben requires a strong focus whenever he is onstage because he is so important in Willy's mind. In the scene where Willy and Charley play cards, Ben should gradually take a stronger focus than Charley because Ben increasingly preoccupies Willy. The Mexican woman who vends tin flowers has little inherent importance in *A Streetcar Named Desire,* but Blanche mysteriously views her as a symbol of death; so the Mexican woman needs sharp focus because of her significance to Blanche.

This method of using light to draw audience attention to the point of a character's concentration must be employed very subtly in a realistic style, but in more symbolic or expressionistic plays the technique may be more overt. With these styles, objective reality is less important than the use of the stage picture to express the subjective reality of the protagonist or the playwright. The concentration camp watchtower remains in focus in Arthur Miller's play *After the Fall* because the protagonist, Quentin, is preoccupied with it as a symbol of human corruption. In Eugene O'Neill's *The Hairy Ape,* the girl Mildred is exposed to the audience as a scheming, brutal young woman, but the only time Yank, the "Hairy Ape," sees her, she is bathed in a brilliant, etheral light which contrasts with the murky, hell-like atmosphere of the ship's furnace room. To Yank she seems a ghostly symbol of a higher form of life who has unjustly rejected him. She never appears again in the play, but Yank remains obsessed with her and what she represents. In a play like Georg Büchner's *Woyzeck,* the audience should see the other characters as Woyzeck sees them. His friend Andre remains compassionate and natural, but Woyzeck's mistress, Marie, grows more alien in his mind as the play progresses, and all of the other characters seem increasingly more demoniac. Unnatural colors, lighting angles, and shadows help to project Woyzeck's view of a threatening world.

What Happens to Each Character? Characters in a play may either remain unchanged, change, or appear to change in the eyes of the audience as more information is revealed. To the extent that theatre is a time art, the principal characters usually undergo change as the play develops, while minor characters, whose function primarily relates to the mechanics of developing plot, theme, or the major characters, frequently remain static. In *The Poetics*, Aristotle stated that changing characters follow two major patterns: from good to bad fortune and the reverse. We should add that in many plays, characters undergo various changes but end pretty much as they began. Even with Aristotle's classic cases, the progression rarely follows such a simple, straightline development, and it is important for the lighting designer to follow every twist and turn because changes in the lighting help to clarify these ups and downs.

A brief analysis of Oedipus' major changes will illustrate these possible links between lighting and the vicissitudes of a character. Because the plot in *Oedipus Rex* links so strongly with changes in the fortunes of Oedipus, the diagram of the play's plot in Figure 10-1 also provides a good schematic for Oedipus' fluctuations.

In the beginning of the play, Oedipus' status is almost godlike. He is the good king, father to his subjects, the healer, the solver of riddles who will find a way to lift the plague. His strength and wholesomeness contrast strongly with the desperate straits of the plagued suppliants, and his first entrance should be as grand as possible. As the suppliants hover in semidarkness, perhaps with lurid colors and shadows cast by the altar fire, the central doors might open to reveal an almost blinding shaft of white light. As Oedipus mounts the entrance ramp, the brilliant back light gives his entire body a halo while his face remains enigmatically in darkness. His shadow looms large across the suppliants, who recoil at the magnificence of his entrance but, after a reverential pause, rush to gather about Oedipus' knees as he moves downstage into an additional key light illuminating his face, masked or not, which reveals dignity, reasonableness, and compassion. This majestic image of man at his highest potential will gradually disintegrate as the play progresses.

Creon's message from the Apollonian oracle gives Oedipus a concrete basis for resolving the plague and arouses all of Oedipus' organizational and rational powers. As he ponders his course of action, he perhaps catches a ray of front light which emphasizes his head, but places his whole body in a clear, almost shadowless light. Here is a man who seems to personify the light of reason, lucid, seeing no apparent ambiguities, only mechanical complications, which he can resolve.

Oedipus leaves the stage to plan while the chorus of Theban elders makes its entrance. His next entrance is quite different from the first. He almost sneaks onto the stage and looms unexpectedly over the chorus. The Oedipus entering now is more cunning and threatening than when we first saw him. This is the Oedipus who lays traps for the unwary and terrible punishments for the disloyal. Oedipus now hovers in the shadows and makes his proclamation standing over the altar fire, which casts unnatural shadows on his face, emphasizing the awesome power of his curses on the murderer or any who withhold information.

Teiresias makes his entrance and for the first time we sense a competing power as great as Oedipus', the power of prophesy and the prophet's god, Apollo. Oedipus loses some of his focus and must struggle to retain his dominance. Teiresias accuses Oedipus of being the murderer, and the king's composure cracks, beginning the process of disintegration. The lighting on Oedipus becomes less strong. He may even move through broken areas of light and shadow, standing in the darkness while bright, eerie colored lights on Teiresias show the blind priest's special vision. After Teiresias' final speech, Oedipus exits silently, confused, threatened, angered, and much weaker. The chorus reflects this confusion during their next ode, but they still side with Oedipus.

The next episode, between Creon and Oedipus, is more restrained than the scene with Teiresias. Even though its tempo rises as the disagreement mounts, the scene has some of the formality of a debate, with the chorus serving as a jury. The important point is that Creon seems the more rational and perhaps the stronger of the two men. Where he was a mere functionary, a messenger, during his first appearance, he is now on an equal footing with Oedipus, more an indication of Oedipus' weakening than Creon's strengthening. As the riddle unravels itself, the darkness of the plague begins to lift and the stage becomes more evenly lit. Strong beams of light no longer give Oedipus special stature; he seems more ordinary, sharing general lighting with Creon.

Jocasta enters to separate the feuding men and scolds them like children. Her attitude toward Oedipus is strongly maternal, and he almost pouts as he relates the conspiracy that he perceives against himself. During the ensuing exposition, when he begins to suspect that he was the murderer at the crossroads, he nearly succumbs to despair and has to be consoled by the chorus. Color shifts are now probably the most effective way of showing Oedipus' further decline. The lights on him may cool in relation to the warmer lighting on the space and figures around him, so that he seems more distant, less sympathetic to the audience.

The news brought by the Corinthian Messenger in the next episode at first marks a minor reversal in Oedipus' decline. Initially Oedipus believes that he has escaped the god's curse, but subsequent information provided by the Corinthian moves Oedipus a step closer to his doom and confirms the awful truth to Jocasta. The next episode, in which Oedipus tortures the Old Shepherd and finally realizes that he, Oedipus, has committed patricide and incest, is probably the lowest point to which Oedipus sinks in

the eyes of the audience, even if he has not reached the depths of his own misfortune. Every means available to the lighting designer could now be used to diminish Oedipus' stature. The space around him should seem much warmer and more pleasant than any space he occupies. Scenery that before had faded off into darkness can now loom over him in its full height. Shafts of top light can seem to bombard him and shorten his figure.

Oedipus reaches the ebb of his affairs within his play when he reenters after having blinded himself, but he also has begun a new climb toward an ancient Greek version of sainthood. His remorse, the unwavering quickness with which he inflicts his own punishment, and the terribleness of his sufferings begin to restore him to the sympathies of the audience. The somewhat maudlin scene with his daughters emphasizes the pathos of his plight and arouses pity. Creon reenters with much of the show of authority and princely power that Oedipus once held, but Oedipus should now possess some of the sacredness that we saw in Teiresias. He slowly acquires the sanctity of the scapegoat whose sufferings relieve Thebes of the plague, a man who has looked upon the terrible power of the gods. An echo of the earlier halo effect may be appropriate here, but with back light that is softer, more luminescent. Hints of the hues used earlier for Teiresias may also be appropriate. The contrast with the new bright surrounding space should be subtle, but Oedipus' light should again be somewhat special and warmer. Oedipus is about to become a superman again, but for reasons entirely different from those that opened the play.

The character development of Oedipus is certainly not the only material on which to base a central lighting design for *Oedipus Rex*. Many directors, for example, take a much more pessimistic view of the play's ending and emphasize the power of the gods and futility of human effort. Some seize on the blindness motif and want to show that progression by the ever-increasing darkness on Oedipus or his surroundings. The play has been popular so long partly because its enigmatic nature opens it to so many possible interpretations. The point of this analysis is simply to demonstrate how changes in one character can provide a basis for structuring the lighting plot.

We also saw that Creon's gain in stature was a reverse image of Oedipus' fall and that Jocasta's decline foreshadowed Oedipus'. Most good plays contain this complex interweaving of changing characters and to the degree that the lighting changes follow these shifts in character, the designer must carefully orchestrate the variations. Each play has its own unique pattern of changing characters, which should emerge from the designer's analysis of the script. A diagram of the changes projected over time often gives a concrete scheme for the lighting plot.

What Impression Should the Character Make on the Audience? The attitude that we desired the audience to take toward Oedipus inevitably influenced our analysis of his changing character. All analysis of characterization ultimately hinges on controlling audience response. Lighting furnishes one of many tools for influencing the way an audience reacts to a character. An extreme example is the use of diffused, pink lights on the heroine, strong highlights on the hero, and low-angled lights which produce unnatural shadows on the face of the villain in melodrama. We can design special lighting for each character in a melodrama which will set up the audience's attitudes just as surely as the introductory musical themes do. In detective plays, much of the fun comes from misdirecting audience suspicions by making progressively different characters seem suspicious. Lighting changes can move focus to different characters and trap the audience into making premature judgments by placing characters in light with unflattering colors and angles. Careful control of the movement of actors in relation to motivated light sources from fireplaces, windows, and lamps can produce these changes even in highly realistic plays.

More sophisticated plays necessitate more subtle effects. For example, interpretations of *A Streetcar Named Desire* vary widely in performance, depending on whether audiences sympathize primarily with Stanley or Blanche or balance between the two. We can depict Blanche as a sensitive person whose positive values cannot survive in a brutal world populated by animals like Stanley, or we can see her as a neurotic, egomaniac who tries to destroy the somewhat idyllic love nest of Stanley and Stella. Williams establishes a strong lighting image for each of the two characters: Stanley lives in the world of clear bright light or the colored lights that he gets going when he makes love with Stella, but Blanche wants the lighting of magic, expressed by candlelight and by the colored shade that she puts over the bedroom lighting fixture, a romantic light which conceals and softens. On the surface, these lighting images suggest a more positive response by the audience to the richer, more variegated lighting of Blanche, but considerable latitude for interpretation remains within each contrasting ambience.

Stanley's light can be either harsh, glaring, and distorting, or it can be clean and sharp with enhancing highlights. Blanche's light can be soft and romantic, but it can also appear distorted and diseased, a florid imposition on an otherwise clear world. Audience response to the characters will vary considerably according to which of these extremes the designer chooses. My own inclination is to retain the ambiguity of William's script and tip the balance neither toward Stanley nor Blanche, emphasizing the positive elements of both lighting images and leaving the audience with the feeling that each of the principal characters is equally right and wrong. The point is that the choices made by the lighting designer can have a strong influence over audience response.

Lighting for Brecht's Epic theatre productions gives the lighting designer a unique opportunity to generate ambiguous audience responses. Even though Brecht proposed performing under worklights to remind the audience of the theatricality of the production, he also allowed the designer to make independent statements on the characters in order to provide audience members with alternative views. Thus a sympathetic character might occasionally appear in an unflattering light, or soft, warm light might accompany a despicable piece of business. Brecht could have solved some of his famous difficulties in alienating his audiences from Mother Courage if he had emphasized unpleasant colors and angles of light on her.

A lighting designer's analysis of the function, relative importance, interrelationships, points of focus, and changes of character, and the desired audience response to characters, should begin with a close reading of the script, but the designer must adjust the approach taken as the production develops. The director's perspective, interpretive contributions by other members of the production team and, more particularly, the evolution of the character as the actor works require periodic adjustments in the original analysis of the script.

Theme

To discover the underlying "meaning" of a play, its theme, the designer interprets the script to discover concepts communicated to the audience by the play's actions, characters, and setting. The production may introduce themes other than those apparent in the text or deemphasize the text's themes as the director's approach takes shape, but the script usually provides a common beginning point for all interpretations of the play. A thematic analysis of the script begins the formulation of a production concept, a statement of the approach used to communicate through the performance the play's meanings and values.

On its most general level, the theme is the message or moral of the play, a truism illustrated by the action of the play. A concise statement of the theme in its most basic form helps to clarify the main thrust of the action and defines the "spine" or core of the play in the same way that describing the superobjective of a character gives a clear sense of purpose to an actor's performance. These thematic statements often seem simplistic because they reduce a complex experience to an elementary form. If an uncomplicated sentence can adequately express a theme, the play may have very little to say to an audience. The complete thematic statement for the most intriguing plays are the plays themselves. Playwrights say what they have to say in the form of a play because that is the most effective form to communicate their ideas. A statement of theme merely isolates the central thought; it does not convey the full complexity of the idea, which only the play itself can express in its entirety.

A complex play also invites varied interpretations of theme, which accounts for the frequent reinterpretation of great plays and for the diversity of production approaches. We might define the theme of *Oedipus Rex* to be "Man cannot control his own fate but obtains nobility through the integrity with which he faces events beyond his control." However, other equally valid statements provide bases for different interpretations: "Human rationality conceals subconscious emotional impulses such as incest and fratricide." "Free will is a self-deception because many human actions are at least partly controlled by outside forces." "The welfare of the group frequently depends on the sacrifice of an individual (scapegoat)." "A rapid change of circumstances quickly destroys fame and honor." "Humans are ultimately helpless in the hands of all-powerful gods." The list could go on. An ideal production, in theory, might convey all of these possibilities, but the need for focus and order would still require the establishment of some priorities. The director, of course, ultimately decides which theme to stress, but the lighting designer should try to be aware of all possibilities by closely reading the text.

Theme and subject differ slightly from one another. A noun usually expresses the subject of a play, but the theme should ideally contain an active verb, reflecting the importance of action in drama. The subject of *Romeo and Juliet* is "Love," but the theme is "Impulsive love can both consume and ennoble lovers." Consumption and ennoblement are two of the primary contradictory actions that contribute to the tragic rhythm in *Romeo and Juliet*. On one level at least, the subject of *A Streetcar Named Desire* is desire, but on that same level the theme is "Strong sexual urges destroy dreamers who cannot adapt their romantic fantasies to the coarser reality of human nature." Blanche destroys herself by her failure to adjust to the strong sexual drives both in herself and in Stanley.

The broad pattern of the lighting design depends on the determination of theme, and the designer's analysis always looks toward the way in which lighting can clarify the theme. For example, whether we see *Oedipus Rex* primarily as Oedipus' descent into the darkness of his own fallibility or emphasize the positive attributes of the lifting of the plague and Oedipus' acquisition of a clearer perception of his own place in his universe, makes a major difference in how the designer handles the lighting for the end of the play.

As we have seen, Tennessee Williams wrote into the script of *A Streetcar Named Desire* lighting effects which express the thematic conflicts in that play. The moment when Mitch tears the colored shade off the bedroom light represents the scripted collision of the unshielded light of Stanley's world and the magic light of Blanche's, but the designer must make decisions regarding the two remaining scenes which depend on the interpretation of the play's theme. Does Blanche restore the shade before the rape scene? Does Stanley turn on an overhead light in the bedroom at some point during that scene? Does the quality of the light in the final scene carry out the pattern established? If Blanche's world has been destroyed, we would expect a brightly lit daytime scene, but the poker game is going on. An afternoon poker game on a weekend day? Williams doesn't specify the time of day. Does Blanche's fantasy about the doctor represent some small recovery? If so, does the lighting suggest this by reintroducing some slight tinge of Blanche's romantic colors? The designer must resolve these questions in terms of the overall thematic statement desired for the play's conclusion.

Symbols

Dramatic symbols are characters, objects, events, or—of particular concern to us—qualities of lighting which represent less tangible ideas. Plays contain symbols on two levels: *literary symbols* which operate primarily in the language of the dialogue, and *theatrical symbols* which exist in a real, concrete form in the setting, costumes, makeup, or lighting. The playwright has greatest control over the literary symbols, but both by stage directions and by references in the dialogue to objects or qualities of light, the playwright also establishes the existence of concrete theatrical symbols. Blanche's references to the colored lamp shade, for example, firmly establish the symbolic importance of that stage prop.

A symbol introduced on a literary level can also provide a basis for theatrical symbols. Shakespeare, for example, had very limited means, if any, for changing the stage lighting in *Romeo and Juliet,* but his frequent use of lighting symbolism in the language of the play opens the possibility for amplifying his literary metaphors with actual stage lighting effects.

The designer, to repeat a caution made in Chapter 8, should carefully avoid imposing symbolic meanings on the script during early readings. A reader in a frame of mind to interpret any event symbolically can induce hidden implications where none were intended. Even the weather report reveals concealed nuances when approached in this fashion. A good playwright usually calls attention to intended symbols by such means as repetition, placing an object or character in an unusual context, or having a character in the play speculate on the possible meaning of something. Later in the process of developing a production concept, the director or designers may add symbolic devices which help to clarify the play or express some special vision of the play, but this should be clearly understood as a step taken beyond what the script provides.

Some plays use lighting symbols, which we discussed in earlier sections on the symbolic function of light, but the lighting designer must also pay attention to other types of theatrical symbols that often require special focus. Also because theatre is a time art, symbols frequently change their importance or meaning during the course of a play, changes which lighting sometimes best makes. For example, in Tennessee Williams' *Summer and Smoke,* a play richly embellished with a variety of theatrical symbols, the central conflicting values, body and soul, are symbolized by an anatomy chart in Dr. John Buchanan's office and the stone Angel of Eternity in the town square. The fact that the Angel is in the center of the stage and the chart off to one side indicates the dominance of the soul as a factor in the play, but both are constantly on stage in this multiple setting and focus shifts back and forth as one element and then the other dominates the two central characters. Williams' stage directions specify lighting on these two symbols at critical moments, but the designer must delicately balance the focus at all times. The Angel also changes from a somewhat warmly lit enigma to a coldly dominating power. Two-step fadeouts specified by Williams end four of the play's twelve scenes by focusing on the Angel, and at the end of one scene, highlight the chart, a way of making an ironic comment on the preceding action. When Alma Winemiller, the protagonist, abandons her commitment to the spiritual dimension in her life for the sake of physical love, Williams provides a tolling bell and the following stage direction: "The light changes, the sun disappearing behind a cloud, fading from the steeple and the stone angel till the bell stops tolling. Then it brightens again," a subtle indication of Alma's major change.[2]

A powerful central image also lies over Peter Shaffer's dramatization of Pizarro's conquest of Peru, *The Royal Hunt of the Sun.* For the opening scenes set in Spain, a huge metal medallion, quartered by sword-shaped black crucifixes, hangs over a bare stage. This emblem does not figure directly in the action at first and should be somewhat unobtrusive, but when the scene moves to Peru, the medallion begins to glow and opens outward to form a gigantic golden sun with the Inca standing in its center (see Plate V). Scenes alternate between the Inca's court and the Spaniards struggling through the jungles. The sun sometimes glares and at other times looms as a shadowy form, an evasive goal for the toiling invaders. After the defeat of the Inca, this sun becomes his prison and finally his death chamber. Stripped of its golden petals, it hovers over the action, a gloomy reminder of the destruction of the Incas. Some of these changes are made by physically altering the emblem, but the more subtle shifts in emphasis and mood are done with lighting.

Not all symbols are as dominant as in these two plays. Hedda Gabler's dueling pistols are a legacy from her father, General Gabler. She threatens to shoot Lovborg at one point with one of the guns and subsequently gives it to him so he can use it to commit a noble suicide, which he bungles. She finally uses the other gun for her own suicide. The pistols represent Hedda's Romantic heritage from her father, an attitude which makes her discontent with her role as a Victorian woman. The naturalistic style of *Hedda Gabler* prevents any artificial highlighting of the pistol case, but its location on stage with respect to realistically motivated lighting sources can provide opportunities to highlight the guns at appropriate moments.

The control of the audience's awareness of the growing significance of theatrical symbols requires careful coordination of effort among the designers and the director. In the best instances, the production allows the audience to make the discovery of meaning for itself, but the astute use of stage lighting can carefully guide audience perception.

Mood and Atmosphere

Properly speaking, a play does not have a mood. It has an atmosphere or ambience which creates a changing mood in the audience, changing because mood, like attention, flags over time if kept at a constant level. In other words, "mood" describes a human emotion, and we are analyzing stimuli in the play which produces that emotional response. As we have seen, lighting conditions have a great capacity to induce emotional reactions; so the lighting designer must be sure that the mood created by the lighting at any moment in the play reinforces the atmosphere appropriate for the script. The genre of a play, whether comedy, tragedy, melodrama, etc., often provides a starting point in identifying the appropriate changes in atmosphere.

Genre. A common maxim in lighting-design theory is that comedy requires brighter, warmer lighting than tragedy. As we noted elsewhere, this type of rule is too broad to be a very useful response to all variation of atmosphere within a single comedy or tragedy. However, if we resist the temptation to use genre as a justification for imposing broad, mechanical schemes of lighting, determining a play's genre can be a valuable first step in deciding the moods the play should evoke and can alert the designer to look for patterns which traditionally recur in plays of a similar type. When we have said that a play is a tragicomedy or a melodrama, we have described very little, but the

implications of those terms do provide a useful beginning.

Tragedy, for example, is not simply a serious play that ends unhappily. Most tragedies generate an ambiguous final response in the audience. What has happened is in some ways good, in others, bad, and the two reactions are inseparable. That which attracts us happens only because of the thing which repels us. Blanch has destroyed herself but Stanley has saved his marriage on new but still acceptable terms. Oedipus leads himself to terrifying suffering but he frees Thebes of the plague and begins the process of attaining a level of divine favor that he could never have reached before. Without this compensating counter movement, tragedy would generate into "pathodrama," the depressing depiction of unrelieved misery. Very few audience members seek such an unmitigatedly depressing experience in the theatre. The lighting designer must therefore seek in a tragedy the conditions for both the downward and the uplifting trends.

Tragicomedy produces similarly mixed responses, but the positive side is more likely to be ludicrous or comic rather than particularly uplifting, or the two extremes are merely linked rather than being interdependent. Madame Ranyevskaya and her family are not particularly ennobled by the events surrounding the loss of their home in *The Cherry Orchard,* but the absurdity of the situation in some ways relieves its seriousness. The farcical antics of the characters in *Waiting for Godot* relieve the tedium of their seriously absurd existence as well as the tedium of the watching audience.

Melodrama also creates contrasting moods, but the final audience response is unambiguously positive. The threats and crises are merely stages leading to the final victory of good over evil, and the very extremity of the contrast assures the audience that no complicating internal ambiguities in the characters will cloud the final issue. Melodrama allows the most extreme counterpoising of antithetical qualities of color and of light and shadow. Audiences enjoy the frightening effects of plays like *Angel Street* or *Dial M for Murder* because they know in the back of their minds that all will work out in the end.

Comedies can have their somber moments as well, and the comic protagonist often struggles against grim adversaries. Northrop Frye observed that comedy runs the gamut from Romantic Comedy, where the quest of the hero or heroine is never seriously threatened, to Ironic Comedy, where the protagonist at best succeeds only in escaping a lunatic world or at worse where the representatives of the old order succeed in blocking the emergence of the usually victorious free society of traditional comedy. The shifts in mood caused by comedy are indicated by the frequency with which comedies contain deaths or at least ritual deaths.[3] Falstaff's sham death in *Henry IV, Part I* even rates a requiem from Hal, and although the audience suspects that the fat knight will pop back to life, the seriousness of Henry, Hal, and Falstaff's near brush with disaster at the hands of Hotspur is best served by using the lighting to stress all of the discord and confusion of war, which also sets up the jubilation of the final victory. In Christopher Fry's comedy *The Dark is Light Enough,* the protagonist actually dies, but her spirit has conquered death itself, the ultimate comic victory.

To simply begin with the artless assumption that comedy requires bright lights misses all the rich complexity of the comic experience, for example, the spectacle of an opportunistic adventurer averting disaster and foiling the best efforts of a ridiculous crew of ludicrous characters. The enchanted forest through which the protagonist passes may be in Brooklyn and peopled with old fathers, bill collectors, and mothers-in-law, but if it isn't at least a little spooky, the comic triumph loses some of its savor and a lot of its fun.

Genres therefore provide a key not so much to static moods as to patterns of experience, stages through which the characters and the audience pass, a journey through which lighting often marks the path.

Atmosphere. The analysis of a script to discover the appropriate atmosphere entails more than a determination of genre. The designer needs to understand each subtle shift in tone and precisely what mood each change evokes. A detailed look at these changes in *A Streetcar Named Desire* will illustrate this method of investigation.

The play opens with a jazz music background that sets a tone of rich indolence. We see figures passing in the streets, women lounging on porches, and Stella lazily fanning herself as she sits in the bedroom. This is the casual life of ease that Blanche will disrupt, the New Orleans of the guidebooks, a little sleazy, but picturesque. "How charming!" is the response we want, and every trick in the lighting designer's repertory should be used to make the setting beautiful, with rich colors, a strong flow of mellow late afternoon sunlight, and interestingly variegated shadows cast by elaborate wrought-iron work.

When Blanche makes her entrance, soon after the establishment of this initial mood, the audience should immediately sense that Blanche is out of place. Something is too high strung, too fragile, too purely crystalline about her to fit into this mellow setting. If we assume that the play's style is at first relatively realistic, we do not want to noticeably change the lighting with her entrance, but gradually, imperceptibly, the lighting should lose some of its charm. Williams helps by setting the scene at dusk. We want the audience gradually to see the setting as Blanche sees it: seedy, run down, a little threatening, "the ghoul-haunted woodland of Weir."[4] Blanche's description of the deaths at Belle Reve should evoke almost gothic horror. The women are in near darkness when Stanley reenters. His first responses to Blanche are pleasant enough, but her anxiety should dominant the scene and foreshow the coming conflict. Stanley can well turn on lights as he moves through the apartment, which allows him to change shirts in full light, emphasizing his animal appeal to Blanche and setting a mood of tension with a strong contrast of light and shadow as Blanche seeks out the darker areas of the room.

Scene two begins on a somewhat brighter note as we see Stanley and Stella engage in playful banter, but the disposition of Belle Reve quickly becomes a point of contention, rising to the sharp encounter between Stanley and Blanche. Except for the possibility of Stella turning off the vanity light as she prepares to leave, there are no opportunities for noticeable lighting changes; so any modification in the lighting to enhance the growing atmosphere of conflict must be slow enough to remain inconspicuous.

Scene three establishes the metaphorical contrast between the sharp, bright lighting of Stanley's poker game and the dappled light from Blanche's paper lantern, but even before Blanche puts the shade on, the scene between Mitch and her should presage romance and be played in the soft half-light which seems to spill from the poker game and outside lighting sources. The atmosphere produced by the poker game depends largely on how much we want the audience to see it from Blanche's view, in which case, the overhead light should be bright, almost glaring, with strong shadows cast by the moving poker players, "the party of apes" as Blanche later describes them. If we choose a more balanced view the effect should be closer to what Renaissance painters called "Tenebrism," a picturesque quality created by a single souce of warm light which accentuates modeling and creates interesting interplays of highlight and shadow. A virtual explosion ends the poker game, and low-angled lights, whose introduction is covered by Stanley's lunge for the radio, create distorted shadows from the milling characters and help to stress the disorderly atmosphere. The mood alters again to a mellower tone when Stanley calls Stella down from upstairs, and the action moves outside where the upstairs porch light silhouettes Stella's return to Stanley. Blanche and Mitch move, somewhat ironically, into this same lighting while Stanley and Stella begin to make love in the bedroom, now dimly but romantically lit by Blanche's lantern. Some of the New Orleans charm begins to return in spite of Blanche's nervous tension.

The morning setting of the next scene indicates the calm following the stormy night before. Bright, cool, low-angled light opens on a contented Stella. Blanche tries immediately to disrupt this mood, but it takes the entire scene for her to have any success at driving a wedge between Stella and Stanley. As the scene turns to a more ominous note, the early morning light shifts to a warmer color and a higher angle, the general lighting in the room dims, and the two women talk in the brightness of an imagined downstage window. During the ape speech, Stanley enters into the other room and stands in a bright overhead shaft of light, like "exhibit A" in Blanche's argument. The separate pools of light help to divide Stanley from the women and, indeed, Blanche comes as close here to alienating Stella from Stanley as she does at any other point in the play. The overhead light on Stanley also creates strong shadows under the brow ridge and neck which suggest an apelike quality. This same brighter light, only perhaps at a lower angle, can emphasize Stella and Stanley's embrace at the end of the scene, and by leaving Blanche in the dimmer perimeter, suggest her exclusion when Stella clearly rejects Blanche's view and takes Stanley, covered with dirt or not.

The fifth scene is again in the afternoon and begins sunnily for a laughing Blanche; however, Stanley soon introduces the first hints that he has learned of Blanche's shady background and the mood of the scene shifts to a more desperate level. Williams punctuates this transaction with a passing thunderstorm, which also justifies changes in the lighting quality to evoke a more threatening atmosphere. Blanche takes refuge in the hope that Mitch will marry her, and the storm passes quickly to allow a major shift of atmosphere for the short scene with The Collector. Here the romantic mood of Blanche's fantasy world must reign. More realistic productions may use that peculiarly luminous quality of light that follows a late-afternoon summer shower and more expressionistic productions might return to a suggestion of Blanche's fantasy light from the paper lantern, but the effect should be almost phantasmal, an impression sustained into Mitch's entrance.

In the next scene, which begins in the melancholy light of deserted streets at two o'clock in the morning, Blanche tries to create "*joie de vivre*," a feeling of delight at being alive, by using candlelight after she and Mitch go inside, but even though the candlelight makes the atmosphere more romantic, the melancholy lingers on. Williams emphasizes this fact by having Blanche say, at the end of the scene, that after her young husband's suicide "the searchlight which had been turned on the world was turned off again and never for one moment since has there been any light stronger than this kitchen candle."

Stanley reveals Blanche's sordid past in full detail in the next scene, and Williams for the first time calls attention to the stifling heat that hovers over the setting through the entire play. The feeling of this scene should be heavy and oppressive, perhaps with washes of light that minimize modeling.

Williams describes the beginning of scene eight as "dismal," a mood that Blanche tries unsuccessfully to dispel. The end of the scene begins the process of destroying Blanche, which culminates with the rape. Three major lighting features provide resources for accentuating this disintegration: the interplay of bright light and shadow, the intrusion of outside lighting, and the distortion of Blanche's "magic" light. The higher contrast lighting should gradually reappear in the eighth scene. Stanley may even snap on the overhead lights before he gives Blanche her bus tickets back to Laurel.

Certainly by the next scene with Mitch, Blanche's desperate attempts to escape reality become a literal effort to avoid bright light, which finally fails when Mitch tears the paper lantern off of the bedroom light and forces Blanche under it.

Throughout the play Williams uses sound effects and music, particularly the Varsuviana, to allow the audience a glimpse of what is going on inside of Blanche's head. This subjective reality becomes more obtrusive as Blanche loses her grip on sanity, and the lighting should help to emphasize her disorientation. The scrim walls reveal events on the street: the passage of the Mexican flower vendor, a mugging, and a police chase. All emphasize the hostile world from which Blanche seeks refuge. Strong shafts of low-angled light coming from different directions should stress the confusion of these disjointed background events. Blanche escapes more and more into her dream world, particularly at the beginning of the scene with Stanley, but now the mood should be more bizarre and tormented. The colors may swirl or cut sharply jagged patterns rather than the softly dappled effect of earlier scenes. All of this crescendos to the rape.

As indicated earlier, the mood of the play's final scene depends on the interpretation of the ending. Either order is restored and we return to the original picturesqueness, or we emphasize the gloom, hypocrisy, and final violence as Mitch erupts while the female attendant pinions Blanche.

Our language contains a rich vocabulary of adjectives to describe mood and atmosphere. The labeling of each major mood shift in the script will alert the designer to these changes. Adjectives used in the dialogue or in stage directions often provide clues to the playwright's intentions. The director and the actors refine these moods in rehearsal, and the designer should adapt the lighting accordingly. Of course, having merely identified the mood wanted from the audience does not solve the problem of designing lighting that will generate the mood, but knowing the desired response is a prerequisite for creating the right lighting. In the earlier sections of this book we examined emotional responses to color, brightness, and composition; these sections provide useful clues for ways to use the lighting to produce specific moods.

Style

We can impose virtually any style on any play, and occasionally valuable new insights result from producing a play in a style other than that in which it was written. Ultimately the director makes the final decision regarding the production style, but even where this departs seriously from the script, a successful adaptation depends on thoroughly understanding the style the playwright originally intended for the play and the important changes that will result when a different style is used.

We discussed the concept of style and the types of style in Chapter 8. A script analysis uses those same categories. Many plays fall neatly into traditional classifications, but many others bridge conventional types or create their own unique styles. These require more careful analysis.

A Streetcar Named Desire, for example, is typical of both Williams and many other post-World-War-II playwrights, in combining realism with more theatrical styles. The fragmented setting with some scrim walls described in the *Streetcar* script forewarn us even before the action begins that the play will not be slavishly realistic. The characters behave realistically, but for one character, Blanche, the staging reflects an inner as well as an outer consciousness. These devices are not handled as extremely as in a strictly expressionistic play, but they are closely akin to expressionism's attempt to dramatize the inner perceptions of the protagonist. A rigidly realistic lighting design would take an approach narrower than the style of the play itself.

Peter Shaffer's *Amadeus*—like his *Royal Hunt of the Sun* and *Equus* or Williams' *The Glass Menagerie,* or a number of other modern plays—uses a present-time narrator to relate past-time events in which the narrator was involved. The major episodes of the play may be relatively realistic, but the narrative passages are very presentational and theatrical. The style is akin to Epic theatre but lacks many of Brecht's "alienation effects" for emphasizing the artifice of the play. Of course the chorus of anthropomorphic horses and the onstage audience in *Equus* do not fit into any traditional category of realism. These are more like features in a pagan ritual.

Understanding the style of a play is a matter of understanding the conventions the playwright assumed the audience would accept when the play was written or first performed. With a period play, these conventions follow accepted practice in the theatre of the time. Of course modern audiences do not necessarily share those expectations; so the problem is adapting the period practices to have a modern appeal. The fact that Shakespeare's theatre had no means to change the lighting does little to console a twentieth-century audience grown to expect elaborate lighting effects for a Shakespearean play. However, the use of chandeliers for a neoclassical play or footlights for a melodrama enhances the sense of period and creates an aura of artificiality which makes the apparent unnaturalness of the acting style more believable. The designer must therefore make a thorough study of changing conventions throughout the history of the theatre.

With modern plays, audiences accept a wide range of conventions as long as the production makes clear what to expect and remains consistently within the established framework. Even though a contemporary playwright may choose from a variety of styles, once the choice is made, stylistic unity is still important. Of course styles change and new styles develop, but even then the designer must understand the new rules and play the game accordingly. A major part of a good designer's preparation is complete familiarity with modern theatre practice.

Given Circumstances

When reading a new script, a lighting designer almost inevitably marks any references to lighting. This is the first step in the process of identifying the given circumstances of the play with respect to the light: historical period, season, time of day, location of setting, light sources, and any special effects called for by the script.

The script provides three sources for this information: direct references in the dialogue, stage directions, and circumstances implied but not directly stated in the dialogue. Of these three, the dialogue is the most compelling, unless we are prepared to change the words of the play. If a character refers to a beautifully moonlit night, about the only question left for the designer is "What kind of beautiful moonlit night would you like?"

Stage directions are another matter. Some directors make a practice of having stage directions marked out of a script before they begin to work, to enable taking a fresh approach to the production. Playwrights are generally unenthusiastic about this practice. As Thornton Wilder observed, there is always something of a struggle between the playwright and those artists involved in the production for control over a play. The best way for the playwright to retain maximum control is to embed all important elements in the dialogue.[5] Nevertheless, stage directions, when written by the playwright, give a valuable clue to the playwright's intentions and, at least at the script analysis stage, should be considered by the designer. Even the stage directions written for many acting editions, which are prepared on the basis of the initial commercial production, provide some insight into the creative collaboration between the playwright and the first production team.

The lack of specific mention of important given circumstances in either dialogue or stage directions does not necessarily imply carelessness. The circumstances may be clear by implication or the staging may have made them clear. Here the designer has to read closely and use a little imagination and common sense. Some plays provide very little explicit information. About all the script of *Oedipus Rex* tells us, for example, is that the play is set in front of Oedipus' palace and that some sort of altar is probably onstage. Even though the time line is strained by the fortuitous appearance of characters on cue, the events could happen in the course of a few hours. Beyond that, we are on our own. Other writers, particularly in the modern theatre, tell us explicitly what they have in mind.

A quick examination of Tennessee Williams' *The Glass Menagerie* demonstrates the importance of the given circumstances in a modern play. Tom, as narrator, tells the audience during his opening monologue that "being a memory play, it is dimly lighted, it is sentimental, it is not realistic."[6] In his initial stage direction, Williams describes the area around the Wingfield apartment at various times as "dark," "grim," "murky," and "sinister." We see the interior of the apartment as first through a scrim, and the dining room appears through transparent gauze portieres, both emphasizing a dreamlike quality, even though the downstage scrim rises out of sight during the first scene. We know from the dialogue that the characters are eating dinner, which establishes the approximate time of day.

During Amanda's first long reminiscence, a stage direction indicates that Tom calls for music and a spot of light on his mother. The scene ends with Amanda behind the portieres and "a shaft of very clear light is thrown on her face against the faded tapestry of the curtains." These are the first of several stage directions calling for spotlights to isolate a specific character. Williams comments further on this device in his "Program Notes," printed with the play:

The lighting in the play is not realistic. In keeping with the atmosphere of memory, the stage is dim. Shafts of light are focued on selected areas of actors, sometimes in contradistinction to what is the apparent center. For instance, in the quarrel scene between Tom and Amanda, in which Laura has no active part, the clearest pool of light is on her figure. This is also true of the supper scene, when her silent figure on the sofa should remain the visual center. The light upon Laura should be distinct from the others, having a peculiar pristine clarity such as light used in early religious portraits of female saints or madonnas. A certain correspondence to light in religious paintings, such as El Greco's, where the figures are radiant in atmosphere that is relatively dusky, could be effectively used throughout the play. (It will also permit a more effective use of the screen.) A free, imaginative use of light can be of enormous value in giving a mobile, plastic quality to plays of a more or less static nature.

The screen Williams mentions refers to stage directions which call for images and titles projected on a section of the living room wall, a device omitted in the original Broadway and most subsequent productions because it usually proved to be distracting and a redundant statement of values already apparent from the dialogue. These projections offer a good example of stage directions frequently ignored in productions.

The spotlights and projections suggest a production style closer to Epic theatre than realism. The lighting not only depicts the locale, it comments on the action. For example, during the argument between Tom and Amanda in scene three, Williams' stage direction calls for a "turgid smoky red glow," in the upstage area, a lighting quality which has no realistic justification but reflects Tom's memory of the event. Similarly the missing father's photograph lights up in the next scene to comment on Tom's search for a way out of Amanda's trap. At the beginning of scene five, Williams specifies that the "shadowy" lights in the upstage area "formalize" Tom and Amanda's movements, "almost as a dance or ritual, their moving forms as pale and silent as moths."

Williams' stage directions call for lighting of almost poetic evocativeness to communicate his attitudes toward the characters. In scene four, Amanda "stands rigidly facing the window on a gloomy gray vault of the areaway. Its light on her face with its aged but childish features is cruelly sharp, satirical as a Daumier print." As Amanda fits the new party dress on Laura in scene six, Williams observes that "a fragile, unearthly prettiness has come out in Laura: she is like a piece of translucent glass, touched by light, given a momentary radiance, not actual, not lasting." In the next scene, "The new floor lamp with its shade of rose-colored silk gives a soft, becoming light to her face, bringing out the fragile, unearthly prettiness which usually escapes attention."

Even on a more realistic level, Williams tries to carefully control the ambience of the lighting contributing to the mood of the play. As the play gathers its attention around Laura's visitor, the Gentleman Caller, Tom stands on the porch and sets a new tone: "On evenings in spring the windows and doors were open and the music came outdoors. Sometimes the lights were turned out except for a large glass sphere that hung from the ceiling. It would turn slowly about and filter the dusk with delicate rainbow colors." Later when Tom and Jim talk on the fire escape porch, Williams indicates that "the incandescent marquees and signs of the first-run movie houses light [Tom's] face from across the alley." Tom and Amanda plan for Jim's arrival while standing outside under "a little silver slipper of a moon." For the next scene, Williams calls for "a delicately lemony light" in the Wingfield apartment for a late spring evening which comes "scattering poems in the sky." Anticipating a device later used so effectively in *A Streetcar Named Desire*, "a colored paper lantern conceals the broken light fixture in the ceiling": Amanda, who has purchased a new rose-colored shade for the lamp, turns it on before announcing that the caller is Jim

O'Connor, and Laura soon turns it off as she retreats in terror from the notion of meeting Jim again.

Amanda realizes that "it isn't dark enough yet" for her to weave the appropriate spell around Laura but, by the time of dinner, a summer storm has come and there is a "deep blue dusk." After the storm, which reflects Laura's inner turmoil, the stage directions tell us that "the air outside becomes pale and luminous as the moon breaks out." The electric lighting in the house flickers off to set the conditions for the candlelight, so important to the mood of the famous scene between Jim and Laura. These candles are also the basis for Tom's final speech: "nowadays the world is lit by lightning! Blow out your candles, Laura—and so goodbye . . . (She blows the candles out)."

On a literal level, Williams handles the passage of time in an extremely fluid manner. The play not only alternates between narrative and dramatic sections but, within a scene, time slows or speeds as the narration requires. Scene four, for example, begins at five o'clock in the morning with the interior of the apartment dark and faint light illuminating the alley. After a few speeches between Tom and Laura, the lights dim out and reopen on early morning light and Amanda's call to "Rise and Shine." The entire play covers a time period from early spring to late summer, a passage of time more important for its symbolic statement than its direct bearing on events.

Williams' consciousness of the dramatic uses of lighting makes him a lighting designer's dream. The problem with his plays is not to discover a lighting image—he provides that—but to find means to translate his almost poetic images into a practical lighting plot. Some designers may even feel that Williams does too much of their work and restricts their artistic freedom, but the richness of his references to lighting reveals how much the lighting designer can glean from a close examination of the given circumstances in a script.

The lighting designer's analysis of these seven elements: structure, characterization, theme, symbol, mood, style, and given circumstances, completes the major examination of the script, but the text of the play for most production situations remains as a constant guide for the evolving production concept. As ideas develop and take concrete form, the lighting designer should always prepare to return to the script to test and retest the appropriateness of the lighting. Departures from the playwright's apparent intentions are justified under certain circumstances, but these should be understood as interpretive variations. At all costs, the designer must avoid lighting mistakes which result from misinterpretation, misunderstanding, or lack of close reading of the play. The designer's bible is not the book of filter samples, or the instrument inventory, or the lighting plot, but that same focus shared by everyone else involved in the production, the play itself. And when we come to control the actual performance of the lighting instruments, the script will also be the basis for the lighting score, the cued production.

11

The Designer's Approach: Analyzing Other Elements of Production

Developing a Lighting Concept

All participants in a production begin with a careful reading and analysis of the script; from this process evolves a production concept, a statement of the principles which guide the interpretation and staging of the script for the audience. The director is ultimately responsible for this concept, and in practice may provide it either orally or in written form at the first production meeting, or evolve it out of discussions with other members of the production team, or develop it with the cooperation of actors, playwright, and designers out of the rehearsal process, or—in the worst possible condition—never clearly formulate it. However, even in the latter case, the lighting designer must form a clear idea of the overall production approach, for from it must grow the more specific lighting concept which gov-

erns the general approach for lighting the production. We will now examine the process by which the lighting concept emerges from the production concept.

A major component in the procedure for developing a lighting design is *communication*. From the script analysis, the lighting designer develops ideas ultimately transformed into stage lighting, but the designer must master an intervening step and communicate these ideas to other members of the production team even before the lighting can be seen. The designer may sketch, draw, and demonstrate, but language, whether in written or oral form, inevitably enters the process. Even though the ultimate language with which the lighting designer communicates is light itself, a language that can never be fully translated into words, the designer who makes a close approximation will find the way more smoothly paved than the designer who has difficulty articulating ideas. This is more than a theoretical consideration. To enter the union of professional lighting designers, for example, the United Scenic Artists of America, an examination requiring a written lighting concept must be taken; more importantly, the lighting designer must constantly "sell" lighting ideas to directors and producers, who are not always adept at visualizing the final lighting from sketches or plots. Particularly when the lighting depends on a major financial investment —instrument rental, professional electricians, etc.—the designer's ability to describe what and why may make a big difference in whether or not the needed equipment will be provided. The designer

needs to develop communication skills just as surely as interpretative and technical skills.

The formulation of the production concept should cover all of the points raised in our discussion of script analysis, plus an explanation of the means to be used for interpreting and applying these ideas in the actual performance. As we have seen, in practice the director usually develops the production concept verbally—and it may be lengthy and detailed.

For the sake of illustrating how one may utilize quite different approaches with equal legitimacy for a single play, we will develop two abbreviated, contrasting production concepts for *Oedipus Rex*, each with its own lighting concept.

Oedipus Rex

Production Concept 1

Oedipus Rex is primarily a drama of religious ritual, confirming the belief that, no matter how inscrutable are the ways of the gods, humans can find lasting meaning and purpose for themselves only by accepting the place ordained for them in a divinely conceived order. In Periclean Athens the play affirmed religious law in an age of humanistic skepticism, and in many respects Oedipus' tragic flaw is the same heresy practiced by many audience members, both ancient and modern: the belief in an anthropocentric universe where human reason controls human fate. The progression in the attitude of the chorus from almost blind faith in Oedipus' power, through a phase of confusion and doubt, to a final recognition of human vulnerability at the hands of the gods provides a guide for the development of the audience's attitude as the play unfolds.

The first apparent major dramatic question, "Will Oedipus discover the murderer of Laius?" quickly transforms into the ques-

tion, "Can Oedipus escape his own fate?" However, because both ancient and modern audiences know the answers to these questions before the play begins, the real issue which holds audience attention is "How will Oedipus respond to the knowledge of his incest and patricide?" The play answers that Oedipus' suffering leads him to a deeper understanding of his dependence on the gods.

Even though Oedipus gains knowledge at the cost of great personal torment and attains his reward only in *Oedipus at Colonus*, Sophocles provides a major positive counterpoint to Oedipus' fall: the lifting of the plague. The suffering of the citizens of Thebes, due to the personal guilt of their ruler, emphasizes the interweaving of personal, social, and religious values, but ironically each step Oedipus takes closer to his personal doom is a step toward a more healthy Thebes. For everyone except members of the house of Labdacus, things are indeed better at the end of the play than at the beginning. The passing of the plague serves as a highly visible sign of the success of Oedipus' ritual of purification.

Just as the breaking of bread and serving of wine in many Christian churches reminds the congregation of Christ's sacrifice of body and blood in order to fulfill the conditions of the Covenant for imperfect man, so the spectacle of Oedipus' fall was a ritual reenacted for the audience of the Dionysian Festival to confirm their dependence on the power of the gods. Even though modern audiences no longer believe in the Olympian gods on any realistic level, they will respond to *Oedipus Rex* as a theatrical fantasy so long as the style of the production avoids any pretensions of realism. The production approach should be analogous to science-fiction fantasy, emphasizing the strangeness of the experience. Masks, costumes, lighting, dreamlike movement, intoned words, even some dialogue in the original Greek should evoke the feeling that the audience is watching a myth, a ritual action with metaphysical implications.

Without commenting on its validity, we can see that this approach takes an interpretation of the overall structure and theme of the play and develops a production method to communicate these ideas to an audience. Staging conventions from the ancient Greek theatre are not used for the sake of historical accuracy but to elicit a specific reaction from a modern audience. The production style does not necessarily violate the script, but it moves beyond textual questions to address the problem of making the play relevant for a contemporary audience.

After close analysis of the play and this production concept, a lighting designer might develop the following lighting concept:

Lighting Concept 1

This production of *Oedipus Rex* emphasizes the protagonist's progression from a seeming superman to a helpless victim of Apollo's power. Oedipus' fall and accompanying acquisition of the knowledge of his proper subordination to the gods causes the gradual lifting of the plague which torments Thebes. The audience should see the play as a mythical fantasy, a symbolic ritual of transformation from a humanistic to a theocentric world view.

Two lighting patterns are dominant in the play: the shift of light on Oedipus himself and the change of light around him to show the passing of the plague. At first low-angled lighting brilliantly lights Oedipus and makes him appear almost supernatural: bright, white back lights halo his body and bottom light from the altar makes his masked face appear powerful and threatening. As his composure begins to crack, the lighting breaks into clearly defined areas of light and shadow through which he moves. As he gradually learns the truth, the lighting becomes more uniform and shifts to higher angles. When he realizes fully what he has done, the stage is bright with strong top light on Oedipus, which shortens him and leaves him without a shadow in which to hide. When he reappears after his blinding, the lights warm noticeably, making him appear softer but more sympathetic.

Gloom dominates Thebes at the opening of the play. Only vague green and chocolate colors sickly illuminate the dimly perceived forms of the suppliants. The only apparent light is a dully greenish amber on the smoke of the altar fire. The light that breaks on the stage when Oedipus enters through the palace door almost blinds in contrast. As the truth of Laius' murder unfolds, shafts of light begin to form, and as the play progresses, shadows fill. By the end of the shepherd's scene, bright, "normal" sunlight bathes the stage, which during Oedipus' final scenes, glows warmly and ethereally.

In addition to this basic scheme, the lighting throughout the body of the play must be unusual enough to remove the play from simple reality. Choral odes particularly should stand apart from the episodes, with very theatrical lighting helping to illustrate specific stories told by the chorus or thematic points they make. As much variety as possible in angle, color, and diffusion allows the static masks to change appearance. The position of particular lighting effects must carefully correlate with actor movement and desired moods as if we were lighting for dance. In general the lighting should create a sense of mystery and magic where actions and characters seem strange and therefore suggest meaning beyond surface appearances.

The tempo of the production should mount to the scene with the Old Shepherd, but more rapid changes in lighting result from Oedipus moving through increasingly variegated lighting rather than from the fast execution of cues. Overall cue timing should maintain the stately tempo of ritual action. The feeling generated by lighting changes should never be hurried but, instead, a stately march toward an inevitable doom.

Despite no mention of specific instrumentation or individual cues, this lighting concept moves a step closer to the final design by outlining the broad approach that will govern the lighting plot. It contains the following essential information: the relationship of the lighting to major themes and symbols, the lighting style, the principles governing the overall pattern of change in the lighting, a statement of mood and tempo, and something about the general treatment of color and angle. The concept may undergo modification as production plans evolve, but it functions as a "working paper" for discussions among the lighting designer, the director, and other designers. The lighting designer may communicate the concept orally, but often the process of writing it forces clarity. Adherence to a clearly formulated lighting concept produces unity and purpose in the final design.

Certainly a director might take a radically different approach to a play like *Oedipus Rex*, and this could result in a lighting concept significantly dissimilar to the one presented above. Let us examine another case.

Production Concept 2

A modern audience only dimly appreciates whatever religious significance *Oedipus Rex* held for the original Greek audience. We associate Oedipus today more with Freud than Apollo. Setting aside the apparently unsolvable issue of determination versus free will, the major theme that we understand is how an apparently rational man can be destroyed by largely subconscious emotional impulses. The fratricide and incest that are committed before the play begins are but two of the more sensational impulses that rack Oedipus. Within the play we see a man weakened by paranoia, uncontrolled anger, and self-righteous pride used as a defense mechanism. For a twentieth-century audience, the operational fate in this play is psychological determinism.

With only minor upward reversals

caused by misconstruing information, Oedipus' disintegration dominates the structure of the play. The destruction of Jocasta merely foreshadows the fall of her husband/son. Sophocles virtually ignores the one possibility for any relief at the end of the play, the lifting of the plague. The chorus does not celebrate the salvation of Thebes but dwells on human vulnerability. Oedipus forsees the suffering of Antigone and Ismene, and the informed audience member knows that even the smug Creon will follow in Oedipus' footsteps. An abandoned, blind, groping Oedipus stumbles into the palace. The only consolation offered by the chorus is to "count no man fortunate until he is dead."

This play attracts us not because it is an ancient tale of a mythical king in a faraway land, but rather because we recognize something of ourselves in Oedipus. Similarly, the trappings of the ancient Greek theatre with its intoning, masked actors only distance us from the drama. This production will endeavor to make the characters as believable as the language of the play will allow. Unmasked actors will use realistic business to make the characters vivid. Rather than the formal, abstract facade associated with classical Greek theatre, this production will use the Mycenean citadel of archaic Thebes—recreated with as much detail as possible—to reinforce the impression that these are real people influenced by a real environment. We should feel the heat and see the dirt on the travelers' feet. Sophocles himself took a step toward greater realism when he made the chorus an assemblage of Theban elders. Each chorus member will have an individual personality. Odes will be divided into speeches for individual voices, a series of discussions, reflections, and observations by a group of old men.

Both our production concepts are based on efforts to make the play relevant for a modern audience, but the first emphasizes theatricality, fantasy, and ritual while the second stresses realism and believability. The first finds a much greater positive statement than the second, and each structures the audience's experience accordingly. What lighting concept would appropriately communicate the second production idea?

Lighting Concept 2

The production emphasizes the erosion of Oedipus' rationality by his subconscious emotional impulses, a personal catastrophe unrelieved by any final compensation. The performance intends to make Oedipus and Thebes as real and believable as possible for a modern audience. Consequently, changes in the realistic lighting environment should motivate any changes in stage lighting.

Within the rigid constraints of this realistically lighted exterior, the lighting design needs to provide visual variety over time, to indicate the decline in Oedipus' fortunes, and to create sufficiently diverse qualities of light to underscore differences in character and mood. The lighting design will emerge from two major premises: that the play takes place in a period of time from midafternoon to late dusk, and that the architectural features on- and offstage produce a wide variety in the brightness, angle, diffusion, and color of light.

In the first case, the gradual darkening of the stage underscores Oedipus' fall, an idea further reinforced by the blindness metaphor in the script. The oppressive heat of brilliantly hot Mediterranean light at the opening can both suggest the sterility of the plague and provide a bright beginning for Oedipus' high starting point. As Oedipus pursues his doom, the dark shadow of the palace facade marches relentlessly down the stage.

To variegate the stage space, parts of the stage are lit differently but all within a unified sense of place. A relatively high-angled wash of light with minimal modeling bathes the open downstage area. Assuming that the palace faces northeast, offstage structures cast broken shafts of shadow up-left. There are deep shadows upstage of the monolithic pillars in front of the palace facade, but the area downstage of the doorway picks up bounce light from the sandstone surface, resulting in a slightly warmer and more diffused light. Light inside the palace comes from torches which produce a smoky, flickering, amber glow when the doors open, particularly after shadows lengthen in front of the palace. The dully glowing altar fire centerstage also becomes more noticeable when shadows pass over it.

The chorus, Creon, and the Corinthian Messenger work mostly in the brighter downstage areas. Teiresias moves in and out of shadows cast by the pillars. Oedipus moves about the stage but primarily in the middle zone. Jocasta remains mostly near the door where the warmer colors and soft modeling emphasize the contours of her body. Back lighting from the palace reveals the human silhouette under the translucent robes worn by Jocasta and Oedipus, calling attention to the sensual bodies under the rational facades of these two characters.

Except for a slight change when the palace door opens, the audience should be unaware of specific shifts in the overall lighting; however, the light on characters will change as they move to different areas of the stage. The director and lighting designer must work together closely as blocking patterns develop.

Realism constrains the second lighting concept much more than the first, but the lighting still helps to shape audience response to the play and the characters. Where symbolism is used conspicuously in the first case, it is carefully tied to otherwise realistic lighting in the second example. The first concept requires an ambiguous response to the ending of the play but is generally much more upbeat than the second. A designer could develop other approaches from these production concepts and could certainly interpret the play in a number of other ways, but these examples illustrate how varying interpretations for a single play interrelate with different lighting concepts.

The development of the lighting concept forces the designer to justify the relationship between the lighting and the production approach. If a performance requires no more than unfiltered overhead floodlights, the designer should be able to explain why this method of lighting suits the production.

In formulating the lighting concept, the lighting designer also begins the process of relating the lighting to other aspects of the production. The lighting concepts above, for example, make suppositions about costumes, scenery, and blocking which require the agreement of other members of the production team. This synthesis between lighting and other production components requires continual revisions in the lighting concept as the production evolves.

ANALYZING OTHER PRODUCTION COMPONENTS

After studying the script and developing an initial lighting concept, the lighting designer turns to a close examination of other production components that influence or are influenced by the lighting, principally scenery, costumes, makeup, sound, and the movement of the performers. If the concern to this point has been to light the play, now we must apply the light to specific objects: scenery, fabric, and the performers' bodies. All of these elements except sound need light to be effective, and all, including sound, affect the way an audience sees the lighting. We will develop a method for analyzing each of these features of the production.

Scenery and Lighting

Professional lighting designers still belong to the United Scenic Artists of America, and only in the last few decades has lighting design clearly separated from the responsibilities of the scenic designer. Some believe this was an unfortunate division and have preempted the term "scenography" to describe an approach encompassing both scenic and lighting design. Certainly these two design areas depend heavily on one another and, even if one person does not undertake both in a production, the scenic and lighting designers must remain in close communication with one another.

The aesthetic precepts developed in earlier chapters on lighting composition supply the tools needed by the lighting designer to assay the lighting requirements of the setting. Without repetition then, we can survey the way these aesthetic considerations apply to lighting scenery and develop a checklist of points the lighting designer should consider when analyzing the scenic design:

color
brightness
surface
visual framework
size and proportion
grounding
part-whole relationships
structure
line
focus and balance
shape

positive-negative space
pattern
flow
gradation and tonal effects
movement and rhythm
harmony and disharmony
style
realistic detail

We will briefly examine each.

Color. Will the color of the scenery change noticeably under the lighting tints being considered and, if so, is this a tolerable change? Do wallpaper patterns or special painting techniques rely upon color differentiation that certain lighting tints might easily obscure? Will multiple reflections from painted surfaces accentuate certain colors in an objectionable way? Even if acting areas and scenery are lit with different tints, will bounce light from the floor influence the color of the scenery? Are there areas of color which the lighting could profitably "punch" or "depress"? Will the color of lights in one area such as a cyclorama noticeably exaggerate complementary colors in another area? Are there strong colors which might produce fatigue or afterimages unless the lighting varies sufficiently? Can changes in lighting tint appropriately modify the color of spattered surfaces (pointillism)? If the scenery changes, should lighting underscore color progressions or contrasts? Does the scenery establish color symbols which the lighting can reintroduce in other contexts? These are but a sample of the questions the lighting designer must ask regarding the use of color in the scene design.

Colored renderings or painter's elevations are close enough approximations of scenery coloring to justify preliminary experimentation with filter colors, but the actual pigments used on the scenery may be slightly different or behave differently under the same light; so the lighting designer should test actual paint samples whenever possible.

The color of light often becomes a bone of contention between the lighting designer and other designers. Of course the director can be the final arbiter, but a good, cooperative working relationship among designers avoids that necessity. The lighting designer should always avoid obscuring the work of any other designer.

Brightness. The lighting intensity suitable for a setting depends partly on reflective and tonal considerations to be discussed later, but it also relates to the question of how much of the setting the scenic designer wants the audience to see. Particularly with three-dimensional objects painted on a two-dimensional surface, or with forced perspective, high levels of illumination expose the artifice. Scene designers frequently treat areas around the perimeter of focus in a fairly sketchy fashion so details will not draw attention away from the focus. They are understandably upset when bright lighting discloses the bareness of these areas. Inversely, dim lighting can obscure painstakingly constructed details. A scene designer who knows that a scene will be lit at a low level or with heavy shadows can often save valuable time and money by eliminating needless embellishments, or knowing that bright lights will be used, the designer may wish to devote more attention to detail.

Surface. Lighting can influence the appearance of surface texture or reflectance. For example, a diffused, relatively low-angled front light enhances the effectiveness of scrumbling, spattering, or drybrush techniques for painting a surface to resemble stone, brick, stucco, or wood. Lights at acute angles to the surface may expose the lack of real three-dimensional detail or betray underlying irregularities in the flattage which belie the surface treatment. As an opposite consideration, textured paints, vacuform molds with highly detailed surfaces, carved rigid foam, and a variety of specialty facing materials introduced into stage use during recent decades offer relatively easy means for reproducing highly realistic three-dimensional textures which are best shown with specular light thrown from fairly sharp angles. Flat, diffused lighting would obscure the fine shadowing needed to emphasize the surface texture contrasts that contribute so much interest to these contemporary settings.

At one time stage paints universally consisted of dry pigments suspended in an animal glue binder; these paints had uniform, predictable reflective properties. The variety of paint vehicles used today possess a wide range of reflective characteristics. For example, many latex binders reflect a slightly larger percentage of lighting color as against surface color than did the old glue-based paints. Careful designers are more likely than before to use semi-gloss coatings where appropriate on marble surfaces, woodwork, or stage-constructed furniture. The growing use of diffusion filters is partially a response to a more "lively" stage picture with more reflective surfaces than before.

The Age of Plastic is also coming slowly to the theatre. Plexiglass, polyvinylchloride tubing, and mylar are but a few of the more common plastic materials in use. The Royal Shakespeare Company's production of *As You Like It* toured with plexiglass scenery, and *Cabaret* calls for a curtain of mylar streamers and a huge mylar mirror suspended over the stage. These and more traditional glass and polished metal surfaces make the lighting designer's task more complicated but, properly approached, they provide rich opportunities for specular effects. The lighting designer must consider the light reflected from surfaces as well as the light cast on the surface.

Visual Framework. What is the outer perimeter of the scenic space? Are the edges sharply defined or do they blend into the surroundings? We can no longer assume that a proscenium arch rigidly defines the playing space. When the Hilberry Theatre opened at Wayne State University with a production of *Antony and Cleopatra*, decorative elements were placed in the auditorium. These were technically part of the scenery. How should they be lit? Picture-frame realism often restricts the scenic area to a very specific space but, at the other extreme, environmental theatre intermixes performance and audience spaces. A whole range of variations exist between these poles, and the lighting design may need to change the scenic framework as the production progresses.

Even with a proscenium production, the scenic designer may make various assumptions about the relationship between the proscenium and the scenery. The proscenium may be a dark frame through which the audience sees a larger space. The scenic area may be considerably smaller than the frame with a vague zone of darkness between the two or with a smaller, clearly defined frame within the larger proscenium. The use of a false proscenium most graphically illustrates this latter case. A forestage or apron may allow the scenery to extend in front of the proscenium. The lighting designer should look at the edges of the scenic design. Where are they, and are they sharp or soft?

Size and Proportion. The treatment of the scenic framework to some extent controls the apparent size of the setting, but size also interrelates with proportion. Increasingly brighter lights on the tops of the palace walls which extend up out of sight in *Oedipus Rex* (Plate VI) make the walls tower and the human figures proportionately smaller. An interior setting without a ceiling and with walls shaded into blackness at the top stresses the horizontal dimension. Brighter lighting from or at the sides further stretches the width of the setting. A scene with clearly differentiated zones of lighting from down- to upstage, particularly if the lights become cooler upstage, appears deeper than if lit uniformly. A scenic design with a "layered" look—for example, a large entryway behind center-stage arches with a large window on the upstage wall re-

vealing a garden, behind which trees can be seen—requires distinct lighting differences for each layer to separate the planes and stress the depth of the composition.

Grounding. Because most stage lighting comes from overhead, the lighting tends to accumulate near the floor, strongly grounding most settings. However, the amount of floor seen by the audience and the treatment of the floor by the designer greatly influence the lighting design. When the audience sits at or below the level of the stage floor, a relatively small amount of brightness near the top of vertical walls can pull the eye up and create distraction. When the auditorium rakes steeply above the stage floor, lighting on the floor itself may generate disturbing glare or make patterns which distract by contradicting patterns in the scenic designer's floor treatment. Only dance productions or plays with open wings allow low-angled side lighting that make possible separate lighting of performers and floor. Otherwise, the lighting designer must carefully watch the floor for unwanted patterns of brightness.

Scenic designs may have cantilevered platforms or other elevated playing areas which need to "float" off of the ground, in which case lights from low angles and lights sharply framed to the playing area can make the stage floor seem to disappear, particularly with high contrast between the lighted and unlighted portions of the stage. Flashbacks, dream or memory scenes, and portions of the setting with symbolic significance frequently profit from this "floating effect."

Part-Whole Relationships. The scenic designer does not necessarily want the audience to see the setting in its entirety at all times. A multiple setting may depict several different locations within a single unit stage, depending on the lighting to frame the specific portion in use at any given moment. Even a somewhat more realistic setting with multiple rooms or playing areas, such as that required for *A Streetcar Named Desire*, may require focus on action within one or more specific portions of the setting while lighting deemphasizes other areas. The designer must make decisions regarding the visual framework of these smaller portions of the setting. In addition, the lighting may indicate the relationship of the part to the whole or of the parts to one another. For example, the restaurant scene in *Death of A Salesman* may require the rest of the setting to virtually disappear, but when Stanley calls for Stella in *A Streetcar Named Desire,* the lights focus strongly on the staircase but the remainder of the setting stays dimly lit. When Blanche and Mitch are on the landing in the following beat, how much of the bedroom where Stella and Stanley are making love should remain in view?

As we saw when we discussed lighting composition, the way lights shift from one portion of a multiple setting to another helps to define relationships. Lights closing down on one section imply inclusion, overlapping fades suggest juxtaposition, and an intervening beat of darkness between a fade and lights coming up on another area connotes separation.

The lighting designer should also determine important relationships between different settings presented with complete scene shifts. Are these two rooms in the same house, another place at the same time, or the same place years later, for example? The audience will confuse scenic relationships unless they are reinforced with similar relationships in the lighting.

Structure. The lighting designer should look for structural features which give the setting character or help to define space and should guarantee that the lighting properly interprets the form of these elements. For example, the wrought-iron work and louvred shutters give the scenery for *A Streetcar Named Desire* much of its New Orleans flavor, but both effects lose their impact without subtle back lighting to accentuate the forms. The columns for the *Oedipus Rex* setting in Plate VI generate most of the visual interest for an otherwise plain facade if sufficient figure/ground differentiation in the lighting prevents the columns from blending into the background. In general, the lighting should be different on each plane when surfaces meet at an angle or when surfaces are layered. Shadowing usually does this naturally except when the axis of the prevailing lights intersects the angle made by meeting surfaces and thus lights them equally or when the axis is perpendicular to receding layered planes. Distinct patterns in the lighting which do not conform to changes in architectural form also confuse the perception of structure. A strong gobo pattern may completely obliterate the structural form of the scenery.

Occasionally large unbroken surfaces in the scenery need variegation in the lighting to break the monotony, or an extremely "busy" scenic background distracts from foreground action unless the lighting blends and "calms" the background. In theory the scenic designer should eliminate these problems by modifications in the design during the planning stages, but in practice the lighting designer must be ready to come to the rescue when unanticipated problems arise.

Line. Does the setting contain important linear features which the lighting should emphasize? For example, Joe Mielziner's setting for *Cat on a Hot Tin Roof* (Figure 6-2) and *Death of a Salesman* (Figure 6-3) or Robert Edmond Jones' design for *Swords* (Figure 7-1) depend strongly on linear elements for their effectiveness. Sufficient figure/ ground differentiation or highlighting is required to call appropriate attention to these design elements.

A lighting designer must be aware of more than components that are conspicuously linear. Compositional unity and flow often depend on the edges of more massive forms, which can be highlighted. The central elliptical shape in the *Winterset* design (Figure 6-15) and the repeated obtuse angles in the setting for *Cat on a Hot Tin Roof* (Figure 6-2) depend on lighting which stresses the edges of large masses.

Focus and Balance. The lighting designer must locate the center of balance for the setting, including elements which balance one another and any additional focus caused by the scenic arrangement. Particularly when a single setting remains onstage for a long time, the use of lighting to shift the apparent balance and focus may provide needed variety. Such settings may be designed intentionally without a dominant center of balance to allow the dynamics of the scenery to vary as the lighting and blocking change. Even when the scene has a strong structural focus, interesting tensions may result when the lights generate a conflicting center of balance.

Symmetrically balanced settings, particularly when linked with a very formal acting style such as that used for neoclassical plays, may demand similar symmetry in the lighting design. In contrast, very dynamic settings with asymmetrical balance or an off-center point of balance encourage similar treatment of the lighting. Also by unduly stressing or deemphasizing one component in the setting, the lighting designer may inadvertently upset balancing features. The lighting designer should think of the setting as an elastic form, changing shape under light, with shifting focus and balance, but not to the extent of abusing the intentions of the scenic design.

Shape. The perception of shape depends on a combination of factors, principally line or contour, color, and figure/ground distinctions, but the scenic designer works with shapes on a variety of levels: the shape created by the vertical mass of the scenery, the shape of the floor space defined by walls, the shape of individual architectural forms, the shape of furniture or decorative elements. To the extent that lighting emphasizes silhouette and models form, it accentuates shape. Lighting gives shape but also takes it away and changes it. Projections can even create shapes which are independent from the scenery. The ability of light to mold shape and change it over time is a tremendous asset in the theatre but requires careful control. Good lighting reveals the setting rather than obscures it.

A good exercise for discovering the important shapes in a scenic design is to lay tracing paper over the design and outline the major shapes, using one color for three-dimensional forms, another color for two-dimensional surfaces. Changes in lighting angle will change the appearance of the three-dimensional forms but generally the two-dimensional surfaces will change only by being partially lit or by having patterns of color projected on them. Shapes that unify the setting, shapes that repeat themselves, or unusual shapes should be preserved or enhanced for at least a good portion of the performance. If this analysis reveals a lack of interesting or varied shapes, then the lighting designer may have more justification for using light to reshape the design. A large, flat, uninteresting surface invites projections, but a rich, interesting interplay of architectural shapes deserves to be set off with light which best enhances the architectural form.

Positive and Negative Space. Does the setting contain importantly shaped negative space which the lighting should accentuate? Look again at the design for *Winterset* (Figure 6-16) and *Hamlet* (Figure 4-5) and imagine how much less effective they would be without the clearly defined central openings. Be particularly aware of negative space when the setting contains large openings, when large areas of the cyclorama or sky drops are visible, or when freestanding units are placed against full-stage black drapes.

The overall appearance of the setting will drastically change if the contrast between postive and negative space changes. Darkening the central opening in Jones' *Hamlet* setting will severely close the stage area; brightening the sky cyc in his design for *Othello* (Figure 6-12) will deemphasize the contour of the wall and open the stage space.

Pattern. Lighting can stress pattern (by consistently illuminating all repeated elements and by accentuating the figure against the background) or it can obscure pattern (by disrupting the consistency, by minimizing the figure/ground contrast, or by imposing another pattern within the lighting itself). Patterns may occur on a small scale such as wallpaper, where lighting tints can either pull out specific colors to exaggerate the pattern or suppress differences of color to obscure it (Figure 11-1). The scenic designer may create larger-scaled patterns by repeating major scenic forms (Figure 7-4). The lights may also enlarge upon vaguely suggested patterns in the scenery by projecting shapes which repeat scenic shapes (Figure 8-2).

Patterning may be a source of unity in a design, but strong patterns demand considerable audience attention and may distract from the action or become monotonous. The lighting designer has the ability to change the effect of the pattern over time and should carefully consider the implications of such a change.

Flow. In analyzing a scenic design, the lighting designer should consider flow on two levels. On one level, the design may have its own flow pattern, an arrangement of lines or shapes which draws the eye in a specific direction (Figure 6-9). This can contribute greatly to the rhythm, mood, and harmony of the design and calls for lighting that both follows the flow and emphasizes scenic elements which establish the flow. However, as with pattern, a rigid, compelling flow may become distracting or compete with action outside of the main current of eye movement, in which case, the lighting design can provide needed variation.

On the second level, the scenic designer often assumes a specific flow of light, which may even be included in the scenic rendering. In other words, the design incorporates light coming from a specific direction. This may be only a suggestion of how the setting will look at a specific moment in the play, but the lighting designer should carefully consider how integral this lighting is to the entire appearance of the setting and discuss with the scenic designer how the appearance of the setting will change with a different flow in the lighting.

When a setting contains faked three-dimensional decorative features, such as molding painted on a flat surface, the chiaroscuro effect assumes light flowing from a specific direction. If the real lighting fails to follow this flow, the painted details may look wrong. When the eye confronts contradictory stimuli, it chooses the more "real" of the two. Even three-dimensional designs for cornice and picture molding, for example, anticipate bottom lighting and look quite different when lit from above (Figure 11-2). Bas-relief sculpture, which has become much more practicable on stage with the introduction of easily carved rigid foams and inexpensive, light-weight plastic molds, is notoriously dependent on directional lighting, and the design may be incomprehensible if lit straight on or at an inappropriate angle. The same principle may hold true on a larger scale for an entire wall containing a large quantity of low-relief detail work.

Gradation and Tonal Effects. As we have discussed, the range of brightness available in pigment is very limited, about one to thirty, and the scenic designer can only hope, using pigment alone, to obtain about ten distinct shades of grey or steps in the brightness of a given hue. Lighting can considerably extend this range. A rendering may therefore be only an approximation of the tonal range which the scenic designer envisions. The designer may wish skies much brighter and shadows much blacker

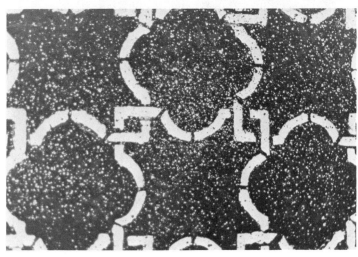

FIGURE 11-1 Different-colored lights on wallpaper patterns radically change their appearance by emphasizing and suppressing various components within the pattern. All three figures show the same pattern: (top) in white light; (middle) in red light; (bottom) in blue light.

FIGURE 11-2 The appearance of mouldings changes drastically depending on the angle of light striking them. The illustration on the left is lit from the top. The illustration on the right is lit from the bottom.

than indicated, or a much more gradual transition between lighter and darker areas. However, for a scenic designer who thinks of a rendering as a literal picture of the setting, the extension of the tonal range with lighting may come as a shock. Again, careful communication between the scenic and lighting designer helps to prevent misunderstandings. Confronted with a rendering such as Gordon Craig's design for *Macbeth* (Figure 6-9), the lighting designer might assume that the relative lack of tonal range results from the limitations of the charcoal medium and may therefore push the range, but the scenic designer might view the overall greying as an essential element—leading to unhappy surprises for both.

The lighting design can also destroy tonal effects obtained in painting the setting by brightly illuminating darker hues or by placing lighter hues in shadow. This may produce needed variety at times, but the lighting designer should be aware of the tonal properties of the scenic design. A useful exercise in analyzing a design's tonal aspects is to take the same overlay used in evaluating shape and number the major tonal shades from one to ten with the brighter shades as the smaller numbers. This calls attention to gradations which may partially govern illumination levels.

Movement and Rhythm. What features of pattern, line, and shape cause a rhythmic movement of the eye over a stationary setting? For example, the progression in size and the spacing of the screen in Gordon Craig's designs in Figures 6-4 and 6-8 establish a definite visual rhythm which the lighting could drastically change by brightening random panels, by obscuring the shape of panels or the spacing between panels, or by imposing an independent rhythm with differently spaced pools of light or different beam angles. The tight curves of Ludwig Sievert's design for *Don Juan* (Figure 7-3) give that setting its sense of elegant tension and pull the eye into a central vortex. Lighting which deemphasized the curves would destroy the rhythmic effect.

A scenic designer can also create rhythm with the actual movement of scenery or the sequence of settings in a play with more than one scene. The rapid shift of wings and drops for a period style Restoration comedy, the smooth interweaving of wagons and flown units in a musical comedy, or the ponderous motion of seemingly massive walls in a historical melodrama contribute to the tempo unique to each style of production and suggest sympathetic rhythms for lighting changes. When examining a series of settings for one play, the lighting designer should look for repeated features which link the sequence and for distinct progressions and contrasts. For instance, a scenic design for a multiset farce might suggest the growing tension and disorder by beginning with smooth flowing lines, moderately large masses, and symmetrical balance for the opening scene and by then using progressively shorter, more tenuous lines, small, overlapping shapes, and increased asymmetry for subsequent scenes. The lighting should both stress these changing elements in the scenic design and follow the overall pattern with the treatment of the lighting itself. A strong, unidirectional key light in the opening scene could gradually shift in following scenes to multidirectional, variegated, broken pools of light.

Harmony and Disharmony. The use of rhythm in a scenic design relates to the interplay of harmony and disharmony. Harmony results from a complex mix: repetition of design elements on any level; the establishment of a broad visual framework on some level such as color, shape, or line,

which consistently encompasses more varied features; or resonance of different design elements which somehow complement, reflect, or reinforce one another. To the extent that drama deals with conflict, harmony, once established, is often intentionally disrupted to underscore dramatic tension. The lighting designer's analysis of the scenic design should aim at discovering the sources of harmony, in order to preserve them when appropriate or disrupt them where justified, and at identifying the bases for disharmony which should be stressed when the production demands. For example, the broken archway which looms over the center of the setting for *A Streetcar Named Desire* in Plate VII is vaguely incongruous with the rest of the architecture. It seems conspicuously unsupported and incomplete and thrusts obtrusively beyond the scenic facade below it. Early in the play, the arch remains indistinct in the overhead shadows, but as Blanche becomes more threatened, lighting could gradually emphasize the arch, reinforcing the feeling that Blanche's environment has become more hostile to her. The scenic designer includes the arch as an element of disharmony to be stressed at the appropriate moment in the play.

Style. What is the scenic style and what style of lighting will be consistent with it? The issues involved here have been discussed at length in Chapters 8 and 9.

Realistic Detail. Does the scenic design assume a particular historical period, time of day or season, or specific sources of light? A baroque interior with chandeliers and candelabra demands a specific lighting ambience. A desert scene, a bleak landscape of leafless trees, or a jungle presuppose different lighting qualities. A range of lighting effects is possible for each of these settings, but a sense of appropriateness limits the range.

Which doors and windows admit light? Where are lighting fixtures? How is the setting oriented toward the compass? Where is the sun or moon? Does a fire burn in the fireplace? The lighting demands incorporated in a design such as Robert Edmond Jones' setting for *The House of Women* (Figure 7-2) must be met by the lighting designer. Jones shows a specific moment in the play, but doors, windows, the fireplace, and candelabra suggest all kinds of possibilities for other moments. The purpose of this search for sources is partly to assure consistency between the scenic and lighting illusion but also to discover lighting possibilities. If the opportunities appear limited, the lighting designer should discuss with the scenic designer the feasibility of adding windows or lighting fixtures.

In summary, a good analysis of the scenic design means examining the setting in terms of most of the principles used for lighting design. The objective is to understand how the scenic design works in order to respect the design intentions, to discover ways that lighting can enhance or appropriately change the appearance of the scene, and to find opportunities which the setting offers for interesting lighting. Remember that the lighting design depends on something to catch the light. The surfaces, shapes, textures, colors, and compositions provided by the scenic designer determine much of what will be possible with the lighting design.

Above all, remain in close communication with the scenic designer throughout the design and execution process so that the final product represents a true synthesis of the best creativity of two artistic specialists.

Costumes and Lighting

The costume designer employs the same design principles as the scenic and lighting designers, but applies them to a different medium and works on a somewhat smaller scale. This smaller scale means the lighting can make fewer differentiations within the design of a single costume than can be made within a setting. It is seldom possible, for example, to differentiate lighting on a skirt from that on a bodice, or to change lighting on one part of a costume without a similar change on another part. In other words, we have to consider the effects of lighting on the costume as a whole.

Costume design consists not of a series of unrelated single costumes, but rather of a composition of costumes combined in space and over the length of the production. In this respect, costumes are like moving scenery and subject to variations in the overall composition of the lighting.

Costume designs deserve the same careful analysis given scenic designs but, rather than repeat every category again, we will examine just four aspects of costumes, ones which depend heavily on variations in lighting design: color, brightness, texture, and modeling.

Color. Because of the assortment of fabrics and dyes used for costumes, color shifts under different lighting tints are hard to predict without testing the effects of various filter colors on the fabric. Where scenery tends to use the same pigment for the same colors throughout, with opaque paints little affected by differences in the underlying material, different costume fabrics of apparently the same color under one light appear a different color under another tint. *Metamerism,* as this is called, considerably complicates filter selection for lighting costumes.

Synthetic dyes occasionally respond to a very narrow portion of the spectrum. This creates no difficulty with full spectrum light, but some filter colors may block virtually all of the light in those wavelengths reflected by the dye. When a desired lighting tint seems to suppress a fabric color, the designer can often obtain the same tint by mixing different colored lights which together improve the appearance of the costume. The eye perceives the same overall tint, but in fact, the light contains a fuller portion of the spectrum which better covers that portion reflected by the fabric.

Some fabrics, particularly satins and a few piles, reflect one color at one angle and another color at another angle. This effect gives the fabric a vibrancy and can be very interesting, but will not work unless both colors are present in the lighting. Many fabrics contain very elaborately colored patterns which change radically in appearance when the light color changes. This can generate interesting variety, but unless carefully controlled, it can be distracting and destroy the appearance of an otherwise attractive pattern. A few synthetic dyes will even fluoresce in response to light of certain wavelengths. This may go unnoticed in full spectrum light, but becomes quite conspicuous when the lighting tint narrows to the wavelengths that produce the fluorescence.

Even when the lighting composition remains unchanged, performers in colored costumes can move through differently tinted areas of light. The resulting changes in the color of the costumes do not always conform to the changes the eye anticipates on the basis of the color of the ambient light. This effect can be interesting or distracting, depending on the circumstances. Generally such effects are better suited for dance or other forms where the attention of the audience is more on the appearance of the performer or on the spectacle rather than on the content of the dialogue.

Costume designers commonly express connections between characters with color relationships. Widely divergent light colors in different areas of the stage can destroy these interconnections since, as characters appear in different areas, the related costume colors change. In general, the lighting designer should pay particular attention to the way lighting influences costume color whenever using highly saturated lighting hues or extreme color variegation.

The color of surrounding scenery greatly affects the color of the costumes. Bounce light from colored surfaces or color contrast can accentuate costume color, and color fatigue or similarity between costume color and background hues can dampen the color of the costume. The lighting design can often eliminate problems by slightly changing background colors to accentuate contrast, by using back lights to separate the costumed performer from the background, by lowering the intensity of the surrounding light in contrast to the light on the performer, or by preceding the appearance of the costume with lights of complementary tint which increase the sensitivity of the audience's eyes to the costume color.

Pervading hues in the lighting tints, particularly washes of red, amber, or blue used for sunlight or night effects, can suppress costume colors. Not only are large portions of the spectrum missing from these washes, but color fatigue and lack of contrast produce insensitivity to the colors that are visible. The lighting designer should be particularly wary of what these washes do to costume color and whenever possible use a separate full spectrum light on the performer.

The costume designer should also accept responsibility for being aware of the way lighting color influences costume color. A few costume designers seem to assume that the lighting will always be full spectrum, and they express dismay when saturated hues are used. As with any production aspect, close communication between the costume and lighting designers early in the production process and throughout rehearsals helps to prevent these "surprises."

Brightness. Not all costumes are constructed with the same attention to detail. The closeness of the audience and the relative lack of scenic background in arena staging may place emphasis on refinements in costuming; such detail would be wasted effort in a dimly lit proscenium production of the Fruma-Sara scene in *Fiddler on the Roof*. However, nothing frustrates a costume designer faster than having spent hours developing a costume with elaborate details which become invisible under dim lighting. An equally frustrated lighting designer is one who creates a subtly mellow lighting atmosphere suddenly disrupted by a troupe of actors in white shirts and spangles. Slight differences in shades of black may be apparent under bright lights and disappear with lower levels, or a color which appears soft in midintensity, diffused lighting glares garishly in bright, specular lighting. Obviously, the effect of lighting intensity on costumes should be discussed early in the design process.

Texture and Modeling. The black-on-black costumes mentioned above were in fact used for a recent production of *Richard III* by The Virginia Shakespeare Festival. The interplay of black satins, velvets, and brocades was interesting when properly lit. Costumers frequently use contrasting textures, either of the same or different hues, to create design variety. The perception of the variations in texture depends on light at a sufficiently high angle to reveal surface texture. Different degrees of absorption may be apparent with flat front lighting, but textures lose their full richness.

Modeling light is important to costumes for other reasons. Even though costume designers may speak in terms of silhouette, they realize that costume design is a three-dimensional art form. The folds, drapes, layers, highlights, and shadows give the costume its feeling of plasticity and require modeling light. The more the costume conforms to or reveals the contours of the body beneath, the more important modeling becomes. Unfamiliar lighting angles can distort the appearance of a costume just as readily as they distort the face or body.

The costume designer also wants to control the degree of opaqueness in a fabric. A translucent material may be used because of its color, texture, or drape, or perhaps simply because of its low cost, and back lighting which exposes its flimsiness may be inappropriate. In other cases, our ability to see through one layer of fabric to another, the silhouette of the body seen under a translucent material, or the actual appearance of the body through a thinly veiling material

may be essential to the design concept and require careful lighting control. For example, the idea of symbolizing the human weaknesses of Oedipus and Jocasta early in *Oedipus Rex* by seeing the bodies of the actors under diaphanous royal robes will work only with strong back lighting that accentuates the transluscence of the fabric (Figure 11-3); otherwise, the robes appear opaque.

Makeup and Lighting

Color, brightness, and modeling are also the principal factors in makeup design influenced by the lighting.

Color. Although mascara and lining colors come in a variety of hues, base colors, which predominate, are primarily tinted red or orange. Any red shift which accompanies lights operated at significantly less than full wattage may accentuate the warm hues in the makeup base. A lighting designer who sets filter tints, particularly with heavy reliance on ambers, without considering makeup color may be in for a shock when actors appear onstage in makeup and appear unnaturally yellow. A change to predominantly red-based makeup colors will help somewhat, but the range of corrective colors available to the makeup artist is considerably more limited than the choice of filter tints.

Most makeup bases are translucent; the color of the actor's skin blends with the makeup color, and there are wide differences in skin coloration. Many makeup designers correct for these differences, but metamerism again complicates matters. Makeup colors which match under one lighting tint may appear different under another. Examining makeup colors by themselves under light will not always reveal these differences; so unless the lighting designer is prepared to pull every performer into the lighting lab to test colors, the designer will have to wait until dress rehearsals, watch for these unnatural shifts in skin color, and then make necessary adjustments.

FIGURE 11-3   On the left, strong back lighting makes Oedipus' robes almost transparent as he first enters. On the right, a higher lighting angle a few moments later emphasizes his flowing cape. [Production by the College of William and Mary. Christopher J. Boll, lighting designer.]

The differences in makeup on the natural skin and on a latex prosthesis can also create difficulties. The blend of colors may be quite successful under dressing room lights and then break down under stage lighting. Differences in the texture and reflective properties of skin and latex accentuate this problem. Using filter colors in dressing room lights may help the makeup artists deal with these complexities, but rarely does the stage lighting tint remain consistent enough or dressing room lights controlled enough to make this any more than a vague approximation of stage-lighting conditions.

Because of dominant warm tones in skin colors, certain lighting tints give the face a deathly pallor, particularly greens and deep blues. Unless this appearance is desired, compensating warm key lights on the performers themselves should be used when these colors light the general stage space. Black skin contains a rich array of warm col-ors, but often appears ashen under some lemony tints.

The lighting designer must also consider hair color. We have already noted how the baby spotlight was invented because of the unnatural appearance of Mrs. Leslie Carter's red hair under the spotlights used in the early decades of the twentieth century. This is perhaps an extreme example, but it demonstrates the responsiveness of hair color to lighting tints. Strongly differentiated colors in down lighting can cause major changes in hair color or produce coloration quite different from that created by a separate tint in the front lighting. Strong tints in the back lights may produce a colored halo effect, particularly for blonde or white hair.

Makeup sometimes entails highly stylized effects: masklike painting such as that used for many forms of oriental theatre, actual masks, metallic or fluorescent bases or liners, sequins, or deeply hued base colors. The interplay with lighting color becomes even more important in these instances.

The effect of lighting color on makeup often helps with characterization. Not only will Count Dracula's pale face appear more macabre in green light or Falstaff's ruddy complexion seem even more sanguine in a rosy hue, but changes in lighting tints can alter the color of makeup to show character changes. A few actors can blush or pale on cue but most need help. Good acting or the imagination of the audience may create the illusion of reality for lines like "Why, you're blushing, Charles!" or "Mrs. Brown, you look absolutely faint," but a subtle shift in makeup color as a result of a gradual lighting change can make the performer's face redden or pale. Slow shifts in modeling and coloration can change facial mood over a longer period of time.

Brightness. Some skin colors absorb more light than others. An audience may have difficulty seeing facial lines on a black actor sharing an area of light with an adequately illuminated white actor. Sometimes better modeling rather than brighter lights will solve this problem or a different lighting tint may reflect more light, but at other times separate lighting on each actor or brighter lights may be necessary.

To convincingly transform a young face to a wizened old face using only highlighting and shadowing requires extreme skill and careful control of brightness and modeling. Lighting that is too dim obscures the chiaroscuro and muddies the entire effect. Extremely bright lighting narrows the difference between highlight and shadows and exposes the artifice. Particularly in college theatre where makeup is extensively used for aging and extreme characterization, lack of brightness control may destroy the good work of the makeup artist.

That makeup corrects for the effect of bright lights is one of the commonplaces of the theatre, probably dating from the time of the unmerciful flat front glare of the limelight and replacing the earlier use of pale bases to compensate for dim lighting. More careful control of intensity and the use of modeling light in today's theatre eliminates the need for heavy toning and modeling in the makeup. However, the general level of illumination does affect the appearance of the face, and knowing the brightness of the lighting influences the makeup designer's plans. Extremely bright lights reflect from the face, lighten skin tones, and expose skin blemishes. Makeup corrections for bright lights may look inappropriate for less intense illumination. The lighting and makeup designers must check signals.

Modeling. Makeup that uses highlighting and shadowing basically employs a chiaroscuro technique for the face's three-dimensional form, either accentuating existing contours or creating the impression of nonexisting features by recreating the tonal gradations that would be present if the features were really there. This technique presupposes key lighting coming from an angle approximately 45° from the horizon, and most stage lighting comforms to this pattern. Even footlights, properly used, provide low-angled fill light without destroying the overhead key light. If the design relies heavily on low side key lights, such as much dance lighting or late afternoon natural light in a play, forewarn the makeup designer not to rely so heavily on chiarscuro and to use prosthetic techniques if the production needs extreme alterations in facial appearance.

Built-up foam or latex pieces applied to the face also require modeling light, but they respond more realistically to a variety of key angles. Diffused front lighting can destroy the effect of time-consuming techniques used to wrinkle a young actor's skin for believable aging. One minor problem the lighting designer should bear in mind is that with repeated use, the boundary between a latex makeup piece and the actor's face becomes increasingly difficult to blend and may be noticeable under high-angled lighting. For example, strong top lighting exposes the line at the edge of a fake bald head.

Lighting designers should not make the mistake of ignoring makeup design when planning the lighting. More than anything, the audience judges what it sees on the basis of the visibility of the actor's face. Even when everything else is well lit, if misunderstanding between makeup and lighting design results in a poor appearance of the performer's face, the audience will notice it faster than anything else.

Sound and Lighting

The interdependence of lighting and other areas of visual design is inevitable. Whether intended or not, they will influence one another. The connection between sound and lighting is more subtle and therefore more easily overlooked, but potentialy of equal importance. The success of well-designed light shows for popular music or the extremely effective European *Son et Lumière* productions demonstrate the opportunity for creative fusion of sound and light.

The more conspicuously a production utilizes sound, the greater its influence on the lighting. Rock concerts, opera, dance, and musicals require special attention in this respect, but even sound effects in straight plays make special demands on the lighting. Nonmusical as well as musical sound merits consideration. A train whistle, breaking glass, or a slammed door may cue a lighting change just as effectively as a transition in the music. The distinction between musical and nonmusical sound is not always clear, particularly in modern works, but the musical sound usually has a structure.

An audience always posits a relationship between juxtaposed changes in lighting and sound, even if the connection is unplanned. You can demonstrate this by designing a brief light "show," with a variety of color, angle, and tempo changes in the lighting on

a three-dimensional stage structure. The lighting board operator should control cues with a stopwatch unless a computerized control system is available that can duplicate complex cues with different time profiles. The point is to replay the "show" with as little variation as possible. Accompany each "run" with different recorded music, using as much variety in tempo and mood as possible. Similar patterns in the lighting and the music create interesting resonances between the two, but even the tension and dissonance produced by unmatched lighting and music has a fascinating appeal. This "indeterminacy" underlay multimedia productions involving the composer John Cage, in which music, light, and dance developed somewhat independent progressions with random interconnections.

Occasionally such disharmony between lighting and sound generates the correct dramatic tension for a specific moment in a play, but generally the lighting designer looks for parallels between lights and sounds, ways of underscoring music with lights or ways of using sound changes to motivate lighting changes. Random juxtapositions are tolerable only without a specific agenda for audience response. In a normal production situation, the lighting and sound together work with other elements of the performance to evoke a particular audience reaction.

In most circumstances, the use of music in a production implies a performance style which frees the lighting from strict adherence to realism and allows it to respond to changes in the musical composition. With ballet or modern dance, the music itself rather than any "situation" motivates most of the movement and can therefore motivate lighting changes as well. Even when the dramatic action of a musical or opera is handled with a relatively high degree of realism, the arias or songs usually stand somewhat apart stylistically, and changes in lighting legitimately underscore major shifts in the mood of the music. In fact, the need to set a song apart from the main action may absolutely mandate a noticeable lighting change. Turning on spotlights blatantly "frames" songs, but without some conspicuous "hype" in the lighting, a performer may have difficulty "selling" a song. Elaborate lighting for rock concerts developed precisely because singers realize how much lighting contributes to the excitement of the occasion and reinforces the impact of the music. Stimulating lighting effects can even make a mediocre song seem good.

When analyzing the music for a production, the lighting designer looks primarily at structure and mood. Lighting cannot respond to note by note differences without becoming distracting or redundant; so the important shifts are noticeable alterations in major features of the music. Like drama and stage lighting, music is a time art which creates texture and interest through changes during the course of the composition. Important modifications in rhythm and tempo, key, dominant pitch, volume, or instrumentation usually signal structural divisions. When lighting dance, any structural feature, no matter how mechanical, will likely influence the movement and therefore have some effect on the lighting, but otherwise we are most interested in musical changes which alter mood.

With the exception of Brecht's Epic theatre, lighting usually tries to reinforce the mood of the music by finding a lighting stimulus that produces a response analogous to the one evoked by the music. The vast majority of songs used in musical theatre build in emotional intensity and require a similar lighting build—increasing intensity, saturation, or movement. Changes frequently come between stanzas of a song but are also appropriate on a vocal swell, a change in tempo, the introduction of additional voices or instruments, or a dance interlude in the song.

Many songs follow familiar patterns, suggesting certain lighting approaches. Characters often "step out" of an action to reveal inner thoughts in song, leaving the main action either frozen or continuing in a low

key. Lighting focus jumps to the singer, and the remainder of the scene either dims or changes to a contrasting color, sometimes with a secondary focus on another character who may be the "object" of the song. Duets, trios, or even quartets may be sung with each character supposedly in a different place, separated in discreet pools of light or by radically different lighting on each character. Characters from the past, whose voices are interwoven in a song, often in a reprise, appear through scrims or in lights of unnatural hues. Lights close in on solo sections by a singer working with a vocal or dancing chorus and open up for the group sections. Kaleidoscopic lighting reflects the musical complexity of catches, rounds, canons, and other contrapuntal songs.

Some of the measurable psychological correlations between light and sound suggest lighting approaches. If a spectator associates low notes with saturated colors and higher pitches with greater brightness and hues in the middle of the spectrum, then perhaps spotlights on the soprano and bass should be colored accordingly or a deepening hue should accompany a descending scale while lights brighten on a long ascending section.

A lighting designer ought to listen to or read the music for a production just as carefully as the script, preferably with a stopwatch in hand. Lighting is often cued by musical changes and timed with measures; so whoever calls and executes cues should understand music. If the production has a composer, he or she should be as involved in the lighting designer's planning as is any other designer. Musical directors and conductors should be consulted regarding musical interpretations which bear on the lighting.

Movement and Lighting

As soon as the choreography and blocking for a production are reasonably fixed, the lighting designer should attend rehearsals to make flow diagrams and time move-

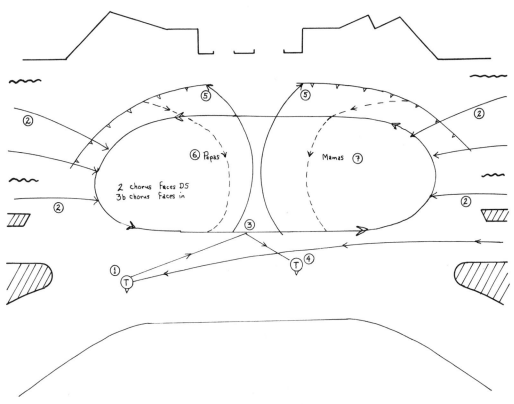

FIGURE 11-4　A lighting designer's flow chart of the movement of performers for the opening few minutes of *Fiddler on the Roof*.

ments. Flow charts are ground plans with basic movement patterns marked on them showing the time required for the movement. Figure 11-4 shows a sample for a production of *Fiddler on the Roof*. These diagrams indicate how the performers use the stage space and suggest patterns for structuring the lighting.

The arrangement of entrances, platforms and stairs, and furniture gives a preliminary indication of the probable areas into which the lighting will be divided, but the actual use of the stage space is a far more accurate indicator. For example, taken by itself, the floor plan in Figure 11-5 suggests a division of lighting areas around furniture groupings and entrances, but rehearsals show intimate scenes which repeatedly bridge these areas. Without sufficient

instruments to light these bridges as additional specials superimposed on the basic pattern, the designer should modify the lighting areas as shown in Figure 11-6.

Particularly on stages with a good deal of variegation in lighting color, intensity, and angle, if major shifts in lighting quality on a moving figure appear objectionable, the predominant flow of movement indicates areas that should be linked with similar lighting. Thus a character can move through a mottled lighting environment while remaining in a fairly constant light.

The directionality of lighting or strong patterns of light exert a pull on movement. The spectator expects the performer to stay in the light and follow the pattern. A marked discrepency between lighting and movement flow may create a desirable ten-

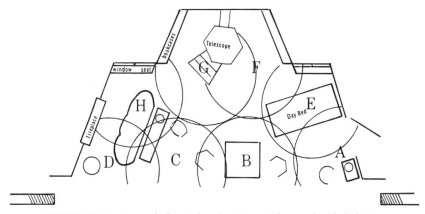

FIGURE 11-5 A rough floor plan for *Venus Observed* with lighting areas shaped by the arrangement of furniture and the entrance.

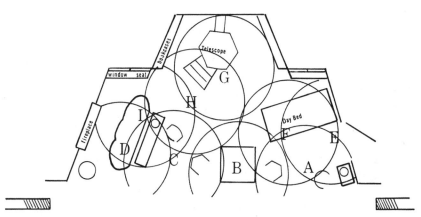

FIGURE 11-6 A rough floor plan for *Venus Observed* with lighting areas modified to reflect actor use of the stage. The differences from the arrangement of areas in Figure 11-5 is slight, but this arrangement reflects a different bridging of furniture groups.

sion in the composition, on one hand, or may seem inappropriate for a more harmonic mood, on the other. For example, side lighting used predominantly for dance or musicals establishes "zones" which separate performers in depth and attracts lateral movement. The clearer the division between zones, the stronger the effect. A performer who moves up or downstage against the grain of the lighting "flashes" through different zones and attracts a good deal of attention. The addition of another light coming along the axis of this movement at an angle to the zones will lessen the tension of this movement. The interplay of side lighting with front or diagonal lighting, particularly when designing for dance, gives a good deal of latitude in varying the mood produced by a movement.

The direction and strength of a movement also influences the progression of lighting qualities. Dancers often make "strong" exits into the wings because they become naturally brighter as they approach closer to the side lights. If the choreographer objects to this effect, the side lights must either be dimmed as the dancer approaches or balancing lights from the onstage side should match the intensity of offstage side lights. Specials used to "punch" an entrance may result in an intensity dip when an actor continues the movement into the stage space unless the path of the cross is equally bright. These same specials should not be used for "weak" exits or entrances. Moving from a darker to a brighter area creates a more "upbeat" mood than the opposite effect. The tendency for frontlit settings to brighten downstage further accentuates the strength of a downstage movement. If a strong upstage movement is required, extra lighting intensity should be added upstage.

Strong linear axes in the lighting imply movement in straight lines. Sinuous, curved, or indefinite movement patterns generate less tension in softer, diffused lighting, which emphasizes the natural curve of individual pools of light.

Where lighting controls the focus, the limits of an area of movement determine the boundary where intensity drops or color changes. Overextension of this area may result in a diffusion of focus. In fact, the audience's assumption is so strong that an area of the stage more brightly lit than the rest will be "used" that failure to do so generates tension, which of course can be dramatically appropriate at times. A bright light on Banquo's unfilled chair in the banquet scene in *Macbeth* emphasizes Banquo's absence.

Because we are accustomed to a changing play of light on a person moving through uneven lighting, actor movement can "cover" a lighting change so the audience does not notice the shifting of the lights *per se*. The speed of the shift, however, must mirror the tempo and energy of the movement, even to the extent of following the time profile of an irregular cross. If a rapid initial movement then tapers off slowly, for example, the majority of the cue is executed during the first part of the cross and the remainder follows slowly. The fact that actors are not automatons and the time of crosses varies from performance to performance attests to the need for manual execution of these cues or manual overrides on computer boards with operators who can see the stage. Even a relatively slight difference between the tempo of the movement and the lighting cue calls attention to the lights.

The execution of lighting cues timed to the performers' moves must also adjust to the fact that the lighting should slightly anticipate the movement to prevent the actor or dancer from stepping into darkness. A properly controlled cue pulls the performer into the new area of light. How closely the cue precedes the cross determines both the inconspicuousness of the lighting change and, to some extent, the mood of the cross. An easy transition establishes a smooth flow. A slight lag in the lighting change dampens energy, and a longer lead time in the cue produces more tension and a greater pull on the performer.

Even though movement through the stage space has the greatest influence on lighting, the designer should also carefully note important motion in place, particularly for dance lighting. Turns, sinuous motions, or moments where multiple dancers intertwine, often work best in a light with modeling strong enough to emphasize three-dimensional composition but without a dominant linear key light which is more suitable for highly directional, straightline motion. The energy of a movement in place may call for similar energy in a lighting change. The relationship here is analogous to the association between lighting and music. Slow, lethargic motion may suggest lower intensities, and either deeper hues or light pastels. More vitality needs brighter lights and a higher level of color saturation. Tightening pools of light can mirror concentric movements where the body closes in, or a widening area of light can underscore eccentric movements where the body opens and fills more space. As always, lighting which contrasts rather than mirrors these movements may produce appropriately theatrical tension and variety.

Lighting can also dramatically reinforce important small movements in a relatively realistic play. For example, a character who has been standing in a beam of light from a window receives a piece of bad news and collapses in a chair, falling out of the beam. Another character persuades him to gather courage to face the crisis, and he resolutely stands, brightening as he rises back into the beam. Often a slight turn of the body or head produces a noticeable change in the brightness or color of the face if lighting comes from a sufficiently high angle overhead or from the sides. The director must block the actors very precisely to the beam of light and the effect should be explained to the actor, who otherwise may be unaware of the difference of brightness or color that results from the turn. In plays that do not adhere to realism, the designer can use more overt links between lighting changes and small movements.

The "homework" is now complete. The designer has carefully analyzed the script, developed a production concept with other members of the creative staff, examined designs for scenery, costumes, and makeup, listened to music and sound effects, watched rehearsals to note movement or choreography, and formulated a lighting concept. Lighting approaches and images evolve out of this process, but the time now comes to combine these insights with a knowledge of instrumentation, control, drafting procedures, psychophysics, and design principles in order to produce a lighting design and, ultimately, a lit production.

Developing
the Final Design

The lighting designer's careful study of the interplay between lighting and other elements of production leads ultimately to a meticulously drafted lighting plot with a plan and sections showing instruments and mounting positions, an instrument and filter schedule, the board hookup sheet, cue sheet, and any other material necessary for the efficient mounting, cueing, and running of the lights for the production. Before drafting the final plot, however, a designer may usefully develop two preliminary pencil-to-paper steps: the lighting score and the rough lighting plot.

THE LIGHTING SCORE

A cue sheet guides the final lighting design, and today, with the timing of cues programmed into the memory of a control console, the lighting board operator primar-

ily needs to know when to push the "go" button. Further details about the instruments controlled by given dimmers and the timing of cues are provided in case of "emergencies": failures of control or instrumentation or unexpected deviations in the performance itself. The stage manager's copy of the script with cues marked in the margins guides these cues. For a simple production with few, widely spaced lighting cues, this is a perfectly adequate way to represent the lighting changes.

For a complicated lighting plot with densely packed, often overlapping cues, the designer profits from a more graphically represented score. Time relations between various lighting changes and other performance elements, the relative brightness or tinting of different moments in relation to one another, interconnections between patterns of lighting, and modifications in the lighting flow need to be seen as a whole, not simply as a number of discrete cues. If time permits, the designer may find it quite useful to develop a detailed lighting score which depicts changes in a schematic fashion. This score is an intermediate step between mental conception and execution. It helps the designer visualize, analyze, and compose the design as a complete entity. Only the designer uses the score. The stage manager and board operators continue to work from a marked script and cue sheets.

The development of a lighting score is not a conventional step in the lighting-design process and, as a consequence, no conventional method of notation has evolved. Many designers, in effect, create a score with a series of sketches, diagrams, and notes on lighting patterns. Modern composers encounter similar difficulties developing a notation system for avant-garde music, due to sounds not usually classed as "musical" or indeterminate relationships between sounds.

Stage lighting does have one constant variable: intensity control. It is a relatively easy matter, particularly with the aid of computers, to produce a series of line graphs showing the changes in dimmer settings through a production. However, unless we translate these graphs into meaningful changes in the perceived quality and distribution of the lighting, they have little relevance to the design process. Given developments in computer technology, these dimmer changes can produce a graphic display of lighting changes on an abstract model of the setting, a sort of time-lapse pictograph of the lighting design; but until such a program becomes easily available, designers must rely on pen-and-pencil techniques to contrive a lighting score.

Notation also varies from one production to another because design factors vary from production to production. For example, the careful modification in direction of key lights and changes of color on a cyclorama that may be important design elements in one production, may not be used at all in another. The opaqueness of the scrim wall

should be charted for *A Streetcar Named Desire* and the modifications in figure/ground relationship between the columns and the palace facade in *Oedipus Rex,* and each requires a notation unique to that production.

The lighting score, therefore, shows transformations in major blocks of lights or groups of lights which together make major changes in the appearance of the stage. The score does not record the variations in each dimmer control but rather the alterations in the appearance of major design elements. Individual dimmer controls may be imbedded in a larger group or may contribute to more than one group. For example, instruments linked to one dimmer may simultaneously influence different lines on the score related to overall color, brightness in one area, and the key/fill relationships on an important character, each charted separately by the score.

To keep the score from becoming impossibly cumbersome, it should show only *important* design features which *change significantly* through the course of the performance. If the key lights always come from the same direction or a color wash remains constant, their inclusion would just clutter the score.

Each major design element should have a separate line on the score. The horizontal axis represents time and should be keyed at the top to minutes and seconds, lines in the play, musical passages, or choreography and movement, depending on the circumstances. Long intervals without lighting changes should be indicated by a hiatus showing the length of the gap in terms of time or pages in the script. All of the important design features should appear on a single piece of paper so the designer can clearly see the relationships at any given moment in the performance.

Changes in the lighting are sometimes shown graphically by variations in the amplitude or vertical dimension of a line. This variable responds to changes in dimmer voltage, but the score usually expresses the variations in terms of perceived brightness, color, diffusion, or direction, rather than dimmer settings. Sometimes interwoven lines show more than one variable on a single scale, but usually each design element has its separate vertical scale. The vertical variable is rarely stated with mathematical accuracy and may be no more than an assumed measure of subjectively perceived variations. Scientific precision is less important than the score's ability to represent to the designer the changes in the lighting quality.

Many changes are shown by better methods than line graphs. Arrows on an assumed vertical picture plane clearly represent the vectors of light flow or dominant key lighting. Sketches of the shape of pools of light show major reshaping of light distribution. Colored pencils may make color shifts more vivid on the score. Sketches of changes in the appearance of major pieces of scenery give a more graphic indication of lighting changes than a series of abstract line graphs.

Figures 12-1 and 12-2 show sample sections of lighting scores developed for productions of *Oedipus Rex* and *Fiddler on the Roof*. In each case, the elements charted were the ones of particular importance in

FIGURE 12-1 A lighting score for the opening of *Oedipus Rex* before the beginning of the first speech. The production opens with a woman kneeling before a low altar on which a fire dimly burns. The suppliants enter from the sides, calling Apollo, followed by the entrance of the Priest who redirects the calls to Oedipus. The king enters through the central doorway.

Oedipus Rex	Opening	Woman holds child DC	Suppliants assemble	Priest enters	Oedipus enters	Oedipus US of altar
Overall Brightness	very dark	altar brightens	brighter	same	blinding	Oed. bright
Use of Stage Floor			side			bottom
Key	vague	silhouette	side	shadowy	silhouette	bottom
Closure	closed	tight	low	same	vertical	same
Contrast	low			→	high	→
Conflict	building					→
Tempo	slow			→	strong	→
Mood	eerie	grotesque	foreboding	expectant	surprising mystical	threatening
Color	grn/amb		add cool sd		wht back	amb bottom
Focus	vague	woman/child	suppliants	Priest	Oedipus	Oed/Priest
Time of day	predawn →		first glimmer			→
Altar fire	dim glow	some bright			→	light
Doorway	dark closed		→	lighten	open/ brilliant	closed

Fiddler on the Roof	Fiddler on roof	Tevye enters	Chorus enters	Circle closes	"Because of"	Papas	Mamas
Overall Brightness	moderate	spot	moderate	dip	spot	brighten	
Use of Stage Floor							
Key							
Closure	above roof	add D	begin opening			entire stage	
Contrast	high ⟶		lower some	higher ⟶			⟶
Conflict	No ⟶					build	
Tempo	moderate ⟶		dignified	slow build	moderate	build	building
Mood	anticipating	friendly	begin build	build	interrupt	swagger	
Color	warm ⟶		warmer ⟶				⟶
Focus	Fiddler	Tev./Fid.	Villagers		Tevye		Mamas
Time of day	dusk ⟶		theatrical ⟶				⟶
Spot	No	Tevye	out on Tev X	No	Tevye	No	No
Cyc	med. blue ⟶		deepen ⟶				⟶
Reality	narrative ⟶		theatrical ⟶		narrative	theatrical ⟶	
Other	Fid. against cyc	Tight on Tev. & Fid.	back lt. cir.	Begin scene lighting	chorus freeze	fill U front	fill C front

FIGURE 12-2 A lighting score for *Fiddler on the Roof* through the "Mama" section of the opening number, "Tradition."

those specific productions. However, because of their consistent importance, certain features commonly recur on lighting scores. Overall brightness is important because of the effects of brightness contrast and brightness adaptation. How long a given intensity level has been sustained or how different brightness levels are juxtaposed becomes immediately apparent by looking at the score. The same holds true for overall tint where color fatigue and color contrast come into play. When large areas of different colors are juxtaposed, as for example, a cyclorama and the major playing area, color relationships are clearly obvious. With realistic plays, it is often useful to chart the location of the sun or times when major artificial lighting sources are turned on and off and correlate these with changes in lighting key.

Charting changes in the shape of the lighting framework shows appropriate correlations with intimate or panoramic moments in the play or with flow patterns in the movement of the performers. Variations between specular and diffused lighting correlate with desired changes in mood. The list goes on.

Exposing time factors is perhaps the greatest value of the lighting score. Only when we see the rate of change in the lighting as a whole does the correlation between the overall rhythm of the performance and the rhythm of the lighting changes become apparent. These rhythms operate on an almost subliminal level and can be easily lost when the designer concentrates on a cue at a time. The score reveals the pattern of change, showing where densely packed cues accelerate the tempo and where slowly executed cues or long periods without change slow the tempo.

Two side benefits are that the lighting score provides a fairly vivid record of a lighting design and offers a means for expressing design ideas short of actually executing the design. The latter is particularly useful for student designers working in a classroom or designers who simply like the exercise of conceptualizing designs for a production they do not have the opportunity to actually light. We can more easily reconstruct a lighting design in the mind from a good score than from trying to mentally synthesize plots, profiles, instrument inventories, cue sheets, and the script. If we had detailed lighting scores of the great twentieth-century lighting designers, we would have a more accessible and lasting record of their work than the mostly anecdotal information currently available.

A lighting score, however, is primarily a working paper for the designer's own use, a way of keeping track of multiple variables, seeing the interrelationships of parts, and viewing the design as a whole entity rather than a collection of separate cues.

THE ROUGH LIGHTING PLOT

Most of the application of design considerations to stage lighting takes place with the roughing out of the plot. The final lighting plot and its accompanying paper work are primarily tools for communicating the designer's concept and intentions to the electricians, lighting crews, and board operators who must hang the design and execute it in performance. The rough plot is where the designer actually develops ideas, experiments, moves and changes instruments and filters, and refines the design.

Some degree of experimentation and discovery is still possible after the lights are turned on, particularly in educational and community theatre, where the cost of time is not as restrictive as it is in the commercial theatre, but careful preconceptualization and planning maximizes the time left, after hanging and focusing, for fine tuning, the polishing that distinguishes an excellent lighting design.

The rough plot takes various forms or may have different forms at progressive stages. The first phase is often a ground plan of the setting over which the designer draws circles and ellipses representing lighting areas and arrows showing the direction of major lighting sources or the principle direction of light flow. The next step is usually a rough approximation of the final plot with instruments lightly penciled in so they can easily be erased and repositioned. This is where the designer translates design ideas into actual instrumentation and simultaneously adjusts for the resources and limitations of equipment, control, and the architecture of the theatre.

Adapting to Available Instruments and Mounting Positions

All lighting systems have limitations. Even if the designer has an unrestricted budget and instrument inventory, the location of mounting positions, space obtainable on the pipes, or the beam characteristics of available instruments narrow options. To what extent should the limitations of the lighting system influence the designer's initial conceptualization? On the one hand, if the designer only visualizes what seems immediately possible with limited resources, the stimulus to invent creative ways to meet ambitious goals may be lost. The design will be no more than what is feasible. On the other hand, a failure to recognize unavoidable limitations early in the design process may result in a missed opportunity to influence other production elements when adjustments could bring about more efficient and flexible use of limited lighting resources. The design process should move from the ideal to the practical, conceiving first of what is desirable and then adjusting that to what is possible. However, a good designer's reach should always slightly exceed his or her grasp; so the final product seems more than what was apparently possible.

Changes in other production aspects can help to stretch lighting resources. For example, a slight adjustment in blocking may enable an instrument to double for two scenes and eliminate the need for additional instruments hung for a slightly different area. A large expanse of cyclorama which consumes a high percentage of available dimmer capacity might be reduced in size by closing in forestage scenery which frames it.

Changing light sources requiring key shifts that serve no other dramatic purpose might be realigned on the same side of the setting. The use of a slightly lighter hued or less absorptive floor covering could result in better bounce light and a brighter stage for a given number of instruments. The redesign of hats to eliminate broad brims might do away with the need for added lights on the balcony rail to fill in shadowed faces, or a better contrast between costume and scenic color could reduce back-lighting requirements. Lighter makeup shades may demand less front light.

Careful consideration of the effect of the lighting on the audience or of the physical attributes of light and color often helps to get maximum results from minimal means. For instance, brightness adaptation often results in some loss of impact for an intensely lit scene. By dimming houselights and beginning the production with a lower level of overall illumination, the audience adjusts to the low level and fewer instruments can generate the impression of greater brightness for a subsequent scene. A higher-angled key light or greater contrast between key and fill, which improves the modeling of the performer's face, often enhances visibility more efficiently than added brightness. Reduction in the brightness of the background accentuates the contrasting brightness on the actors. Back, side, and top lighting, disregarding other functions, produce less visibility than light from the front of the house and may need to be sacrificed

first when the number of instruments is limited. However, angling side lights slightly upstage so their beams overlap on the downstage side of a figure can eliminate the need for added front light.

Utilization of principles of color contrast can produce the same effect as double-hung crosslighting, but with three rather than four instruments on each area. If a single instrument with a neutral tint hangs opposite two instruments, one with a warmer and one with a cooler tint, the neutral instrument will seem to provide a warmer key or a cooler fill depending on which of the other two is used in combination with it. We can obtain a range of color washes otherwise provided by separate sets of instruments for each tint if we mix light from two sets of instruments with carefully selected filters. With a limited number of instruments, a designer should avoid color mixes using combinations of deeply hued filters because of the considerably lower efficiency of the darker tints. The careful matching of filter tint with costume, makeup, or scenic color often results in a higher level of reflection from the lit surface and, consequently, a brighter stage for a given quantity of light. Remember that the important factor is how the audience uses the light that reaches its eyes, not the output of the instruments *per se*.

In selecting lighting instruments and mounting position, the designer has but six static variables to consider: intensity, color, direction, form, diffusion, and luminousness, all of which relate to one another. Knowing the lighting characteristics of a specific instrument mounted in a specific position is a fundamental step to designing the plot. Intensity is a product of wattage but also depends on the age of the lamp, the efficiency of the instrument and filter, and the distance of the throw. It is not wise to simply use the most powerful instrument available, assuming that it can be dimmed to the required level of brightness, because the red shift that occurs when lamps are operated at less than full capacity may distort color fidelity. Filters, lamp types, and the percentage of capacity at which the lamp is operated influence color. Direction depends on mounting position. Form largely results from the shape and characteristics of individual beams of light and beam combinations from a number of instruments. Even when different types of instruments produce beams of comparable size and intensity, the distribution of light within the beam varies. For instance, one instrument may have a brighter center or a sharper edge than another. Slight differences between lenses, lamps, or the adjustment of instruments of the same type may even produce significant differences in the appearance of the beams. One of the reasons for numbering instruments in a house with a permanent lighting inventory is to quickly identify units with specific "personalities." The shape of the beam depends on the type of lens, shuttering or masking devices, and, as a practical consideration, on the mounting position. Even though the beam itself is not influenced by the location of the instrument, the intersection of the cone of light with floors, walls, or performers obviously changes according to the beam axis. The degree of diffusion depends on instrument type or the use of diffusion filters.

Grouping Instruments According to Dimmer Resources

Ideally each lighting instrument should be thought of as a separate "unit" in the composition and should be capable of separate dimmer control and linkage with any other instrument in any combination of instruments. Except for computerized control systems with a separate dimmer for each instrument, limitations in the number of dimmers and the mechanical restrictions of board operations (particularly with manually controlled boards), often force the designer to group instruments under a single control. How instruments are grouped greatly influences the execution of the design. When such arrangements become necessary, the designer has to think in terms of larger "units," lighting characteristics created by a number of instruments but viewed as a whole, and these units vary from design to design. In one instance we may need separate control for each of a number of separate areas with a fixed balance of crosslighting. In another the designer may divide the stage space into larger areas and change key/fill configurations, in which case the multiple instruments providing key light for the larger area are thought of as a single unit.

When it becomes necessary to group a number of instruments under a single control, the balancing of separate instruments or planned variegation becomes very important because further adjustments cannot be made by varying dimmer settings within the group. A few control boards contain "trimmers" which allow intensity reduction for instruments within a unit, but the designer must usually make corrections with mismatched instruments, hanging distances, or filtration which reduces intensity without affecting color or diffusion. One problem here is that mismatched instruments in combination, which produce one balance at a given dimmer level, may create a radically different balance at another level. If carefully planned, these shifts may give needed variety in an otherwise static unit. For example, a 500-watt instrument paired with a 1000-watt instrument at a greater throw may produce the same intensity level on stage at full capacity, but as the lights are dimmed the lower-wattage instrument will seem to lose brightness and shift to red at a faster rate. As lights grouped this way dim, that portion of the area covered by the stronger instrument will take slightly greater focus, a way of shifting the focus with lights otherwise locked into a fixed relationship.

Developing the Plot

Where do we begin the process of translating all the information we have accumulated into a workable lighting plot? Experienced lighting designers evolve their own strategies for developing the plot. For many the plot ultimately emerges full-blown from the imagination, like Athena coming from the thigh of Zeus. A thorough process of preparation, investigation, and conceptualization stimulates images of light which, from the beginning, are associated with specific instrumentation in the mind of a skilled designer. Until this "second nature" develops, more mundane and practical strategies are available.

Most apprentice lighting designers begin with a "building block" approach, adding separate lighting functions one by one. Once the acting areas have been determined (see Figure 11-6), the designer chooses instruments to cover them. This usually entails determining the direction of light sources and light flow to establish warm/cool relationships or the direction of key lights. Provisions for multiple coverage allow for changes in the direction of dominant light sources or key lights and for major toning changes. Depending on the design system used (see Chapter 9), fixing the area lighting may entail crosslights from the front, front and side combinations, key/fill combinations, or some mixture of these. If needed, back lighting is added next. The designer then turns to "specials," lights focused on particular areas of the stage, such as entrances or scenic features of symbolic importance, and lights to accentuate realistic illumination sources or design highlights, such as beams coming through windows or a pool of light around a lamp. Finally, if not covered by area, back, or special lights, the scenery and ground receive separate attention with instruments designated specifically to light and color floors and walls.

At worst, this approach results in a mechanical lighting grid imposed on all productions with the same "look" from production to production. At best, the designer makes interpretative, compositional, and stylistic decisions at each step which tailor the lighting to the particular needs of the production and maintain the values developed in the lighting concept.

The notion of a lighting grid adaptable for more than one production can be a positive asset when designing lighting for rotating repertory or stock theatre with limited instruments and a short turnover time between productions. In such a situation, the designer may aim for a "palette" approach with areas designated to cover all productions and with double-hung complementary colors and opposing key lights to provide as full a range as possible in lighting color and flow.

Any design process must deal with all aspects of lighting covered in the "building block" approach, but the lighting concept and lighting score provide bases for developing a lighting plot more overtly from compositional and design considerations. In this case we start with the principal design features articulated in the lighting concept or developed in the score. For *Oedipus Rex*, as an example (see Lighting Concept 1, Chapter 11, and Figure 12-1), we could begin with the progression of lighting angles on Oedipus himself: from brilliant back light, to a macabre bottom light, to high-angled key light, to broken shafts of light and shadow, to a wash of unflattering color with strong top light, to a warmer, more sympathetically colored wash. This becomes the spine of the lighting design, which we establish first and around which we build lighting to cover the special needs of other characters, the setting, any realistic or symbolic demands, and additional changes in mood. The final lighting plot may look very much like the one developed from the "building block" method, but we know that design and interpretative values determine the final product rather than the requirements of a lighting "system." We have the confidence of building from lighting ideas which grew out of our careful analysis of the play and all of the elements of this particular production, a design shaped uniquely for this one theatrical experience.

THE FINAL DESIGN

From the rough plot, the designer drafts the final lighting plot,[1] but this plot is not the design. It is a schematic representation of an array of lights, used in various combinations and intensities, to produce the actual design, which is the arrangement of lighting seen by the audience (Figure 12-3 and 12-4). To a great extent, all that has gone before is preliminary to the final act of design, the setting of cues. The designer may need to contend with followspots and manual or motorized filter changes, but most of cueing is a matter of setting dimmer intensities and timing; yet this requires all of the *art* of lighting design.

Using the plot and accompanying schedules, the equipment is mounted and circuited, then focused. Regardless of how detailed written instructions have been, the designer usually needs to supervise the fine focusing. A matter of inches in the centering or shuttering of an instrument may make a critical difference to the effectiveness of the design. After focusing, the instruments receive any necessary filters.

To expedite technical rehearsals, the designer usually writes "blind" cues without the benefit of actually seeing the lighting, except in the imagination. With experience, the designer frequently creates a close approximation to the final cue. "Dry" lighting rehearsals with only board operators and someone to "walk" the stage also provide an opportunity to write preliminary cues from the actual lighting, but even here prewritten blind cues speed the process. Directors frequently want to see "dry" lighting rehearsals before full technical rehearsals. Particularly with the director present, the designer should have prewritten preliminary cues in

order to present as close an approximation to the actual design as possible. Otherwise the director may be tempted to play with the lights and the designer will lose control of the design. Under no circumstances does the designer merely present an array of lighting from which the director chooses what he or she wants. This is a complete abrogation of the lighting designer's responsibilities.

A carefully developed lighting score greatly aids the process of setting cues. If the designer constructs the score in sufficient detail, the location and timing of cues has already been decided, and the only problem is to translate the relatively abstract design values on the score into specific combinations of instruments and intensities.

Throughout the cueing process, the designer must apply all of the design principles we have discussed to the lighting concept and must constantly view the product from the perspective of the audience member. Is the scene bright enough for sufficient visual acuity? What is the brightness adaptation level? Do tonal variations produce desired brightness contrast? Is there objectionable fatigue produced by glare, afterimages, or flashing light? Do brightness and color generate the desired emotional response? Do color contrasts and lighting angles create good modeling? Are colors inappropriately distorted in costumes, scenery, or makeup because of lack of color contrast, color fatigue, or the narrow spectral profile of filter hues? Does the light reveal appropriate textures and conceal unwanted blemishes? Does the audience have the desired perception of stage depth, proportion, or edge sharpness? Are important shapes or patterns emphasized? Do lighting changes conform to structural changes in visual planes in the setting? The list should go on to cover the major topics that we have studied.

The final design is in the eye and mind of the spectator, and the design process is com-

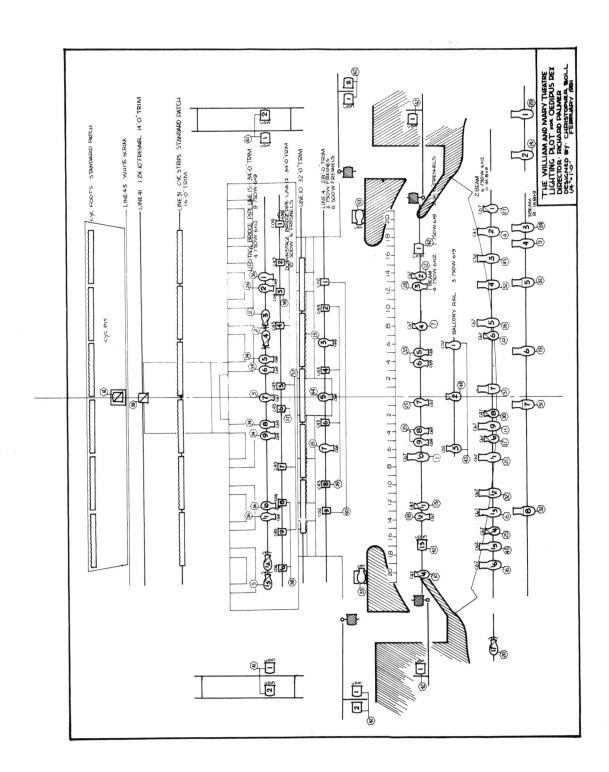

OEDIPUS REX Instrument Schedule

Position		Type	Focus	Dimmer	Color	Notes
3rd beam	1	8×9 ellip	Area 6	29	C47	
	2	8×9 ellip	3	14	C47	
	3	8×9 ellip	5	24	C47	
	4	8×9 ellip	2	9	C47	
	5	8×9 ellip	Lft.	32	NC	Template
	6	8×9 ellip	Area 4	19	C47	
	7	8×9 ellip	Cntr.	31	NC	Template
	8	8×9 ellip	Rt.	32	NC	Template
2nd beam	1	6×12 ellip	Area 6	27	C67	
	2	8×9 ellip	1	4	C47	
	3	8×9 ellip	Spec.	45	C52	
	4	8×9 ellip	Lft.	32	NC	Template
	5	8×9 ellip	Area 6	26	C67	
	6	6×12 ellip	5	22	C67	
	7	8×9 ellip	Cntr.	31	NC	Template
	8	6×12 ellip	Area 6	30	C47	
	9	8×9 ellip	3	11	C67	
	10	6×12 ellip	4	17	C67	
	11	8×9 ellip	5	21	C67	
	12	8×9 ellip	Rt.	32		Template
	13	8×9 ellip	Area 2	6	C27	
	14	6×12 ellip	5	25	C67	
	15	8×9 ellip	Spec.	45	C62	
	16	8×9 ellip	Area 4	16	C67	
	17	6×12 ellip	4	20	C47	
1st beam	1	8 fresnel	'Wm. Wsh	42	C03	
	2	6×12 ellip	Area 3	12	C67	
	3	6×9 ellip	6 top	28	C67	
	4	6×12 ellip	Area 2	7	C67	
	5	6×9 ellip	DS back	35	C69	
	6	6×9 ellip	DS back	35	C69	
	7	6×9 ellip	5 top	23	C67	
	8	6×9 ellip	DS back	35	C69	
	9	6×9 ellip	DS back	35	C69	
	10	8×9 ellip	Area 1	1	C67	
	11	6×12 ellip	3	15	C47	
	12	6×9 ellip	4 top	18	C67	
	13	8 fresnel	Wm. Wsh	42	C03	
	14	6×12 ellip	Area 2	10	C47	
Pipe 1	1	6 fresnel	Columns	40	C02	Barndoor
	2	6 fresnel	Columns	39	C43	Barndoor
	3	6×9 ellip	3 top	13	C69	
	4	6 fresnel	Columns	39	C44	Barndoor

OEDIPUS REX Instrument Schedule

Position		Type	Focus	Dimmer	Color	Notes
	5	6×9 ellip	Spec.	44	C69	
	6	6 fresnel	Columns	39	C43	Barndoor
	7	6×9 ellip	2 top	8	C69	
	8	6 fresnel	Columns	39	C43	Barndoor
	9	6 fresnel	Columns	40	C02	Barndoor
Bridge DS	1	6 fresnel	Columns	38	C04	Barndoor
	2	6 fresnel	Columns	37	C43	Barndoor
	3	6 fresnel	Columns	38	C04	Barndoor
	4	6 fresnel	Columns	37	C43	Barndoor
	5	6 fresnel	Columns	37	C43	Barndoor
	6	6 fresnel	Columns	37	C43	Barndoor
	7	6 fresnel	Columns	37	C43	Barndoor
	8	6 fresnel	Columns	37	C04	Barndoor
	9	6 fresnel	Columns	38	C43	Barndoor
	10	6 fresnel	Columns	37	C04	Barndoor
Bridge DS	1	6×9 ellip	Back L	36	C69	
	2	6×9 ellip	Back L	36	C69	
	3	6×12 ellip	Area 1	2	C67	
	4	6×12 ellip	Area 1	2	C67	
	5	6×9 ellip	Back C	34	C69	
	6	6×9 ellip	Back C	34	C69	
	7	6×9 ellip	1 top	3	C67	
	8	6×9 ellip	Back C	34	C69	
	9	6×9 ellip	Back C	34	C69	
	10	6×9 ellip	Back R	36	C69	
	11	6×9 ellip	Back R	36	C69	
	12	6×12 ellip	Area 1	5	C47	
	13	6×12 ellip	Area 1	5	C47	
Balcony rail	1	6×9 ellip	Wash	45	C02	
	2	6×9 ellip	Warmer	44	NC	
	3	6×9 ellip	Wash	45	C02	
Box L	1	8 fresnel	Wash	41	C03	
	2	8 fresnel	Wash	41	C03	
Box R	1	8 fresnel	Wash	41	C03	
	2	8 fresnel	Wash	41	C03	
Torm L	1	8 fresnel	Wash	42	C03	
	2	8 fresnel	Wash	42	C03	
Torm R	1	8 fresnel	Wash	42	C03	
	2	8 fresnel	Wash	42	C03	
Cove L	1	8 fresnel	Wash	42	C03	
Cove R	1	8 fresnel	Wash	42	C03	

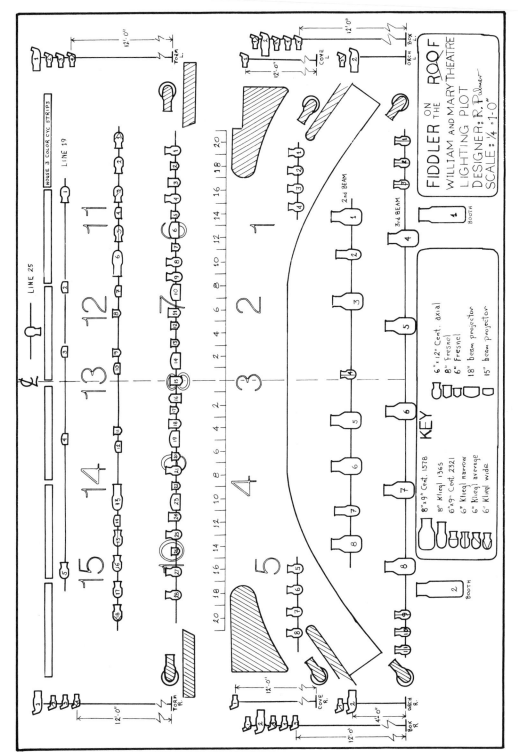

FIGURE 12-4

INSTRUMENT SCHEDULE
FIDDLER ON THE ROOF

Position	#	Type	Color	Focus	Circuit	Dimmer	Function
Booth	1	Follow spot					
	2	Follow spot					
Beam 3	1	6″ K narrow	RX65	A	20	32	Tev. house L
	2	6″ K narrow	805	B	6	34	Tev. house L
	3	6″ K narrow	805	C	20	32	Tev. house L
	4	8×9″ Cent.	C54	1	18	1	Fill
	5	8×9″ Cent.	C54	2	15	2	Fill
	6	8×9″ Cent.	C54	3	13	3	Fill
	7	8×9″ Cent.	C54	4	10	4	Fill
	8	8×9″ Cent.	C54	5	8	5	Fill
	9	6″ K narrow	RX65	A	5	33	Tev. house R
	10	6″ K narrow	RX65	B	6	34	Tev. house R
	11	6″ K narrow	805	C	5	33	Tev. house R
Beam 2	1	8×9″ Cent.	C54	7	19	7	Fill
	2	8″ Kliegl	849	inn dr.	17	42	Special
	3	8×9″ Cent.	C54	6	16	6	Fill
	4	6″ K narrow	805	Tev dr	14	35	Special
	5	8×9″ Cent.	C54	8	12	8	Fill
	6	8×9″ Cent.	C54	10	11	10	Fill
	7	8″ K	NC	Ta. dr	9	41	Special
	8	8×9″ Cent.	C54	9	7	9	Fill
Beam 1	1	6×12″ axial	G32	7	24	28	Key L
	2	6×12″ axial	G32	8	23	29	Key L
	3	6×12″ axial	G32	9	22	30	Key L
	4	6×12″ axial	G32	10	21	31	Key L
	5	6×12″ axial	G80	6	4	27	Key R
	6	6×12″ axial	G80	7	3	26	Key R
	7	6×12″ axial	G80	8	2	25	Key R
	8	6×12″ axial	G80	9	1	24	Key R
Electric 1	1	6×12″ axial	810	12	A24	A24	Key L
	2	6″ fresnel	RX17	6	64	37B	Sabbath
	3	8″ fresnel	C54	11	65	11	Fill
	4	6×12″ axial	810	13	A24	A24	Key L
	5	6″ fresnel	RX17	6	66	41B	Sabbath
	6	18″ beam proj.	NC	1	A1	A1	Back
	7	6″ fresnel	RX03		68	43	Inn
	8	6×12″ axial	810	14	A25	A25	Key L
	9	6×12″ axial	810	15	A25	A25	Key L
	10	18″ beam	NC	2	A2	A2	Back
	11	8″ fresnel	C54	12	71	11	Fill
	12	6″ fresnel	RX03		72	43	Inn
	13	6″ fresnel	RX03		73	43	Inn
	14	18″ beam	NC	3	A3	A3	Back
	15	8″ fresnel	C54	13	74	12	Fill
	16	8″ fresnel	RX17	3	75	36B	Sabbath

INSTRUMENT SCHEDULE
FIDDLER ON THE ROOF

Position	#	Type	Color	Focus	Circuit	Dimmer	Function
Electric 1	17	6″ fresnel	RX03		78	44	Tailor shop
	18	8″ fresnel	C54	14	77	13	Fill
	19	18″ beam	NC	4	A4	A4	Back
	20	6″ fresnel	RX03		78	44	Tailor shop
	21	6×12″ axial	G86	11	A23	A23	Key R
	22	6″ fresnel	RX17	5	79	37B	Sabbath
	23	18″ beam	NC	5	A5	A5	Back
	24	8″ fresnel	C54	15	80	13	Fill
	25	6×12″ axial	G86	12	A23	A23	Key R
	26	6″ fresnel	RX17	5	81	37B	Sabbath
	27	6×12″ axial	G86	13	A22	A22	Key R
	28	6×12″ axial	G86	14	A22	A22	Key R
Electric 2	1	6″ K wide	839	11/12	A19	A19	Side L
	2	6×12″ axial	838	12/13	A19	A19	Side L
	3	6″ K aver.	838	13/14	A21	A21	Side L
	4	15″ beam	NC	6	A6	A6	Back
	5	6″ K nar.	RX91	13	A31	A31	Fruma Sara
	6	8″ Kliegl	838	14/15	A21	A21	Side L
	7	15″ beam	NC	7	A7	A7	Back
	8	6″ fresnel	RX03		A30	A30	Tev. house
	9	6″ fresnel	RX03		A30	A30	Tev. house
	10	15″ beam	NC	8	A8	A8	Back
	11	6″ fresnel	RX03		A30	A30	Tev. house
	12	15″ beam	NC	9	A9	A9	Back
	13	8″ Kliegl	811	11/12	A17	A17	Side R
	14	15″ beam	NC	10	A10	A10	Back
	15	6″ K nar.	RX91	13	A31	A31	Fruma Sara
	16	6″ K aver.	811	12/13	A17	A17	Side R
	17	6×12″ axial	811	13/14	A15	A15	Side R
	18	6″ K wide	811	14/15	A15	A15	Side R
Electric 3	1	6″ K nar.	G80	13	A27	A27	Fiddler
	2	15″ beam	NC	12	A11	A11	Back
	3	15″ beam	NC	13	A12	A12	Back
	4	15″ beam	NC	14	A13	A13	Back
	5	6″ K nar.	G82	13	A27	A27	Fiddler
Electric 4		3 col. strip				46-48	Cyc
Electric 5	1	6″ K nar.	NC	13	A26	A26	Fid. back
Orch. L	1	6″ K aver.	RX91	2	57	44B	Pattern
	2	8″ Kliegl	RX91	3	56	44B	Pattern
Orch. R	1	6″ K aver.	RX91	4	49	45	Pattern
	2	8″ Kliegl	RX91	3	48	45	Pattern
Box L	1	6″ K wide	RX17	1/2	62	42	Sabbath
	2	8″ Kliegl	G32	5	61	23	Side L
	3	6″ K aver.	G32	4	60	22	Side L
	4	6×12″ axial	G32	3	59	21	Side L
	5	6×12″ axial	G32	2	58	20	Side L

INSTRUMENT SCHEDULE
FIDDLER ON THE ROOF

Position	#	Type	Color	Focus	Circuit	Dimmer	Function
Box R	1	6″ K wide	RX17	5/4	54	42	Sabbath
	2	8″ Kliegl	RX51	1	53	18	Side R
	3	6″ K aver.	RX51	2	52	17	Side R
	4	6×12″ axial	RX51	3	51	16	Side R
	5	6×12″ axial	RX51	4	50	15	Side R
Cove L	1	6×9″ Cent.	810	1	63	19	Side L
Cove R	1	6×9″ Cent.	G80	5	55	14	Side R
Torm L	1	8″ Kliegl	G82	9/10	A20	A20	Side L
	2	6″ K aver.	G82	8/9	A20	A20	Side L
	3	6×12″ axial	G82	7/8	A18	A18	Side L
	4	6″ K wide	G82	6/7	A18	A18	Side L
Torm R	1	8″ Kliegl	G32	7/6	A16	A16	Side R
	2	6″ K aver.	G32	8/7	A16	A16	Side R
	3	6×12 axial	G32	9/8	A14	A14	Side R
	4	6″ K wide	G32	10/9	A14	A14	Side R

Note — beam projectors 2K; 8″ spots 1K; all else 750 w

plete only when the designer has aroused the appropriate response from the audience member.

When we add all of the knowledge of related subjects not discussed in this book—electricity, optics, instrumentation, lighting control, drafting procedures—to all that we have investigated here—psychophysics, principles of composition and design, style, analysis of the play text, and other production elements—the art of stage lighting design may seem impossibly complex. Complex it is, but not impossibly so. Theatrical lighting is an art, and like other arts, we can learn its principles.

Most people can easily learn the workings of the few instrument types used for the majority of stage lighting or can operate the increasingly foolproof dimmer systems—and can, therefore, quickly acquire the skills needed to provide basic stage illumination. This approach resembles the art of lighting design no more than painting-by-numbers resembles the work of Rembrandt.

Stage lighting provides a remarkably subtle, versatile, and pliant artistic medium, capable of marvelous nuances as well as powerful mind-bending effects. To control its full range of expression we must fully comprehend the nature of lighting, the effect of lighting on objects, the mechanisms by which we perceive and interpret lighting, and the aesthetic principles governing the use of lighting. Because stage lighting is a cooperative art form that depends on other stage arts, we must understand the intertwining artistic principles of all aspects of theatre. Only then can we use our lighting equipment with an eye toward the creative effect, subtlety, precision, and control of the master artist.

In one respect, the more we investigate stage lighting, the more complex its possibilities become. In another, the more we inquire and learn, the more easily we control all the variables of theatrical lighting. Investigation, however, is but the first step in acquiring knowledge. You must now practice, test, and observe, gaining the understanding that comes to an artist only through years of applying aesthetic principles to practical experience.

Bibliography

Stage Lighting

Bellman, Willard F. *Lighting the Stage: Art and Practice* (2nd ed.). New York: Crowell, 1974. A detailed text on the technology of stage lighting. Bibliography.

Benthan, Frederick. *The Art of Stage Lighting* (2nd ed.). New York: Theatre Arts Book, 1976. An introductory text with emphasis on British lighting practice.

Bergman, Gosta M. *Lighting in the Theatre.* Totowa, N.J.: Rowman and Littlefield, 1977. A detailed survey of the history of stage lighting with a short introductory section on optics and psychology. Well illustrated and contains a detailed bibliography.

Burian, Jarka. *The Scenography of Josef Svobada.* Middleton, Conn.: Wesleyan University Press, 1971. A well-illustrated examination of the work of one of the most influential contemporary designers.

Gillette, J. Michael. *Designing with Light.* Palo Alto, Calif.: Mayfield Publishing, 1978. A clear, elementary text for the beginning lighting designer.

Jones, Robert Edmond. *The Dramatic Imagination.* New York: Theatre Arts Books, 1941. A brief, almost poetic statement of principle which has become a spiritual touchstone for contemporary designers.

McCandless, Stanley. *A Method of Lighting the Stage* (4th ed.). New York: Theatre Arts Books, 1958. From its first publication in 1932, this was a standard source for much lighting in educational theatre.

Parker, W. Oren and Harvey K. Smith. *Scene Design and Stage Lighting* (4th ed.). New York: Holt, Rinehart and Winston, 1979. A clearly illustrated basic text on technology and design procedures.

Penzel, Frederick. *Theatre Lighting Before Electricity.* Middletown, Conn.: Wesleyan University Press, 1978. A history of stage lighting from the beginning through the use of gas. Extensive written and pictorial documentation and a bibliography.

Pilbrow, Richard. *Stage Lighting* (rev. ed.). New York: Drama Book Specialists, 1979. A well-illustrated elementary text with emphasis on British practice.

Rosenthal, Jean and Lael Wertenbaker. *The Magic of Light.* Boston: Little, Brown and Co., 1972. A mixture of lighting text and autobiography, this is the most detailed record available of the design methods of a successful theatre lighting designer. Contains useful illustrations and lighting plots.

Rubin, Joel E. and Leland H. Watson. *Theatrical Lighting Practice.* New York: Theatre Arts Books, 1954. A concise overview of lighting design for commercial, arena, and open-air productions, puppetry and television. Sample lighting plots and bibliography.

Sellman, Hunton D. and Merrill Lessley. *Essentials of Stage Lighting* (2nd ed.). Englewood Cliffs, N.J.: Prentice-Hall, 1982. An introduction to the history of stage lighting, instrumentation, control, and stage practice. Bibliography.

Warfel, William B. *Handbook of Stage Lighting Graphics.* New York: Drama Book Specialists Publishers, 1974. This 41 pp. booklet sets a standard for lighting graphics.

Warfel, William B. and Walter A. Klappert. *Color Science for Lighting the Stage.* New Haven: Yale University Press, 1981. An analysis of color filters using the C.I.E. Chromaticity Diagram.

Psychophysics

Beck, Jacob. *Surface Color Perception.* Ithaca, N.Y.: Cornell University Press, 1972. An investigation of research concerning the perception of surface color with particular attention to color constancy under changing illuminants. Bibliography.

Billmeyer, Fred W. and Max Saltzman. *Principles of Color Technology.* New York: Interscience Publications, 1966. A graphic presentation of color theory, color order systems, color measurement, and the use of color in industry. Bibliography.

Birren, Faber. *Color & Human Response.* New York: Van Nostrand Reinhold Co., 1978. A somewhat mystical but interesting discussion of human response to light and color. Bibliography.

———. *Color Psychology and Color Therapy* (rev. ed.). New Hyde Park, N.Y.: University Books, 1961. A mixture of science and mysticism by a leading exponent of color therapy.

———. *Light, Color and Environment.* New York: Van Nostrand Reinhold Co., 1969. A discussion of the psychological effects of color design for work and domestic environments. Bibliography.

Burnham, Robert W., Randall M. Hanes, and C. James Bartleson. *Color: A Guide to Basic Facts and Concepts.* New York: John Wiley & Sons, 1963. A good outline of basic ideas.

Committee on Colorimetry of the Optical Society of America. *The Science of Color.* New York: Thomas Y. Crowell, 1953. A well-illustrated and documented description of the psychological, physiological, and physical concepts relating to color perception. Bibliography.

Cornsweet, Tom N. *Visual Perception.* New York: Academic Press, 1970. A detailed investigation, amply illustrated, of the psychophysiology of brightness and color, the physics of light, and the visual system. Bibliography.

Erhardt, Louis. *Radiation, Light and Illumination* (adapted from an original text by Charles P. Steinmetz [1909]). Camarillo, Calif.: Camarillo Reproduction Center, 1977. A graphic survey of basic concepts with a final chapter on the aesthetics of lighting.

Evans, Ralph. *An Introduction to Color.* (2nd ed.). New York: John Wiley & Sons, 1959. A thorough and fundamental study of the scientific bases for light and color perception. Bibliography.

———. *The Perception of Color.* New York: John Wiley & Sons, 1974. An updated and somewhat more technical discussion of topics examined in Evan's *An Introduction to Color.* Bibliography.

Hopkinson, R. G. *Architectural Physics: Lighting.* London: Her Majesty's Stationery Office, 1963. A thorough and technical investigation of the bases for illumination engineering.

Hurvich, Leo M. and Dorothea Jameson. *The Perception of Brightness and Darkness.* Boston: Allyn and Bacon, 1966. A technical but readable survey of psychological experiments in brightness perception. Bibliography.

Illuminating Engineering Society of North America. *I.E.S. Lighting Handbook.* New York, 1981. A reference book for the lighting industry with data on light, vision, color, illumination, and the application of lighting principles to living environments.

LeGrand, Yves. *Light, Color and Vision,* trans. R.W.G. Hunt, J.W.T. Walsh, F.R.W. Hunt. London: Chapman & Hall, 1957. A very thorough technical survey. Bibliography.

Levine, Michael W. and Jeremy M. Shefner. *Fundamentals of Sensation and Perception.* Reading, Mass.: Addison-Wesley Publishing Co., 1981. A textbook on biological and psychological bases of perception with primary emphasis on vision. Bibliography.

Luckiesh, Matthew. *Color and Its Application.* New York: D. Van Nostrand, 1915. An excellent book, limited only by its age, written by a pioneer in the scientific investigation of vision.

Luckiesh, Matthew and Frank K. Moss. *The Science of Seeing.* New York: D. Van Nostrand, 1937. An examination of all aspects of vision and illumination, thoroughly grounded in scientific data but quite readable.

MacAdam, Daniel L. (ed.). *Sources of Color Science.* Boston: MIT Press, 1970. A collection of writings on color from Plato, through Newton, to Helmholz.

Mueller, Conrad G. and Mae Rudolph. *Light and Vision.* New York: Time Inc., 1966. An easily understood presentation of basic information with ample graphic and pictorial material. Part of the Life Science Library.

Padgham, C. A. and J. E. Saunders. *The Perception of Light and Colour.* New York: Academic Press, 1975. A technical but clearly written survey of fundamental principles. Bibliography.

Pirenne, M. H. *Vision and the Eye* (2nd ed.). London: Chapman and Hall, 1967. A survey of physiological and psychophysical bases for vision, primarily visual acuity and color vision. Bibliography.

Rainwater, Clarence. *Light and Color.* New York: Golden Press, 1971. An elementary but graphic presentation of basic facts for the general reader.

Sheppard, Joseph J., Jr. *Human Color Perception: A Critical Study of the Experimental Foundation.* New York: American Elsevier Publishing Co., 1968. A detailed discussion of the physiological and psychophysical aspects of color perception.

Wright, W. D. *Researches on Normal and Defective Colour Vision.* St. Louis: C. V. Mosby Co., 1947. An investigation of scientific research on all aspects of visual perception relating to color vision.

Wyszecki, Gunter and W. S. Stiles. *Color Science: Concepts and Methods, Quantitative Data and Formulas.* New York: John Wiley & Sons, 1967. A sourcebook of experimental data. Bibliography.

Lighting and Design in Nontheatrical Arts

Adams, Ansel. *Artificial Light Photography.* Hastings-on-Hudson, N.Y.: Morgan & Morgan, 1968. A theoretical and practical study of the use of lighting in photography by a master photographer.

Arnheim, Rudolf. *Art and Visual Perception.* Berkeley and Los Angeles: University of California Press, 1969. A study of psychological bases for the perception of space, light, and color, among other factors, in two-dimensional art.

Feininger, Andreas. *Light and Lighting in Photography.* Garden City, N.Y.: American Photographic Book Publishing Co. (Prentice-Hall), 1976. Develops standards for "ordinary," "unusual," and "fantastic" illumination.

Graves, Maitland. *Color Fundamentals.* New York: McGraw-Hill, 1952. A study of the psychophysics of color with special reference to the visual arts.

Hattersley, Ralph. *Photographic Lighting.* Englewood Cliffs, N.J.: Prentice-Hall, 1979. A survey of lighting composition in photography with detailed projects for mastering lighting techniques.

Hopkinson, R. G. and J. D. Kay. *The Lighting of Buildings* (rev. ed.). London: Faber and Faber, 1972. Contains some aesthetic and psychological material, but this is primarily a practical consideration of the lighting of living spaces.

Klein, Adrian. *Coloured Light.* London: The Technical Press, 1957. A discussion of associations between color and music.

Lam, William M. C. *Perception and Lighting as Formgivers for Architecture.* New York:

McGraw-Hill, 1977. A well-illustrated examination of perceptual factors influencing the use of lighting in architecture. Bibliography.

Mason, Robert G. (ed.). *Color*. New York: Times Inc., 1970. A volume in the Life Library of Photography concerned with color photography, this book provides useful visual examples of the relationship between color and light.

Mortensen, William. *Pictorial Lighting*. San Francisco: Camera Craft Publishing Co., 1935. A perceptive discussion of aesthetic principles of lighting by a prominent portrait and "art" photographer of the pre-World War II era.

Time-Life Books. *Light and Film*. New York: Time Inc., 1970. An entertaining and attractive introduction to the use of light in photography.

Williams, Rollo Gillespie. *Lighting for Color and Form*. New York: Pitman Publishing Co., 1954. A survey of basic scientific data concerning light, color, and light sources in relation to architectural, display, stage, media, and exterior lighting.

Periodicals

Lighting Design & Application. A publication of the Illuminating Engineering Society of North America, which replaced the earlier *Illuminating Engineering* in 1971. Contains a variety of articles on topics relevant to the lighting industry.

Lighting Dimensions. A magazine for lighting designers in the entertainment industry. Articles on media-, show-, and theatre-lighting design and equipment.

Journal of the Illuminating Engineering Society. A quarterly publication of I.E.S. standards, recommended practices, testing and measurement guides, and research.

Journal of the Optical Society of America. Publication of much of the basic research on vision, light, and any optical phenomenon, principle, or method.

Tabs. A quarterly publication between 1943 and 1973 of Strand Electric Co., the leading British manufacturer of lighting equipment. Describes lighting installations in theatres throughout the United Kingdom.

Theatre Crafts. A popular-format magazine on theatre technology, frequently containing articles on lighting design practice.

Theatre Design and Technology. A publication of the U.S. Institute of Theatre Technology. Contains occasional articles on lighting and instrumentation.

Footnotes

chapter 1

1. Most writers follow Stanley McCandless, *A Method of Lighting the Stage* (New York: Theatre Arts Books, 1932) and isolate only four properties: intensity, color, form, and movement.
2. Again, most writers follow McCandless and describe only four functions: visibility, naturalism, composition, and mood. Hunton D. Sellman and Merrill Lessley, *Essentials of Stage Lighting*, 2nd ed. (Englewood Cliffs, N.J.: Prentice-Hall, 1982) adds "revelation of form."
3. Robert Edmond Jones, *The Dramatic Imagination* (New York: Theatre Arts Books, 1941), p. 115.

chapter 2

1. Matthew Luckiesh and Frank K. Moss, *The Science of Seeing* (New York: D. Van Nostrand, 1937), p. 377.
2. R. G. Hopkinson, *Architectural Physics: Lighting* (London: Stationery Office, 1963), p. 107.
3. Ibid., p. 99.
4. Ibid., p. 216.
5. Faber Birren, *Light, Color and Environment* (New York: Van Nostrand Reinhold Co., 1969), p. 48.
6. Luckiesh and Moss, *The Science of Seeing*, p. 111.
7. Faber Birren, *Color and Human Response* (New York: Van Nostrand Reinhold Co., 1978), p. 34.
8. Yves LeGrand, *Light, Colour, and Vision*, trans. R.W.G. Hunt, J.W.T. Walsh, and F.R.W. Hunt (London: Chapman & Hall, 1957), p. 296; and Birren, *Light, Color and Environment*, p. 27.
9. LeGrand, *Light, Colour, and Vision*, p. 294.
10. C. A. Padgham and J. E. Saunders, *The Perception of Light and Colour* (New York: Academic Press, 1975), pp. 137–39.

11. Tom N. Cornsweet, *Visual Perception* (New York: Academic Press, 1970), p. 237.
12. Ibid.
13. Birren, *Light, Color and Environment,* pp. 74–5.

chapter 3

1. W. D. Wright, *Researches on Normal and Defective Colour Vision* (St. Louis: C. V. Mosby Co., 1947), pp. 220–55.
2. W.E.K. Middleton and M. C. Holmes, "The Apparent Colors of Surfaces of Small Subtense—A Preliminary Report," *Journal of the Optical Society of America* 39 (1949), pp. 582–92.
3. Fred W. Billmeyer and Max Saltzman, *Principles of Color Technology* (New York: Interscience Publishers, 1966), p. 32.
4. For further discussion see Michael W. Levine and Jeremy M. Shefner, *Fundamentals of Sensation and Perception* (Reading, Mass.: Addison-Wesley Publishing Co., 1981), particularly pp. 360–62.
5. H. Helson, "Fundamental Problems in Color Vision," *Journal of Experimental Psychology* 23 (1938), pp. 439–76.
6. Robert W. Burnham, Randall M. Hanes, and James Bartleson, *Color: A Guide to Basic Facts and Concepts* (New York: John Wiley & Sons, 1963), pp. 88–90.
7. Faber Birren, *Light, Color and Environment* (New York: Van Nostrand Reinhold Co., 1969), p. 47.
8. Burnham et al., *Color,* pp. 208–10.
9. Faber Birren, *Color and Human Response* (New York: Van Nostrand Reinhold Co., 1978), p. 24.
10. Ibid., pp. 23–24.
11. Burnham et al., *Color,* p. 211.
12. Robert Gerard, "Differential Effects of Colored Light on Psychophysiological Functions," Ph.D. dissertation, UCLA, 1957, cited by Birren, *Light, Color and Environment,* p. 19.
13. Felix Deutsh, "Psycho-Physical Reactions of the Vascular System to Influence of Light and to Impression Gained Through Light," *Folia Clinica Orientalia* I (1937), Fasc. 3 & 4, cited by Birren, *Color and Human Response,* p. 47.

14. Birren, *Light, Color and Environment,* p. 49.
15. Lorraine Dusky, "Startling New Theories on Light and Color," *Popular Mechanics* 150 (Sept., 1978), p. 184.
16. See Johann Wolfgang von Goethe, *Theory of Colors,* trans. Charles Lock Eastlake (Cambridge, Mass.: MIT Press, 1970); and *Goethe's Color Theory,* trans. Herb Aach (New York: Van Nostrand Reinhold Co., 1971).
17. See *Light, Color and Environment* and *Color and Human Response.*
18. Richard Kavner and Lorraine Dusky, *Total Vision* (New York: Addison & Wesley Publishers, 1978), p. 97.
19. Birren, *Color and Human Response,* p. 18.

chapter 4

1. R. G. Hopkinson, *Architectural Physics: Lighting* (London: Her Majesty's Stationery Office, 1963), p. 8.
2. Stanley McCandless, *A Method of Lighting the Stage,* 4th ed., (New York: Theatre Arts Books, 1958).

chapter 6

1. Maitland Graves, *Color Fundamentals* (New York: McGraw-Hill, 1952), p. 170.
2. G. W. Granger, " 'Colour Harmony' in Science and Art" in *Colour 73* (New York: John Wiley & Sons, 1973), pp. 504–505.
3. Ralph M. Evans, *An Introduction to Color* (New York: John Wiley & Sons, 1948), p. 321.
4. P. Moon and D. E. Spencer, "Aesthetic Measure Applied to Color Harmony," *Journal of the Optical Society of America* 34 (1944), pp. 234–42.
5. Robert Edmond Jones, *The Dramatic Imagination* (New York: Theatre Arts Books, 1941), p. 69.
6. Ibid., p. 116.

chapter 8

1. Robert Edmond Jones, *The Dramatic Imagination* (New York: Theatre Arts Books, 1941), p. 25.
2. Ibid., p. 26.

3. Christopher Fry, *A Phoenix Too Frequent* (Oxford: Oxford University Press, 1949).

4. Jones, *The Dramatic Imagination,* pp. 115–16.

5. Jo Mielziner, *Designing for the Theatre* (New York: Bramhall House, 1965), p. 172.

6. Antonin Artaud, *The Theatre and Its Double,* trans. Mary Caroline Richards (New York: Grove Press, 1958), p. 94.

7. Ibid., p. 95.

8. See Brecht's "Noitzen uber die Zurcher Erstauffuhrung" of *Puntilla* in *Versuche* X (Berlin, 1950), p. 110.

9. Jerzy Grotowski, *Towards a Poor Theatre* (New York: Simon and Schuster, 1968), p. 20.

chapter 9

1. The most complete history of stage lighting is Gosta M. Bergman, *Lighting in the Theatre* (Stockholm: Almqvist & Wiksell International, 1977).

2. Howard Bay, *Stage Design* (New York: Drama Book Specialists, 1974), p. 135.

3. Ibid., p. 136.

chapter 10

1. One of the best studies of dramatic structure and characterization is Northrop Frye, *The Anatomy of Criticism* (Princeton: Princeton University Press, 1957).

2. Tennessee Williams, *Summer and Smoke* (New York: New Directions Books, 1948).

3. Frye, *The Anatomy of Criticism,* pp. 163–86.

4. Tennessee Williams, *A Streetcar Named Desire* (New York: New Directions Books, 1947).

5. Thornton Wilder, "Some Thoughts on Playwriting," in *The Intent of the Artist,* ed. Augusto Centeno (Princeton: Princeton University Press, 1941), pp. 83–98.

6. Tennessee Williams, *The Glass Menagerie* (New York: Random House, 1945).

chapter 12

1. The best source of information on drafting a lighting plot is William B. Warfel, *Handbook of Stage Lighting Graphics,* 2nd ed. (New York: Drama Book Specialists/Publishers, 1974).

Index

*Terms are defined on pages indicated in bold face type.